IRISH

*Charles G. Halpine in
Civil War America*

IRISH

*Charles G. Halpine in
Civil War America*

WILLIAM HANCHETT

FOREWORD BY ALLAN NEVINS

SYRACUSE UNIVERSITY PRESS

To Tom and Em

WILLIAM HANCHETT is professor of history at San Diego State College, San Diego, California. He received the B.A. from Southern Methodist University and the M.A. and Ph.D. from the University of California at Berkeley. His articles have been published in the leading historical journals. He discovered Charles G. Halpine while conducting research on the poetry of the Civil War years as a source of social history.

Contents

Foreword

PROFESSOR HANCHETT has enriched the biographical and critical materials available upon American journalism, humor, military life, and Irish-American politics by the first truly searching and thorough treatment ever accorded the witty Irishman, Charles G. Halpine. After writing extensively for most of the major New York newspapers and achieving a national reputation for some widely quoted stanzas on "Sambo's Right To Be Kilt," happily seconding Lincoln's decision to give southern freedmen a place in the uniformed forces, and after becoming an active propagandist for the Union party during the last years of the Civil War and for the Johnson administration during the beginnings of the struggle over Reconstruction, Halpine died, just on the apparent threshold of a busy career as an officeholder, party lieutenant, and satirical commentator of some real originality. A contemporary of Petroleum V. Nasby and Artemus Ward, who delighted Lincoln and entertained large audiences, he rivaled them in invention, wit, and ability to pen apt hoaxes, burlesques, and penetrating poetic hits. He also gave promise of ability to promote the causes of the Democratic party nationally and of political and social reform in New York, with cleverness, variety, and occasionally memorable felicity.

This book, the product of years of industrious research and a tireless collection of manuscripts, quite supersedes the earlier sketches of Halpine (better known by his pen name "Miles O'Reilly") by Robert B. Roosevelt and others. It merits attention and preservation for a variety of reasons: first, as an engaging character study of an unusually amusing, talented, and beguiling writer with an uneven but sunny gift for brightening the pages of the press and lifting the hearts of many contemporaries and friends. By his pungent bits of analysis and description, and his penetrating improvisations upon passing events, Halpine was able to turn out striking paragraphs and couplets whenever occasion offered, and to rise at times above the mundane world of ordinary journalism with brief flashes of genuine shrewdness and poetic talent. He had qualities of personal magnetism and an exuberant talent for friendship which seemed to equip him for a worthy role in the political life of New York and the Union. Unquestionably, he enlivened many newspaper pages and a wide circle of spirited comrades as an irrepressible adventurer of the pen and a *franc-tireur* of the Lincolnian party. At times excitingly adventurous, Halpine's life was darkened by episodes of undeserved misfortune and was closed by a sadly premature and sudden death.

Students will value this book for its careful use of a varied array of letters and other manuscripts illustrating Halpine's career, which the author has gathered from a large number of the newspapers and magazines of the period and from private citizens. After using these materials, Professor Hanchett has placed historians under an additional debt by depositing the hundreds of letters and other papers he had collected in the Henry E. Huntington Library, where, along with many rare personal papers acquired by the library from Halpine's descendants, they are available to all scholars interested in the life and literary or political activities of the Civil War years. Particular attention may be directed to the materials relating to Halpine's service in Missouri as a staff officer with General David Hunter, and to his subsequent Civil War service with Hunter in South Carolina and the Shenandoah Valley.

An especially attractive portion of Halpine's career relates his close and confidential friendship with Horace Greeley, James Gordon Bennett, Henry J. Raymond, and other distinguished editors of his time.

Professor Hanchett notes that Halpine's life descended into misfortune, partly because some of his friends were unfortunately chosen, and partly because he was unable to control his own appetite for drink. Association with politics and Tammany Hall in New York led to familiarity with such machine politicians as William Marcy Tweed and Peter B. Sweeny. General Hunter, though a brave officer, disgraced himself by his brutality in laying much of Virginia waste in the Shenandoah Valley campaign, and he outraged Americans both North and South by burning down the Virginia Military Institute, where Stonewall Jackson had taught. No doubt influenced by the warmth of Halpine's feeling for Hunter, Professor Hanchett has described the General's operations in more favorable terms than is usually the case, a fact which will be of special interest to Civil War military historians.

This biography gives keenly perceptive portraits of not only the men mentioned, but of such striking personalities as John C. Fremont, Thurlow Weed, and John Hay. Robert B. Roosevelt, who knew Halpine well and was associated with him in the creditable work of the Citizens'

Association, an organization devoted to constructive reform in New York, predicted that he would be remembered as a "brilliant genius and an uncommon intellect." Rather, he will be remembered as an erratic and lovable spirit who was associated with many of the most important men and events in a crucial era in the history of his adopted country, but whose gifts were squandered, whose full potentialities remained tragically unfulfilled.

Halpine possessed some true poetic impulses which unfortunately withered in the hot atmosphere of political struggle, but which occasionally enabled him to strike some genuinely creative phrases, as in his impassioned outburst in 1854 upon the federal rendition of the fugitive slave, Anthony Burns, to bondage. Entitled "The Flaunting Lie," he wrote of the American flag:

> Tear down the flaunting lie!
> Half-mast the starry flag!
> Insult no sunny sky
> With this polluted rag!

Had this poem, published and republished with spirited commentary in the New York press, been followed by others as good, Halpine might have made a more enduring mark upon the effervescent literary and political life of the Civil War era, and might have wasted less time upon the sparkling drink and conversations of Pfaff's Restaurant on lower Broadway.

As it was, Halpine's brief and abortive career included chapters of high achievement well worthy of the distinguished and conscientious chronicle now given him and his crowded years in this admirably written and exhaustively documented biography.

San Marino, California
Summer 1970

ALLAN NEVINS

Preface

THE NAME CHARLES G. HALPINE (or that of his fictional alter ego, Private Miles O'Reilly) was well known to the people of the United States during the Civil War. As a satirist and commentator on literary, military, and political affairs, Halpine's burlesques and hoaxes enlightened, entertained, and occasionally outraged his contemporaries. They are still capable of bright flashes of illumination, and their humor has not entirely disappeared, as has that of the better known Artemus Ward (Charles Farrar Browne) and Petroleum V. Nasby (David Ross Locke).

As a War Democrat, Halpine, at the request of his good friend John Hay, aggressively backed the efforts of Lincoln's administration to build up popular support for the war, especially among the New York Irish after the July, 1863, riots. As an army officer and aide to General David Hunter, Halpine helped compile the bill of particulars which resulted in the removal of General John C. Fremont from command in Missouri, accepted the Confederate surrender of Fort Pulaski, Georgia, and witnessed and later defended the unsuccessful attack of the monitors on Charleston, South Carolina. He also helped to justify and make palatable to prejudiced northern whites Hunter's pioneering experiment with Negro soldiers in the nearby Port Royal area. He participated in Hunter's expedition up the Shenandoah Valley to Lynchburg, Virginia, and in the disastrous retreat through the mountains of West Virginia, an adventure which has hitherto been described only in terms unflattering to Hunter.

As a journalist, Halpine wrote extensively for the major New York newspapers, and edited two of his own. As a Democratic party propagandist and office holder, he was active in New York politics and in the Reconstruction program of President Andrew Johnson. His largely fictional portrait of Jefferson Davis' life in prison helped rehabilitate the reputation of the rebel leader and has had a major influence upon

Davis' position in history. As an immigrant and professional Irishman (though a Protestant), Halpine supported the radical Fenian movement and sought to improve the image of the Irish among native-born Americans. In short, the story of his life provides new material and new perspectives on many individuals and events in the history of the 1850's and 1860's. It also recalls from near-oblivion a man—colorful, appealing, tragically flawed—who deserves recognition as one of the major minor figures of American history.

Since Halpine was a writer, and a prolific one, there are abundant sources for a critical biography. Among the most important are his two books of poetry—*Lyrics by the Letter H.* (New York, 1854) and *The Poetical Works of Charles G. Halpine* (New York, 1869), edited by his friend Robert B. Roosevelt; his two collections of essays, satires, and reminiscences—*The Life and Adventures of Private Miles O'Reilly* (New York, 1864) and *Baked Meats of the Funeral* (New York, 1866); his seven novels published serially in the New York *Irish-American;* the files of his newspapers, the New York *Leader* and the New York *Citizen;* and identifiable articles in the Boston *Carpet-Bag,* the New York *Times,* the New York *Tribune,* and the New York *Herald.* There are, as well, one box and five scrapbooks of miscellaneous clippings in the Library of Congress. In addition, over two hundred Halpine Letters, miscellaneous and, for the most part, unused components of widely scattered manuscript collections, have been photocopied and brought together, and it is a pleasure to thank the following libraries for their cooperation and for permission to reprint or quote: Boston Public Library, Brown University Library, Chicago Historical Society, Columbia University Library, Harvard College Library, Henry E. Huntington Library, Library of Congress, Massachusetts Historical Society, Eleutherian Mills Historical Library, Pierpont Morgan Library, New-York Historical Society, New York Public Library, New York State Library, Historical Society of Pennsylvania, University of Rochester Library, University of Virginia Library, and Yale University Library.

Most important of all is a fabulous and until recently unknown collection of Halpine manuscripts and papers, including some two hundred letters from Halpine to his wife and to Halpine from such men as Horace Greeley, John Hay, David Hunter, Andrew Johnson, and many others. For nearly a century, these priceless papers remained the cherished possession of Halpine's family, the present generation of which not only allowed me to study them but entertained me as a guest for a week in Annapolis, Maryland, while I did so. In particular, the widow of Halpine's grandson and namesake, Mrs. Charles G. Halpine, provided me with privacy, showed me Halpine's uniform, books, and personal belongings, over-fed me from his own china, and treated me as if I had been one of his personal friends. To her, and to Mr. and Mrs. Sidney K. Smith and the late Mrs. Kenneth M. Halpine, I am indebted for one of the most pleasant and rewarding experiences of my life.

The Halpine papers are now owned by the Henry E. Huntington Library, San Marino, California, where I have had additional opportunity to study them, and where, like so many other researchers, I have experienced the inspirational effects of Allan Nevins' interest and example.

Through the years, I have received research assistance from Clay M. Fechter, Marian Browne, John J. Kern, and especially Nancy Prager Levin. I am happy to thank them, and also Pat Wood, who drew the map, and Mrs. Mildred H. LeCompte, who located and borrowed a great many books through inter-library loan. I am indebted for a variety of information and favors to Frederick M. Anderson, Chester D. Bradley, Susan Haber, Thomas F. Hanchett, E. B. Long, Robert L. Munter, and Martin Ridge. My friends and colleagues Alvin D. Coox, Richard T. Ruetten, and C. R. Webb, Jr., of San Diego State, and Stanley I. Kutler, of the University of Wisconsin, have helped me in more ways than they may realize. The portion of Chapter 10 dealing with *The Prison Life of Jefferson Davis* was originally published in the *Journal of American History,* and is reprinted by permission. The San Diego State College Foundation has been generous to me with financial grants and with a semester's leave of absence, for which I am most grateful.

WILLIAM HANCHETT

San Diego, California
Summer 1970

CHAPTER 1

Carpetbagger

IT RAINED on and off all morning, August 7, 1868, upon the two or three hundred people who stood quietly beneath their umbrellas looking at the emotionless brownstone front of the big house at 58 West Forty-Seventh Street, New York City. Inside, the air was oppressively humid with the crowd of mourners and the summer heat, and the presence of death hushed voices and straightened faces. The rosewood coffin was placed before the fireplace in the drawing room, its lower length topped with floral wreaths—one of them inscribed "Ireland's Loss"—an officer's dress hat and sword, and an American flag. Through a glass window which exposed the upper part of his body, stunned friends looked for the last time upon the features of Charles G. Halpine, suddenly dead at the age of thirty-eight years, and about to be buried in the uniform (which he had not worn during the Civil War) of a major general.

At 11:00 A.M. the pallbearers grouped themselves about the coffin. Among them was the mayor of New York, John T. Hoffman, and the real rulers of the city—William Marcy Tweed and Peter B. Sweeny. Tweed and Sweeny had been the dead man's enemies, but they looked through the glass at his face with respect for power mingled with an affectionate understanding of his weaknesses. Also at the coffin were the sportsman-reformer Robert B. Roosevelt, the controversial Major General David Hunter, and the editor of the New York *Tribune,* Horace Greeley, who had been the dead man's patrons and friends. Nearby were other friends—Henry J. Raymond of the *Times,* James Gordon Bennett of the *Herald,* the members of the New York Common Council, important persons from the city, men from the Odd Fellows Lodge, men from uptown, and men from downtown. Their wives were there, too, some of them (who had seen looks of admiration and invitation in the eyes which would never open again) with a secret grief their husbands would not approve. Three sisters were present, but Halpine's wife and six children, still too much crushed by their unexpected bereavement to accept sympathy for it, remained upstairs.

1

The service was conventional. The Reverend E. O. Flagg, of the Church of the Resurrection, read the Episcopalian burial service and delivered a sermon on the perishability of earthly fame and power. A hymn was read, the benediction proclaimed, the coffin shut. The mourners (the women now with handkerchiefs to their faces) backed away, and the coffin was carried out of the house and down the steps. It was raining as the pallbearers placed it in the hearse, but the people in the street uncovered, and the soldiers presented arms. A section of police from the Nineteenth Precinct led a drum corps and the band of the Sixty-Ninth New York—the famous Irish Regiment in which Halpine had briefly served—down Fifth Avenue to Broadway. Behind them marched a hundred men from the various Fire Department companies, the Sixty-Ninth Regiment, and detachments from New York regiments of cavalry and artillery, their colors draped in black, their arms reversed. The hearse was escorted by an honor guard, followed by the pallbearers and city officials in carriages, and a large number of friends and associates on foot. Stretching for blocks, the procession moved down Broadway and through the Irish section of the lower east side to the Brooklyn ferry. Despite the weather, the sidewalks were crowded with spectators, mostly lunch-hour parade watchers, no doubt, attracted by the drums and the band's funereal music. But they knew the man who was being buried, and thousands of them felt a personal loss. For during the Civil War, when there had been more tears than laughter, he had made them laugh.

At the ferry slip the procession disbanded, and only the pallbearers, family, and most intimate friends accompanied the hearse across the East River to Cypress Hill Cemetery. Besides the comfort of the more-than-ordinarily flattering obituary notices—most of them written by the deceased's friends—they shared the conviction expressed by Robert Roosevelt that his position in history was secure. "That Charles G. Halpine was a great man," said Roosevelt, "a brilliant genius, and an uncommon intellect, his contemporaries have conceded, and posterity will confirm by more deliberate decision." [1]

But Roosevelt was wrong. When the rosewood coffin was lowered into the earth, more than a century of darkness closed over Halpine. He was quickly forgotten. His name, to be sure, may be found in the standard biographical directories, which (with many errors and omissions) recite the bare outline of his life, and in various literary histories, where he is mentioned as a poet or humorist. As a prominent newspaperman and soldier, he is referred to in some histories of the Civil War. But there has been no "deliberate decision." Far from confirming Halpine's genius, posterity has all but ignored him.

Born November 20, 1829, in the quiet country parish of his father, near Oldcastle, County Meath, Ireland, he was christened Charles Boyton Halpin. His father, Nicholas John Halpin, was educated at Trinity College, Dublin University, where he wrote the University Prize Poem honoring George III upon the completion of the fiftieth year of his reign, took orders in the Church of Ireland (Episcopal), and, at about the time of his marriage to Ann Grehan in 1817, was given the parish where Charles was born and raised.[2]

The duties of a Protestant clergyman in Catholic Ireland were not burdensome (or overpaid), and the senior Halpin was able to devote much of his time to the education of his sons. By the time he was ten years old, Charles was an accomplished scholar in Latin and French, and he aspired to be a poet. He would be "the pen of the Halpin family," his father declared, and the father lost no opportunity to make his prediction come true, even writing letters to his son in verse. Once, when the boy was away visiting cousins, the father wrote:

> I'm delighted to hear you are learning to ride,
> Tho' it is but a donkey you have to bestride. . . .
> 'Tis in riding the same as in writing and reading,
> A gradual, progressive, and steady proceeding. . . .
> And he that on horseback the muster would pass,
> Must graduate by entering at first on an ass.[3]

Charles inherited the gift for light verse and published a romantic poem in *Punch* before he was twenty. He saw rhymes everywhere, continuously, effortlessly. Rhyming couplets, sometimes clever and shrewd but more often merely amusing, came to him like sentences to most men, and he dashed off impromptu stanzas as quickly and often as most men write letters—and with as little revision. Making rhymes was the easiest thing he did, and neither he nor a great many of his admirers ever fully recognized that it was not always the same thing as writing poetry.

About 1840, Nicholas Halpin moved his family to Dublin, where he became managing editor of the *Evening Mail*, Dublin's principal Protestant newspaper. Vigorously anti-Roman Catholic, Halpin raised his editorial voice against Daniel O'Connell, who, having achieved Catholic emancipation in 1829, was working in the 1840's for repeal of the Act of Union between England and Ireland. But journalism and politics occupied only part of his time. He published two books on Shakespeare and wrote articles on theology and Elizabethan literature. Many years later, Charles published an article based on his notes on Edmund Spenser, and encouraged by praise from James Russell Lowell, sent to Ireland for additional notes and unfinished manuscripts left by "the best of fathers." [4] Scholar, versifier, and journalist-politician, Nicholas Halpin's influence upon his son's life was profound, and Charles always acknowledged the debt with admiration, gratitude, and love.

There was perhaps some fear mixed with the love. In a sonnet written in America in 1852, two years after the father's death, Charles recalled the Sunday mornings of his childhood, the church bells ringing, and his father standing high in his pulpit, Bible in hand, white hair flowing backwards, his face glowing alternately with benevolence and zeal. To have such a father and teacher was an inspiration and a source of pride, but a source of apprehension, too. What if one proved unworthy? What if one's best efforts and highest achievements should prove disappointing to so magisterial a figure? Until the end of his life, Charles was afraid that he would fail to measure up to what others expected of him, and the fear was perhaps responsible for the stammer which was often, according to his friends, "painfully apparent," and made it necessary for him to assume the role of a comic. To keep others from laughing at him, he had to laugh at himself, and there were times when it was not funny.

Fear, apprehension of failure or disapproval, is something he lived with all his life, and even in America there were several men—Horace Greeley, Thurlow Weed, David Hunter—who stood above him in the equivalent of his father's pulpit and supervised his progress as if he were an especially bright and promising son who could have a brilliant career if only he lived up to his potential. Toward them all, as toward his father, he felt the most sincere affection and respect. But on various occasions he was desperate with fear that he would disappoint them, lose their good opinions, lose their patronage. In one way or another, he was dependent upon them all, and yet, like an *enfant terrible* asserting his independence and his individuality, he disagreed violently with each over some important matter of public policy.

In this respect, too, his relations with his American father replacements paralleled his relations with his father. For Charles and his father disagreed on a subject of the greatest possible moment to them both—the future of Ireland. Where the father was a member of the pro-English minority and fought O'Connell for being too radical, the son hated England and denounced O'Connell for being too conservative. Where the Protestant father considered anti-Catholicism a virtue and an act of patriotism, it bothered the son not at all to be taken for a Catholic. Where the father's loyalties were associated with the established church and crown, the son numbered among his close friends John Mitchell,

Thomas Francis Meagher, and John Savage, leaders of the revolutionary Young Ireland organization. The intensity of Charles' Irish nationalism was unmodified by his migration to America, and he was among the first to give sympathetic publicity to the Fenians in the United States. It was in America, too, that he made the supreme demonstration of his independence of his father by adding the "e" to his surname, radically changing its pronunciation. At the same time, he took the middle name "Graham" after a deceased brother.[5]

In 1844, shortly before his fifteenth birthday, Charles enrolled at his father's alma mater, Trinity College, and began the study of medicine. He found it uncongenial, however, and left Dublin before graduation to read law at Lincoln's Inn, London. Through family influence, he also held a minor political office at Somerset House, and he wrote for a variety of English newspapers and magazines. On January 25, 1849, he married a childhood sweetheart, Margaret G. Milligan, daughter of a surgeon with the Inniskilling Dragoons, who was living in retirement in Warwickshire, England. The marriage of the two nineteen-year-olds had the approval of their parents, but not that of the Lord Chancellor in Ireland, who refused to convey to them a legacy Margaret was to have received upon her marriage. They fought for it in the courts, only to have it largely consumed by legal fees.[6] The judge's reasoning was that Margaret and Charles were still "infants in the eyes of the law," but it is possible that he was influenced by the politics of the groom. If so, Charles had a personal reason for hating the English. In February, 1850, Margaret gave birth to a daughter, Syble. Charles wrote that when bathed and bundled and lying next to her mother, the baby

> smelt so much like chicken broth
> That all the neighboring hens grew wroth,
> And cackled loud with angry look,
> Denouncing vengeance on the cook.[7]

A few months later, he left his wife and child with Margaret's parents, and, like 164,003 other Irishmen in 1850, sailed for America.

The record of his new life under his new name begins at the end of September, when he became friends with a young newspaperman, John T. Trowbridge, later to be a prominent editor and author of novels for boys. At the time he emerges from the nameless throng of immigrants, Halpine was an employee of Phineas T. Barnum, and he was in Boston to publicize the concert appearance of Jenny Lind. Trowbridge found him to be a little above medium height, with a florid complexion and a superabundance of youthful animal spirits. At the same time, Trowbridge recalled in a 1903 article in the *Independent*, he displayed "a maturity of mind and manner astonishingly beyond his years, then barely twenty-one." Looking at his eyes, deepset and intense, Trowbridge sensed a personality determined and powerful, yet restless and worldly. Halpine wanted to leave "B-B-Barnum," he told his new friend, who found his stammer "engaging," and very soon he did. Taking a small office on Tremont Row, he began to write poems and stories for the Boston newspapers, and advertising copy for business firms.

Through Trowbridge, Halpine met Benjamin P. Shillaber, a printer and writer for the Boston *Post*, who in March, 1851, brought out the first issue of his imaginative but short-lived weekly paper, the *Carpet-Bag*. As its name suggests, the *Carpet-Bag* was a literary catch-all of jokes, stories, poems, essays, reviews, cartoons, and such burlesques and hoaxes as chatty letters to the editor from Prince Albert. ("P.S. Victoria and the children send their kindest regards to you.") Shillaber's own sketches of Mrs. Ruth Partington, her nephew Ike, and her misadventures (mostly with the English language) attained a popularity difficult for another century to explain, and were published as a book in 1854. Mrs. Partington and Ike have been called the prototypes of Aunt Polly and Tom Sawyer, and indeed Mark Twain's first published story appeared in the *Carpet-Bag*, May 1, 1852. Signed S. L. C. and entitled "The Dandy Frightening the Squatter," it tells of the riverboat dandy who tries to impress some ladies by frightening a resident of Hannibal, Missouri, who impassively knocks him into the Mississippi. Other *Carpet-Bag* writers and humorists included Charles Farrar Browne (Artemus Ward), George H. Derby (John Phoenix), and, most regularly, Trowbridge and Halpine. The young men let their imaginations and their pens run wild, and, using an endless variety of pseudonyms and datelining their stories from distant cities, gave the illusion that the paper had vast numbers of readers and contributors. It did not; it sold only a few hundred copies per issue. But that was Boston's fault and Boston's loss. The *Carpet-Bag*, like its writers, was original, vital, and entertaining. Near the end, when Halpine was in charge, it also became caustic beyond the limits of literary criticism acceptable at the time.[8]

Halpine's connection with it, apparently casual at first, began with the very first issue, March 29, 1851, to which he contributed a little story about two men who accidentally exchanged reading glasses, and then wondered at their inability to read their own handwriting. Two weeks later he had another story on a subject which he could discuss (and often did), but his friends could not. It was about a storekeeper and his friend who stammered. When each, in succession, was unable to speak in answer to the question of a stranger, the man left in anger, believing they were making fun of him. Soon, under a variety of pseudonyms, he was contributing a major portion of most issues. As "Charles Broadbent," he published many of his own poems and original translations of verses from Horace, whose urbanity and good-humored cynicism appealed to him. The Latin was "Freely Translated," he admitted, until the editor of an out-of-state newspaper (possibly a hoax) complained of the inaccuracies, after which Broadbent labeled them "Very Freely Translated," and in subsequent issues took even greater liberties with them. In addition, Halpine often published poems under the initial "H," and there is evidence to prove or suggest that he wrote the articles and poems signed "Trismegistus," "Vinum Myrrhatum," "Oscar G. Hughan," "Ex-Editor," "Charles H. Haynes," who liked to translate from the French, and "Charles C. Hazewell," who wrote, among other pieces, an article on the ague, "By One of the Shakers." Without doubt, many unsigned articles and editorials were also Halpine's, including, quite possibly, a critique of *Othello*, which treated the play as if it had been recently written by a radical abolitionist capitalizing upon the popularity of *Uncle Tom's Cabin*.

His most important contribution to the *Carpet-Bag* was a mythical personality, one "Jehiel Stebbings," whose character and activities seem more amusing to modern readers than Mrs. Partington's, and are far more significant.

It was an era of aggressive foreign policy. After the easy conquest of Mexico, many Americans favored the annexation of additional parts of Latin America, and responded sympathetically to the appeals for help against Austrian tyranny of the visiting Hungarian revolutionary, Lajos Kossuth. They also applauded Secretary of State Daniel Webster's famous announcement of 21 December 1850 to the Austrian Emperor that, compared to the United States, "the possessions of the House of Hapsburg are but as a patch on the earth's surface." Jehiel Stebbings, living quietly in his cottage in the country near Spunkville when Halpine "discovered" him, was a caricature of belligerent national patriotism.

A grim-faced naval officer, whose lowly rank of ensign was supposed to suggest that the country did not appreciate his principles (and to provide a contrast to all the generals currently popular), Stebbings was a talented yet modest man, whose character was "warm, patriotic, resolute, daring, defiant and untamed." His conduct was ever guided by the documents he had reverently placed on his mantel, next to the flag—the Bible, the Psalter, the *Federalist,* the *True American,* Steuben's *Tactics,*

Jackson's Proclamation to the Nullifiers, and Webster's 7th of March speech.

The Ensign was a quick improviser, and upon occasion would burst into patriotic song. Once, when a neighbor used the word *disunion* in his presence, Stebbings was so aroused he composed on the spot a hymn to the Stars and Stripes. His "The American Flag" bore a resemblance, it was admitted, to a well-known poem of the same name by another writer, but perhaps the other writer had stolen it from Stebbings! (Halpine thus acknowledged his debt to Joseph Rodman Drake's famous "The American Flag," written in 1835.) The poem described how Freedom, standing on a mountain peak, had created the flag out of the sky, the stars, the milky way, and the sunrise, and entrusted it to the Bald Eagle to be carried to points specified in the last verse, which switches the parody from Drake to John L. O'Sullivan, the prophet of Manifest Destiny.

> That flag shall wave in the east
>   Where sunrise paints the sky,
> And its limits shall be in the west,
>   Where the setting sun doth die.
> It shall gleam o'er the frozen north,
>   Where the pole sticks up through the snow,
> And its bounds shall be in the south,
>   As far as we choose to go.

So ardent an expansionist (and so anti-British) was Stebbings, so determined was he that the flag move only onward, that his friends, fearful of the effect of the truth upon his sanity, denied the United States had settled its northwest boundary dispute with England back in 1846 by compromising. To the end, the Ensign believed the nation held Oregon all the way north to 54°40'!

In the summer of 1851, many decades before it became commonplace for humorists to stage mock-serious political campaigns, Halpine entered his hero in the race for President of the United States. Judging from reports in the *Carpet-Bag,* the Stebbings candidacy was greeted with enthusiasm from the beginning, but as the man and the details of his program became better known, the number of his supporters became enormous, and their ardor and dedication complete. Stebbings favored, in summary, the annexation of Cuba, a high protective tariff (except on munitions), cheap postage, cheap beef, and wages of two dollars a day. At all costs he would preserve the Union, even if it had to be "smoked and dried, salted down, [and] pickled."

Influential endorsements of "The People's Candidate" quickly followed. One newspaper, reliably quoted in the *Carpet-Bag,* announced it was backing Stebbings because he would call out 2,500,000 men to wage a war against tyranny in Europe, and thus bring an end to talk of secession at home. "Stebbings and War!" it cried, urging its readers to the polls. Another paper reported a growing conviction among the Irish that Stebbings meant to bring about their liberation from England, and the London *Times* (as quoted in the *Carpet-Bag*) announced the reorganization of the Admiralty and the strengthening of defenses at Quebec and Gibraltar. There were, of course, dissenting voices. In the New York *Tribune,* Horace Greeley (whom Halpine must have known by this time) opposed the annexation of Cuba and was quoted as saying that before supporting Stebbings he would consent to become President himself.

In his speech formally accepting the people's nomination, Stebbings told the cheering crowd of patriots before his house that "All things to all men" would be his motto. It was his opinion, he said, that "the smell of gunpowder is the true presidential perfume," and "military glory . . . the only true national glory."

The Stebbings program for America and the Stebbings integrity and strength of character, which caused him during the campaign to announce his refusal to equivocate and straddle issues (although he did tell the people of Maine that he favored their law against liquor but was opposed to its being enforced) were so attractive to the voters that as the 1852 election approached a Stebbings victory seemed almost certain. Even the opposition press appeared to concede it. The New York *Post,* supporting the Democratic candidate, General Franklin Pierce, predicted this distribution of electoral votes: Pierce, 214; Scott, 25; Doubtful, 57. The New York *Tribune,* supporting the Whig candidate, General Winfield Scott, predicted this distribution of electoral votes: Pierce, 82; Scott, 134; Doubtful, 80.

Without Halpine's explanation, it would perhaps be difficult to interpret these numbers. The Doubtful votes were in reality for Stebbings, giving the hero of Spunkville a total of 137 certain votes. When added to the 214 votes allotted to Pierce by the *Post,* Stebbings had a total of 351, and a landslide victory over the highest total which could be claimed for Scott. On the other hand, if the certain Stebbings votes were added to the 134 predicted for Scott by the *Tribune,* Stebbings would have 271 to Pierce's 214, the most which even the *Post* could scrape together for the Democratic candidate. Either way, Stebbings was the sure victor, and the next President of the United States.

But statistics in the American sport of president-making are often wrong, even when given the most judicious analysis. The *Carpet-Bag* took Stebbings' defeat with good grace—by ignoring it, although it printed one story that the Ensign's neighbors had almost been able to send him to Congress by way of compensation. Shortly after Pierce's inauguration, Stebbings himself wrote that he had been appointed postmaster at Spunkville. His spirit and patriotism unchanged by defeat, he was well pleased with the new President, having arranged with him for moving the old Secretary of War to the State Department, and for appointing another military hero, Jefferson Davis, to the War Department.

These were the appearances, however, of a ghost. The fact was that Stebbings was dead, and that Shillaber had paid him a formal goodbye right after the election. Stebbings had been intended, wrote Shillaber, as a rebuke through satire of "the gunpowder spirit which invariably attends our Presidential elections." But readers who had not understood that it was a hoax, and thin-skinned politicians who believed themselves the victims of it, had complained, and the *Carpet-Bag* was forced to discontinue the character. It was a great misfortune, Shillaber concluded in the issue for 13 November 1852, for he considered Stebbings the best public myth since the days of the *Spectator*.

It was no doubt good public relations for Shillaber to say that the spoof on American politics had been abandoned because it was so realistic that people took it seriously, and so deadly accurate in its satire that politicians were embarrassed by it. But why were inquiries and protests not welcomed as proof that the parody was a success? Why was such a good thing not continued? The most probable answer is that Jehiel Stebbings offended more than a few politicians. It is likely that many readers resented the burlesque of their nation's leaders, political institutions, and foreign policy, that the blustering kind of patriotism which Halpine was satirizing was incapable of laughing at itself, that, in short, Jehiel Stebbings was considered unpatriotic. If so, it would be necessary to sacrifice him, for the *Carpet-Bag* had already antagonized too many readers.

During the middle of the Stebbings campaign, Halpine purchased a quarter interest in the *Carpet-Bag* (evidently he had resources of his own, or was assisted by Margaret's father or by an Aunt Eliza in Brooklyn), and beginning with the July 3, 1852, issue, was listed with Shillaber as editor. No change in editorial policy resulted until late in August, when Shillaber departed for a vacation in his native New Hampshire, leaving Halpine in charge.

In the character of Jehiel Stebbings, Halpine had created an outlet for his dislike of American patriotic arrogance. But in his cosmopolitan though immature mind there were strong opinions on other subjects still unexpressed. Feeling newly authoritative in his capacity of editor-proprietor, he began to express them when Shillaber went away.

In particular, he expressed his disgust with the level of public taste which gave so much popularity to "Blood and Thunder" romantic novels and inferior sentimental poetry, and with the writers who pandered to it. The readers of novels, he claimed, were not interested in the development of character; they did not want to be led step by step through the operations of a real human passion, but preferred "to have their feelings roused as by the bursting of a mine." They were entertained by the sensational and the grotesque, no matter how unrealistic, and were moved more by contradictions in character, no matter how absurd, than by logic and consistency. Thus, a murderer was presented as a highly moral man, a savage as a student of theology, a temperance advocate as an opponent of the Maine law. The writing of such novels, Halpine declared, could be reduced to fixed rules and be performed by anybody. A few years later, he proved it.

To satirize this genre of popular literature, which, unlike the dime novels of later decades, appealed to latent snobbery by describing the adventures of aristocrats, Halpine published in September issues of the *Carpet-Bag* what purported to be excerpts from a novel entitled *The Parricide's Pardon: A Thrilling Narrative,* by "Terrible Horrofed, C. G. H."

The story tells of the love of Reginald de Montmorency and Madeline de Mowbray. Because his father opposed their marriage, Reginald decapitates him and takes his head in a valise as a present to Madeline. He is forced to fight a duel with a rival suitor, however, and while preoccupied with sword-play, the valise is stolen by a Jew, who applies a secret salve and reattaches the head to the body of the senior Montmorency. In the meantime, Madeline's Nubian servant reveals himself as a French marquis who had long loved her and become her slave in order to be near her. At first repulsed by the black man's profession of love, Madeline is impressed with his rank, and upon proof that his color was only burnt cork, agrees to marry him instead of Reginald. Meeting Reginald as she emerges from the church on the arm of her new husband, Madeline says, "Guess you've missed it this time."

"And it is for this," exclaims Reginald, "that I murdered the best of fathers, and carried his head in a valise!"

"Weep not, my son," says his father, who had been standing behind a nearby pillar, "weep not dear Reginald, your father lives to forgive and bless you for your thoughtless deed."

Because of his refined sensibilities, the shock of seeing his father alive causes Reginald temporarily to lose his sanity. But he recovers, learns that the Marquis had fallen and broken his neck the morning of his wedding, is reunited with Madeline, and lives happily ever after with her.

Longer excerpts from a similar burlesque (which also dealt with the subject of parricide) were published during the fall months. Although Halpine's criticism of trashy romantic novels would not be considered particularly objectionable today, it was so overdrawn that at the time of publication some readers found it more offensive than amusing. Halpine alienated them by maliciously ridiculing their taste in light reading, just as through Jehiel Stebbings he had offended one segment of the public by ridiculing its most sacred patriotic sentiments. No doubt Halpine also lost friends for the *Carpet-Bag* among the writers of fiction (in Boston especially, one may suppose), just as the Stebbings sketches had lost them among politicians.

But it was in his sarcastic attacks on minor New England newspaper poets that Halpine did most to change the character of the *Carpet-Bag*. It was published "For the Amusement of the Reader," the paper regularly announced beneath its masthead—until October 16, 1852, when "For the Week Ending . . ." was substituted. By then the change was several weeks overdue.

One poet whose work Halpine subjected to a scorching critique was "Lilian May," whose incompetent and insipid verse he had been willing to forgive only while he believed her to be a simple school-girl. When she turned out to be, instead, "a long-faced, sickly-looking, narrow-headed youth, with a feeble attempt at a corsair expression of face, hair sedulously brushed back to develop his 'ample brow,' and his collar turned down a la Byron," Halpine announced that his patience was exhausted. "Endurance has its limit," he said. Two weeks later he again referred to the poetry of Lilian May, but refrained from additional criticism because "we have already wasted too much time on this grasshopper of absurdity." And he never did tell his readers who the poet really was.

Of another aspiring poet, Halpine wrote: "Somewhere up in the neighborhood of Worcester lives a young person called Jillson, who believes himself possessed with the spirit of poetry; and, not content with the satisfaction of the private belief, seeks to induce the public into a similar mistake." An analysis of some of his metaphors and rhymes pretty well proved that Jillson was indeed mistaken.

It is by no means impossible that such critiques were hoaxes, that Halpine published some of his own inferior verses under the pseudonyms Lilian May and C. Jillson, and then gratified his taste for deception by giving an identity to the mythical poets and proceeding to tear his own work apart. In a July, 1852, article he demonstrated with playful seriousness that Coleridge's "The Ancient Mariner" was much inferior to the creations of modern poets "like the Jillsons, Handiboes, Wideswarths, Bones, Broadbents, and Lilian Mays." Since Wideswarth was one of Shillaber's pseudonyms and Broadbent one of Halpine's, it is not farfetched to believe that the other names, too, might have been used by either or both of the editors. But Handiboe was almost certainly somebody else, and therefore Jillson and Lilian May might also have been the names or pseudonyms of other persons. In any case, the spirit of the articles involving them, more venomous than amusing, was new to the *Carpet-Bag*.

Recalling Halpine's literary critiques, the publisher J. C. Derby declared that Halpine was "a remorseless writer," who "dashed among people right and left, impaling them upon his pen-point and showing them no mercy." [9] The man who felt the stab of Halpine's steel most keenly was Edward J. Handiboe, the pseudonym of the author of stories and poems published in many newspapers and magazines, including the *Carpet-Bag*. In a September, 1852, essay entitled "The Pirate's Doom," Halpine called him a plagiarist, accusing him of searching for stories in obscure English journals, giving them new titles, adding a certain amount of bombast and bad grammar to appeal to popular taste in romantic fiction, and passing them off as his own. When his piracies were discovered, he fled to New York, Halpine continued, but he was exposed there, too, and had recently returned to Boston. A young man "of superficial education, and a capacity not much below the ordinary level," Handiboe possessed one virtue: "He is ashamed of his conduct, and conceals his name." Two weeks later, when Halpine reported that a number of writers had combined to help each other combat *Carpet-Bag* criticism, he said their articles would expose them for fools more certainly "than we could do, if, after having exhausted the dictionary of literary abuse, we were even to go to the extreme of calling them each a Handiboe."

It was more than Handiboe could stand. According to Trowbridge, who wrote of the affair in his *Independent* article a half-century later,

Handiboe (Trowbridge remembered his name as "Hardiboe") determined to punish Halpine on the field of honor, if not in the courtroom.
Seconds were chosen, Trowbridge representing Halpine, and preparations made for a trip across the Canadian border. The seconds had con-
spired to prevent casualties, but before the duel could be held, Trowbridge wrote, the matter "was precipitated to a most unlooked for
calamitous conclusion, the circumstances of which, although I was
deeply concerned in it, cannot be related here." Whatever happened,
whether Handiboe committed suicide or experienced a breakdown of
some kind, it had a deep effect upon Halpine, and brought his brief
career as associate editor of the *Carpet-Bag* to a sudden end.

It also caused him within a short time to leave Boston and take up
residence in Brooklyn with his Aunt Eliza, whom he had visited the
previous July in order to greet his sisters, who had apparently just
arrived from Ireland. In letters to the *Carpet-Bag,* he had then described
the joyful family reunion and a busy July 4 in Manhattan, including visits
to Central Park, Barnum's Museum, and the City Hall, where Henry
Clay's body was lying in state. New York, he had reported, "is for
Stebbings to a man."

As a New Yorker, Halpine continued with decreasing frequency to
send pieces to Shillaber for the *Carpet-Bag,* most often using the name
"David Goldthwaite." In a few of them, his mood was light and happy.
His "Vision of the Letters" in the 11 December 1852 issue describes a
dream of "A Lazy Correspondent" about his mail.

> Epistles full of solid sense,
>   And billets full of fun,
> Long letters from his reverence,
>   And short ones from a dun;
>
> Some notes that make my bosom bleed,
>   And some that make my pocket,
> One with a sermon on the creed,
>   And one that brings a locket.
>
> This says my uncle has the gout,
>   And that, my cousin's seedy,
> And here are half a score about
>   The widowed and the needy.
>
> Letters of every sort and size,
>   Sad, solemn, bright, and funny,

"But ah!" my soul, despairing, cries,
"Not one that covers money!"

More reflective of his state of mind during his first months in New York was his letter describing Christmas Day. Feeling depressed and much older, he portrayed David Goldthwaite as a middle-aged man who recalled the happiness with which as a youth he had left the school of Didymus Dunderhead to spend the Christmas holiday at home, how he and his friends had felt the stinging cold of the coach ride, how they had been warmed by brandy, the coachman's rough stories, and their own high spirits, how they had reveled in warm welcomes, and stuffed themselves with delicacies. Today it was different. There was still mistletoe above the door, but the bespectacled woman who sat opposite and called him "my dear" could not really be "the blue-eyed fairy in pink silk" he had once so longed to kiss. And the beef was tougher than it used to be. Even the sports were different. That morning as he walked across the dirty snow, he had witnessed a group of men taking turns shooting at a chicken tied to a log. "At every discharge the poor bird tumbled over, and a handful of feathers were scattered; she got on her legs again and the next—Man—fired. This was repeated some thirty times, until the mangled carcass lay quiet in the sleep of death.

"A merrie Christmas to you, gentlemen," concluded David Goldthwaite.

Charles G. Halpine survived, but the *Carpet-Bag* did not. At the end of its second year, March 26, 1853, Shillaber announced his intention—never fulfilled—to convert it into a monthly magazine, the *Pocket Carpet-Bag.* The change was necessary, he said, because his refusal to publish the trash that was submitted to him had offended those who contributed it, and caused them to withdraw their patronage. "We have received more insults from boorish and vulgar subscribers with regard to our course than we ever thought we could stand," he declared.

If Shillaber really believed it was Halpine's intemperate criticism of local writers which turned readers against the *Carpet-Bag,* he never said so publicly, and he remained a good friend for the rest of his headstrong junior editor's life.

CHAPTER 2

A Literary Swiss

IT IS IMPOSSIBLE to say when Halpine began to drink excessively. Perhaps it was when he could not allow himself to escape responsibility for whatever it was that happened to Handiboe. Perhaps it was while a student at Dublin, or while studying law and writing for the papers in London. Perhaps it was early in his long separation from Margaret and his infant daughter, still waiting in England for him to make good in America. Whenever it was, and whether it was because of a sense of guilt or loneliness or his fear of failure, he drank compulsively for the rest of his life. In later years he experienced acute headaches and trouble with his eyes, and he drank to relieve these maladies, as well. Periodically, he suffered attacks of what was called "brain fever," an interacting combination of physical disorders, psychological tensions, and alcohol. He drank heavily and suffered mightily while the attacks lasted, and swore never to touch another drop when they were over. One of his worst attacks, during which he was cared for by Trowbridge, took place just before he left Boston.[1]

That liquor was the principal cause of his illnesses and that it was certain to interfere with his career, his friends told him and he told himself, repeatedly. When Trowbridge received a copy of Halpine's first book of poems, he wrote to him that he hoped the spirit revealed in the poetry would someday be free. "That spirit I love & reverence," he said, "—for I know what it is capable of: it's a spirit such as not one man in thousands ever dreamed of—& I want to see it free to soar. You yourself can have no conception of what you would be able to do in moving the hearts of men to true, great & noble aspirations, if—" [2] The implications of the "if—" were enough to drive Halpine back to the bottle.

Halpine's arrival in New York coincided with the peak of anti-foreign sentiment, and it was difficult for an Irishman, even a Protestant Irishman, to find a job.

16

During the years between 1820 and 1846, 500,000 immigrants arrived in the United States from Ireland. Most of them were able to find jobs, though by the middle 1840's the labor shortage which had characterized America from the time of Columbus was being replaced by a labor surplus, and there was an inevitable decline in wages and the quality of working conditions. The decline approached a collapse by the 1850's. Between 1847 and 1854 alone, well over one million Irishmen fled the famine resulting from the failure of the Irish potato crop for three successive years, and arrived in the eastern industrial centers hungry and desperate for work. It was not only the competition for jobs which made them unpopular. Their presence in such large numbers profoundly changed the character of the cities where they concentrated by introducing problems like crime, disease, and tenement slums, for which they were held personally responsible. Their religion, too, and their accents, were resented by the native-born, many of whom saw them as a foreign subversive influence in American society. A nativist reaction against them and against other immigrant groups, as well, was only natural. It was a subject which occupied Halpine's attention during the Civil War, when Irishmen were sometimes more disliked than southern rebels.

Through Charles W. Greene, founder and editor of the Boston *Post,* New England's leading Democratic newspaper, Halpine might have obtained a patronage position of some kind, but, he wrote to Margaret in December, 1852, "I have thrown myself upon the pen for support, and mean to sink or swim as a simple author." That he had already made something of a splash (if not much money), was demonstrated by the large bundle of his published poems, stories, essays, and political pamphlets which he prepared to send her. His pamphlets, he said, had "worked miracles in my favor among the democratic party." As a "simple author," he kept himself busy writing New York correspondence for the Boston *Post* and Boston *Evening Traveller*—his pieces were entertaining and much talked about, wrote Shillaber in 1853, adding a newspaperman's advice to "give 'em gossip"—and he sold occasional articles to the New York papers.

He also tried to promote a gigantic panoramic painting of the Crystal Palace erected on Sixth Avenue as the main attraction of the international fair held in New York in 1853. At the peak of their popularity in mid-century, panoramic lectures featured long canvas paintings moved across a stage from one roller to another, while a speaker explained the passing spectacle. A panoramic lecture devoted to the Crystal Palace and New York City was bound to be popular with hinterland Americans,

Halpine believed, and he wanted to tour the country with it. An explanatory guidebook, in which advertising space could be sold, would be an additional source of income. He found two backers who said they were willing to put up a few thousand dollars and give him a full partnership in exchange for the idea and the writing of the guidebook, but apparently the money did not materialize, for the panorama was not completed.[3]

While working on the project in a small office on Nassau Street, Halpine lived with Aunt Eliza in South Brooklyn, devoting his evenings to collecting and revising some of his poems for book publication. The household consisted of admiring women: Aunt Eliza, his sisters, with whom he joked and sang for an hour or two after dinner, and his mother, who had either joined her daughters or accompanied them from Ireland. Still absent after two and one-half years was his wife.

It was no simple lack of funds which kept Margaret so long in England. In all likelihood, she felt deep reservations about joining her young and erratic husband in a strange land across the ocean. A member of a family which was proud of its descent from Colonel John Lane and his wife, Lady Jane, who had assisted in the escape of Charles II following his defeat by Cromwell at Worcester in 1650, and after the Restoration enjoyed the honor, rewards, and prestige of royal favor, Margaret had led a life sheltered by the satisfactions and securities of wealth and social position. She already possessed the good life which most emigrants went to America to seek; if she went, she would be giving it up. No doubt her parents, anxious to hold on to their daughter and granddaughter, played upon her fears and contributed to her reluctance to leave. Whether deliberately or not, Halpine himself must have done so, for he told Margaret soon after moving to Brooklyn that one member of his family would not be happy to see her. Aunt Eliza had opposed their marriage, was hoping to prevent their reunion, and had sworn never to live in the same house with Margaret. His mother and sisters were very angry with her, Halpine wrote, but he himself would always be grateful for her kindnesses to him.

Unquestionably, Halpine wanted Margaret to be with him. In long letters written during the winter he told her how he liked to imagine himself seated at a large table piled high with manuscripts, while Margaret read aloud before a blazing fire and the baby played on the hearth rug. He carried some of his wife's hair in a locket on his key chain, and he had her initials and Syble's engraved on the inside of his signet ring. And yet, he too had reservations, for during the months they had lived together, he had found her cold, a disturbing fact for a more-than-ordinarily amorous young man. Shillaber, with whom he had discussed the problem and who was anxious for his younger friend to have the steadying influence of a wife at his side, tried to be reassuring. Margaret's coldness, he told Halpine, was probably only a kind of protection against his excesses. *"You* are impetuous," he said, "—too much so, perhaps— and you must curb that passion which has brought you sorrow, and . . . *she* may become warmer." Margaret was certainly too conscious of rank and family, Shillaber conceded in a fatherly letter, 27 November 1852, but she would soon learn that America was different from the Old World and adjust to it.

Margaret came to the United States in February, 1853, and remained with her husband ever after. She bore him seven children (all but one of whom survived their father), managed his household, nursed him during his attacks of brain fever, forgave his infidelities, and through a long widowhood revered his memory. Halpine was devoted to Margaret (although a family tradition says he did not always treat her well), adored his children, reproached himself for his lapses, resolved continually to reform, and drove himself to make a name and fortune to redeem his shortcomings. One of his poems, "Duet for the Breakfast Table," between the Romantic Husband and the Sensible Wife, reads like a very nearly literal transcription of what must have been a frequently held conversation.

> Thou art my love!—I have none other,
>   But only thee,—but only thee—
>   Now Charles, do stop this silly bother,
>   And drink your tea,—your cooling tea!
>
> Your eyes are diamonds,—gems refined,—
>   Your teeth are pearl,—your hair is gold,—
>   O nonsense now!—I know you'll find
>   Your cutlets cold,—exceeding cold.
>
> Where'er thou art, my passions burn;
>   I envy not the monarch's crown!
>   Put some hot water in the urn,
>   And toast this bread, and toast it brown!
>
> Had I Golconda's wealth, I say,
>   'Twere thine at will, 'twere thine at will;
>   Then let me have a check to pay
>   The dry-goods bill—that tedious bill!

O heed it not, my trembling flower!—
  If want should press us, let it come!
    And, apropos, the bill for flour
      Is quite a sum,—an unpaid sum.

So rich in love—so rich in joy—
  No change our cup of bliss can spill.
    Now do be quiet:—you destroy
      My cambric frill,—my well-starched frill.

Ha! senseless, soulless, loveless girl,
  To sympathy and passion dead!
    A moment since I was your pearl,
      Your only love—at least, you said.

I spoke it in the bitter jest
  Of one his own deep sadness scorning.
    Well, candor is at all times best;
      I wish you, sir, a fair good morning! [4]

Looking back on her first months in America, when she was faced
with so much that was new and different, and her husband was struggling
to establish himself as a writer, Margaret remembered that things had
been "very hard." [5] They remained very hard until the spring of 1854,
when one of Halpine's poems inspired by the Anthony Burns case made
a favorable impression on Horace Greeley and launched Halpine's
career in New York journalism.

Burns was a slave in Richmond, Virginia; he had stowed away on a
ship and landed in Boston, where he was discovered by his owner. Under
the terms of the Fugitive Slave Act of 1850, his master was able to re-
claim him in a simple hearing before a United States Commissioner, take
him through the streets of Boston to the docks with an escort of United
States soldiers, and carry him back to slavery in a United States naval
vessel. The employment of the United States government as a slave-
catching and slave-delivering agency caused indignation all over the
North, even among many men previously uninvolved in the slavery
controversy. It prompted Halpine, who was shocked to find the United
States cast in England's role of oppressor, to write four angry poems,
which were published anonymously in Henry Ward Beecher's *Independent* and the New York *Tribune*. One of them in particular, "Hail to
the Stars and Stripes," but more often referred to as "The Flaunting
Lie," attracted Greeley.

Tear down the flaunting Lie!
Half-mast the starry flag!
Insult no sunny sky
With this polluted rag!
Destroy it, ye who can!
Deep sink it in the waves!
It bears a fellow-man
To groan with fellow-slaves.[6]

These lines, so utterly unlike those of Jehiel Stebbings, expressed Greeley's own sense of outrage at slavery's desecration of the American flag, and aroused the editor's professional interest in the young writer. As the years passed, his interest became increasingly personal and paternal, and there came to be a room in the house on West Forty-Seventh Street—"Uncle Horace's room," Syble called it—where Greeley sometimes spent the night when his wife was away at their country home.

At about the same time that Halpine found the doors of the New York newspaper offices opening to him, his stature as a writer was enhanced by the publication of his book of poems by J. C. Derby of New York. *Lyrics by the Letter H.,* published anonymously, was almost universally well-received. Reviews in the Boston and New York press were enthusiastic. The July, 1854, *Harper's New Monthly Magazine* called the poems "gay, sparkling, and humorous," said they possessed "true poetic fire," and declared that their author showed great "satirical power, a quick, glancing wit, and an uncommon grace and facility of versification. His more earnest efforts betray noble humanitarian sympathies, and indicate a generous and impulsive nature. The contents of this volume prove that he possesses genius worthy of the severest culture; and," continued the reviewer in a passage which makes it practically certain he knew the author's identity, "if he is not seduced by the perilous ease with which he apparently produces his best things, we shall look for riper and still more delicious fruits from its maturity."

If the enthusiasm of some reviewers makes one suspect personal friendship for the author, there is no doubt whatsoever about the personal enmity of the reviewer for *Putnam's Monthly,* identified by Francis Wolle as FitzJames O'Brien, another young Irish immigrant and writer.[7] Most of the *Lyrics,* O'Brien pointed out in the August issue, had been previously published in the newspapers, "in which place," he declared, "they ought to have remained. We look in vain through this volume for any evidence of imagination or taste." O'Brien accused "H" of imitating Edgar Allan Poe, Thomas Moore, and Charles Mackay, and said he lacked boldness, knowledge of life, dramatic fire, and enthusiasm. He did not possess "even the slight qualifications of cultivation and elegance." The frequency of references in his verse to wine and overflowing flagons, O'Brien continued, revealed "H" to be a "bacchanal." When in one poem he spoke instead of "a pail of ocean brine," it must have been because "H. G[reeley].—or some other prophet of temperance, was seated in the next box, and in such a neighborhood, 'H' durst not call for his usual bottle of Asmanhausen." The poems were "trashy newspaper squibs." In the entire volume, there was "nothing to charm, nothing to teach." Why was such a book inflicted upon the public? O'Brien, pretending ignorance of "H's" name, imagined a brash young man appearing with his manuscript at the publisher's office and overcoming the publisher's natural caution and good judgment with sheer arrogance and persistence. He expressed his indignation at the audacity of the scene, and concluded his review with some advice to the author: "If he is young, we would seriously advise him to turn his attention to something else."

It was, of course, not *Lyrics by the Letter H.* which inspired this devastating review, but the stinging literary criticism which Halpine had published in the *Carpet-Bag*. Indeed, O'Brien might himself have been the Lilian May, the C. Jillson, or even the Edward J. Handiboe whose works Halpine so cruelly ridiculed. If not, he might have been a friend of one of those writers, or for some reason have wished to avenge them by giving their critic a massive dose of his own medicine. O'Brien's hatred for Halpine might also have been political; Halpine wrote for the Democrats, O'Brien for the Whigs. Halpine was a professional Irishman, and O'Brien, according to Augustus Maverick, who knew him, "was absurdly ashamed of his Irish birth." [8]

Derby's own account of how he happened to publish Halpine's book is quite different from the confrontation between author and publisher imagined by O'Brien. Halpine appeared at his office one day, Derby wrote, with a letter of reference from Shillaber, which described him as a brilliant writer on any subject, but a born poet and a genius in wit and humor. The letter was just another of Mrs. Partington's jokes, said Halpine, as he handed his manuscript across the desk. Derby said he published *Lyrics* because "I liked the man and his verses." [9]

It was untrue that Halpine's need for drink was betrayed by his poetry, but the number of his poems about beautiful women does reveal his very great need for love. Like other sensual men married to cold

women, he fell a little bit in love with every beautiful woman he saw.
His love poems, both those in *Lyrics by the Letter H.* and those written
later, dealt not with love in the abstract, but with the passions ignited
within him by particular women, whose anatomy he dared to describe
in terms more specific and graphic than was customary in his time. The
maddening appeal of a woman's form, and the incredible good fortune
of the clothing and either bath or sea water which caressed it were recurring themes in his verse. Nor was the attraction only a matter of
fantasy; he yielded to temptation with women exactly as he did with
liquor, and was equally contrite and self-disapproving of the weakness.
As he put it in "Passion,"

> Could woman's peerless form convey
>   Its beauty only to the brain,
> How many a cheek were dry today,
>   Down which the tides of anguish rain!
>
> It may not be! The inner fire
> Defies reproof's exterior flood;
> It is in the marrow of the bone—
>   The surging current of the blood!

Many of the *Lyrics* possessed the qualities which O'Brien said they
lacked, especially boldness, dramatic fire, and knowledge of the world.
What they really lacked was originality, finish, and maturity, qualities
which might have developed as the author grew in self-confidence. But
self-confidence was something in which Halpine, for all his aggressive-
ness, was pathetically deficient. In "We Might Have Been," he described
the whisper which tormented his sleepless nights:

> As memory bids the past arise,
> The soaring hopes that swept the skies,
> (Each in its narrow grave now lies,)
> We hear, and not with tearless eyes,
>   "You might have been—you might have been."
>
> We might have won the meed of fame,
> Essayed and reached a worthier aim—
> Had more of joy and less of shame,
> Nor heard, as from a tongue of flame,
>   "You might have been—you might have been."

At the age of twenty-five, the just-published poet believed he was a
failure.

His enormous vitality, his warmth of character, and his Irishman's
wit and volubility won Halpine an ever-widening circle of friends among
the writers and journalists of New York, and he was a popular member
of the group of bright young men who used to gather for sparkling drink
and conversation at Pfaff's on lower Broadway. Nothing perishes more
quickly than a barroom witticism, but it is easy to imagine the happy
tumult Halpine caused when he replied to a reference to a certain English aristocrat who was a Knight of the Garter, a Knight of the Bath,
and a Knight of the Golden Fleece, by exclaiming that his name was
Michael Murphy, "night before last, night before that, last night, tonight,
and every domed night—Michael Murphy." On another occasion, he
convulsed the house at Pfaff's with a reference to "H-H-Harriet Be-
seecher Bestowe." [10]

The city's major editors also recognized his extraordinary abilities.
James Gordon Bennett, editor and publisher of the *Herald,* took very
nearly as personal an interest in him as Horace Greeley, and it was in
the pages of the *Herald* that Halpine became famous. Among his other
special friends were Henry J. Raymond of the *Times,* Charles A. Dana
of the *Tribune,* and Frederic Hudson of the *Herald.* For them all and
others, he dashed off copy on an astonishing range of subjects. "As a
translator of the continental languages he was employed by one paper,"
wrote the *Herald* a decade later, "while for another he discussed in a
masterly manner leading general and local political questions of the day,
and at the same time he would prepare a severe criticism on some professional subject for a monthly and then turn his attention to a pathetic
poem or rolicking song for one weekly, while for another he would
illustrate its columns with a stirring story founded on some legend or
historical statement."

In order to maintain such a frenetic pace, Halpine was forced to
write rapidly, feverishly, and he seldom took time to revise or polish.
He cared nothing for style, wrote Roosevelt, but "worked for a purpose."
Putting an idea on paper was the important thing for him, and once it
was down, he hurried on to the next. As the reviewer of *Lyrics* in *Harper's* observed, that was no way to write poetry! But he had a gift for
words which flowed in easy cascades from his pen, and he quickly rose
to the top ranks of New York journalism. Driven on by his nervous
energy, by his wide-ranging mind, and by his ambition, he wrote for
long stretches at a time, filling up page after anonymous page until he
became physically exhausted.[11] He wrote as he drank, compulsively. "I
weary of my pen," he once said.

I weary of my pen,
And write not of mine own accord;
It was my slave, and I was happy then;
'Tis now my lord.[12]

Often his physical exhaustion was accompanied by such nervous restlessness that relaxation became impossible, and he would feel it necessary to drink himself into unconsciousness. Then he would awake with an attack of brain fever, and drink more to escape its torments. Eventually he would recover, and with genuine contrition and resolution for future good behavior, begin writing again.

It may have been after such an attack early in 1856 that Halpine left the deadly pace and pressure of the metropolis, and moved his family—a second daughter had been born in November, 1853—to the rural quiet of Astoria, Long Island. Probably he considered the move as no more than a means of recovering his health and making a fresh start on his career in New York, but Margaret may have hoped that he would be content to remain in the country. The *Irish-American,* New York's leading weekly for the Irish-born, had agreed to publish stories dealing with Irish history and the experiences of Irish immigrants in America. If these proved sufficiently popular, her husband might decide to give up journalism and politics, and settle down to the life of a country gentleman and novelist. In the meantime, he was close enough to the city to write occasionally for the papers and to maintain his political friendships in the Democratic organization, Tammany Hall.

Between May, 1856, and December, 1857, Halpine published serially in the *Irish-American* a total of six novels and a novelette under the pseudonym "An Irish Collegian." Four of them [13] dealt with incidents in Irish history, and were designed to keep hatred for England and hope for Ireland's ultimate liberation alive in the hearts of Irish-Americans. To counteract the perversions of English history, which treated Englishmen as superior beings and Irishmen as mere barbarians, he personalized the burning, pillaging, raping, spying, blackmail, and betrayal which characterized English tyranny. Of course his characters were oversimplified representations of good and evil, and his plots over-involved romances of devotion, deception, sacrifice, love, and war—all of them with unhappy endings.

The three American novels, by way of contrast, had happy endings.[14] Each had its full complement of villains (one of them, "Knightly Fitz-James," bearing the name of Halpine's bitter enemy), but all were in the end exposed and destroyed, and the heroes and heroines lived happily ever after. In *Us Here, or A Glimpse Behind Know-Nothingism,* the major villain is the English minister to the United States, anti-Catholicism is called a revival of Orangeism, and the whole anti-foreign movement is said to be "armed to the teeth with English weapons, and breathing English hate and English blasphemy, and with an English thirst for Irish blood," but there is little propaganda or even social commentary in the other two. For the most part, they are pure romance adventures involving mysteries, secrets, crimes, treasures, and true love.

The novels are innocent of some of the literary crimes which Halpine condemned so vigorously in his *Carpet-Bag* essays, but they are guilty of others, and in general are probably almost as routine and formalized as most of the work he criticized. To the biographer, however, they are important for the passages suggestive of Halpine's own character and experience. In the *Willows of the Golden Vale,* for example, which was later published as a book under the title *The Patriot Brothers* (Dublin, 1869), the hero, John Sheares, speaks to the mother of his sweetheart, who wants him to give up his anti-English politics. "I tell you once and for all, Mrs. Steele," declares the young man,

> that so long as I remain in Ireland—so long as I am forced to witness the oppression without a parallel in history, to which my countrymen are forced to submit at the bayonet's point—so long as the cry of the injured and the innocent rings in my ears through all the hours of the day, and all the watches of the night—so long as my path is beset by perjured spies and paid stiletto men—so long as I see nobility of soul rewarded with the dungeon and the rope, while infamy is exalted to the seats of power, and rules as best it pleases—so long, in fact, as I see around me the picture Ireland now presents, so long must I remain an active and untiring opponent of the policy by which this country is misgoverned.

It is easy to imagine this speech as the echo of one delivered on some impassioned occasion to Margaret's ardently pro-English parents.

The hero of *Us Here,* Stephen St. George, is an undisguised self-portrait of the author. An Irishman of education but no fortune, St. George made his living as a free-lance writer. He was, Halpine explains, "a literary Swiss—if you have ever heard of that profession; [he] edits books and newspapers, writes verses, novelettes, reviews, political essays and sermons, and is political tutor and spoon-feeder to sucking candidates of the kind described in the conclusion of the preceding chapter. He is a Swiss, we must confess; but like the Swiss, his arms are never turned against the country of his birth." Among the politicians for whom St. George writes speeches is one with whose principles he strongly disagrees. "Whichever way you decide," St. George tells him with reference to a particular policy, "I will find reasons to sustain your course to the best of my ability." But when he learns that the politician was involved with the American, or Know-Nothing, party, the political expression of the prevalent anti-Irish, anti-foreign, sentiment, he resolves never again to use his pen in behalf of a man or a cause in which he did not believe. A "literary Swiss" Halpine remained for the rest of his life. If he did not always remember St. George's resolution, he did not forget it in matters which involved the position of the Irish in America or the ultimate liberation of Ireland from England.

There is a tradition, perpetuated in various articles and biographical directories,[15] that as "Nicaraguan correspondent" for the New York *Times* Halpine reported the filibustering expedition of William Walker in 1855. Although he might easily have written on the subject for the *Times*, it is almost certain that it was not as a correspondent on the scene. There is nothing in any of his known published writings or in any of the hundreds of his private letters which have survived to suggest that he had ever been in Nicaragua, and Margaret, in her biographical sketch of his life, makes no mention of his having been in Central America, a most unlikely omission if he had in fact been there. But, curiously, the latter half of his last novel, *The Title Deeds,* takes place in Nicaragua, and includes a great deal of seemingly authentic detail about the country's politics and geography. If Halpine never went to Nicaragua, he read about it extensively, perhaps as the anonymous "Voice of Nicaragua," whose letters critical of Walker were carried in the *Times* in 1856–57. Indeed, one reader complained to the *Times* that "Voice's" knowledge of Nicaragua seemed based exclusively on second-hand reports.

According to Margaret, Halpine always remembered the time spent at Astoria as the happiest and most peaceful of his life. Certainly, he loved the countryside. His nature walks with his father through rural Ireland were such pleasant memories for him that in the next century his great-grandchildren would hear about them from his grandchildren, and one of the poems in *Lyrics by the Letter H.* describes a conversation between a country breeze and a breeze from New York City and reveals how much he preferred the former.

But by the end of 1857 he seems to have had enough, and perhaps the readers of his novels had had enough, too. With solemn promises to Margaret and a sincere determination to keep them, he moved his growing family—he had a son now, Nicholas John Lane Trowbridge Halpine—back to the city, and reentered upon full-time participation in the world of New York journalism and politics. But it was a different world for him, for he had purchased, at what must have been a bargain price, a one-third interest in a declining Democratic weekly, the New York *Leader.*

The editor of the *Leader* at the time was John Clancy, born in New York of Irish parents, and educated in the rough and tumble of city politics in the Sixth Ward, where he grew up. He studied law in the office of one of the cleverest leaders of Tammany Hall, Peter B. Sweeny, and wrote for the *Leader* from its founding as a pro-Stephen A. Douglas organ. With Sweeny's backing, he simultaneously engaged in politics, serving on both the Board of Councilmen and the Board of Aldermen, in 1859 being elected to the valuable office of County Clerk.[16]

Clancy's political career flourished, but under his editorship the *Leader* did not. Its circulation was only a few hundred when Halpine was brought in to build it up. He soon did so, presenting his readers each week with a lively smorgasbord of literary and political features, serialized novels, personality sketches, travel letters, commentaries upon local, state, and national politics, and a variety of other general interest articles. Within a year or two, circulation had increased to 11,000, and the *Leader* had become a respected and influential journal.[17] If most of its readers were Irishmen, they were the educated leaders of the New York Irish community rather than the unfortunate tenement-dwellers crowded into the lower east side.

For the ghetto Irish, who were perhaps more attracted to the *Irish-American* than to the *Leader,* America meant not freedom and an opportunity to better themselves, but continued poverty and persecution. From the unscrupulous politician Fernando Wood and his ward representatives, however, they received kindly attention and some jobs and favors, and in return they willingly delivered their votes on election day. What difference did it make that Wood was corrupt and a demagogue? He seemed to be on their side at a time when few others were, and they helped elect him Mayor of New York in 1853 and again in 1855.

The masses looked upon Wood as their friend because they could not see that his shameless pillaging of the city would be damaging to themselves in the long run. In the ghetto, after all, there is no long run. But middle-class reformers in the nineteenth century never doubted that the secret of good government was simply a matter of voting dishonest leaders out of office and putting honest men in their place. As a member of the Tammany executive committee, Halpine was one of the reformers who expelled Wood from the Tammany Society and in 1857 nominated Daniel F. Tiemann, a wealthy paint manufacturer, for mayor. Although Wood promptly turned his personal machine into a new organization, Mozart Hall, and fought for a third term, Tiemann had the advantage of general voter alarm over crime and misgovernment, and with Republican support was elected.[18]

The reform administration, anxious to build up its own base of power among the Irish, recognized Halpine's potential influence. Mayor Tiemann employed him as a speech writer and occasional aide, and rewarded him for his support in the *Leader* with a variety of patronage positions. "There was hardly a subordinate office in the city that he did not fill," recalled one associate. He held, among other positions, that of secretary in the Post Office, clerk of indictments, secretary of the Street Department, clerk of chancery records, and commissioner of deeds.[19] The duties of these offices must have been close to nominal, for at the same time he held them, Halpine was doing most of the political writing for the *Leader,* assuming more and more editorial responsibility for the paper, and publishing articles in the big dailies. Fernando Wood may have wondered how the reformers differed from those who had to be reformed, but respectable New Yorkers were sure there was a difference and that it was a significant one.

The common purpose which held Republicans and reform-minded Tammany Democrats together in the mayoralty campaign of 1857 had dissipated by 1859, and in that year both groups put up candidates for mayor. The result was victory for Wood and Mozart Hall. Two years later, Wood was again defeated, but by then the Civil War had distracted the attentions of reformers, or taken them out of the city as soldiers, and William Marcy Tweed and his friends, even greedier and more resourceful than the spoilsmen led by Wood, were able to seize control of Tammany and the city. When Halpine returned to New York in 1864, after three years in the Army, his personal power vastly increased by his national reputation, he once again became a leader in the fight for good government in New York.

If the *Leader*'s chief villain was Fernando Wood, its chief hero was Senator Douglas. Like so many other Democrats, Halpine fell under the spell of the Little Giant, whose captivating personality and inner drive and intensity were much like his own, and he would have sacrificed anything to make him president. Douglas must have liked and respected his young editor, too, for on several occasions he sent him as an emissary to President Buchanan, with whom Douglas had broken over Kansas affairs.

At the 1860 Democratic National Nominating Convention in

Charleston, to which Clancy and Halpine's closest friend, John Savage, were official delegates, Douglas was unable to reunite his party, and the convention adjourned for a month without making any nominations. Ever the optimist and believer in the destiny of his hero, Halpine was sure it was only a temporary setback, that when the convention reconvened in Baltimore Douglas would yet receive the support of southern moderates and go on to win the nomination of the whole party. Somewhat prematurely, as it turned out, he described it happening in a political poem published in the *Leader,* 5 May 1860. Single-handed, the Little Giant overcame his enemies, as the cheers of the American people, recorded at the end of each verse, echoed through the convention hall like an irresistible battle cry from the mountains of Scotland, "A Douglas and a Douglas!"

Despite his devotion to Douglas and the Democratic party, Halpine became a close friend of one of the most powerful leaders of the Republican party, Thurlow Weed, owner and editor of the Albany *Evening Journal.* It began as a relationship between two "literary Swiss." Weed found it convenient to have a friendly Democratic editor in New York City, and planted various stories in the *Leader* which he then reprinted in the *Evening Journal* as indicative of Democratic sentiment. For his part, Halpine was delighted to have such an important contact with the inner circle of Republicanism, and displayed to the future readers of his letters a not very attractive eagerness to please Weed and be of service to him.[20]

And yet it would be wrong to accuse Halpine of simple insincerity and opportunism. His experience with his father, with whom he disagreed violently on the subject which was of more importance to him than any other, had taught him that men could oppose, even fight, each other like gentlemen, without loss of mutual respect or self-respect, and without sacrifice of principle. Halpine could find and keep friends on both sides of most issues and elections, and there is no reason to doubt the sincerity of his often expressed admiration for Weed. Besides, it was only party affiliation which divided these two men of the world, and when the long-standing feud between Weed and Horace Greeley erupted in the presidential campaign of 1860, Halpine deliberately and unnecessarily lined himself up behind Greeley. By doing so, he not only alienated Weed temporarily, but lost an opportunity to go down in history as the first biographer of Abraham Lincoln.

In 1840 and 1848, Weed had been a president-maker, and he expected to be one again in 1860, with his friend and partner, William H. Seward, as his candidate. One of the reasons why he was not was that he and Seward had offended Horace Greeley. As editor of their campaign journals in the 1830's, Greeley had made a major contribution to their achievement of political power, but believed that his services had never been properly acknowledged or rewarded. His sense of injustice turned to humiliation and hatred in 1854, when Seward and Weed supported his rival, Henry J. Raymond of the New York *Times,* for nomination to the political office which he coveted for himself. Following Raymond's election to the office—lieutenant-governor of New York—Greeley wrote a long letter to Seward detailing the wrongs and slights he had suffered, and formally breaking off the old political alliance. Now, in 1860, with the presidential prize for which the two partners so desperately yearned seemingly as good as won, Greeley got his revenge by going to the Republican convention in Chicago and using every power at his command to deprive Seward of the nomination.[21]

Weed quickly recovered from his disappointment, and within a week traveled to Springfield to mend fence rails with the Rail Splitter and to advise him on the campaign. Among other things, he recommended that Lincoln have his biography written by a bright young friend of his in New York, Charles G. Halpine. The next day, Lincoln's friend Leonard Swett, who was present at the interview, advised Lincoln to accept the suggestion.[22] Halpine did not get the chance to write the book because Greeley, to complete his triumph over Seward and Weed, published the text of his own 1854 letter outlining his grievances against them, and Halpine commented favorably upon it in the *Leader,* 16 June 1860.

Greeley, Weed, and Seward, wrote Halpine, had entered politics in partnership. Two of the partners had prospered beyond their fondest hopes, but had left the third behind, a mere private in the ranks, with "no right to draw checks on the joint political bank account." They ignored Greeley. They treated him as if he were "such a good fellow—such a true fellow—such an industrious and contented hack—such a warm-hearted, unselfish friend, that any favor due to him might be better employed in purchasing some venal enemy." Although Halpine did not accept all of Greeley's allegations of betrayal, the tone of his article was decidedly sympathetic to him, and that could only mean that it was antagonistic to Weed. The article would displease Weed, he wrote to Greeley, but he would publish it anyway, because "it is the truth." To Weed, he apologized for anything that might sound "unkind." [23]

Weed did not respond, and the old contacts with him ceased. The two men met once, but Halpine, not knowing what to say about the subject which had come between them, said nothing, and the meeting ended in confusion and embarrassment. The summer passed, and Halpine, distressed at the apparent loss of so agreeable and so powerful a friend, wrote to him to ask "that if you have *ever* found me of the slightest service to you, and I certainly tried my best, you will give me an interview of [a] quarter of an hour at your earliest convenience. I have no other request in the world to make to you." Weed replied that he held no grievance, and the friendship was promptly renewed on a new and more intimate basis. Before long, Weed—like his enemy Horace Greeley—came to look upon Halpine with some of the affection and indulgence of a father for an impulsive son.[24]

CHAPTER 3

Adjutant

HALPINE was among the Democratic editors who scoffed at Lincoln's appearance and belittled his abilities. Adding his own picturesque details, he published in the *Leader* a poetic version—"The Night Ride of Ancient Abe"—of Joseph Howard, Jr.'s, fictitious story that the President-elect had sneaked into Washington in disguise. Two weeks after the inauguration he wrote that the country had already had enough of "ancient Abe, . . . poor bewildered Abe." But Fort Sumter had an impact like Pearl Harbor upon public opinion, and Halpine's pettiness, though not his partisanship, ceased immediately. In fact, he was one of the first to respond to Lincoln's call to arms, and on April 23 marched off to war as a ninety-day volunteer with New York's regiment of Irish militiamen, the famous Sixty-Ninth.

It was an exciting day when the Sixty-Ninth marched down Broadway, its bands playing and the flag of Ireland flying next to that of the United States. New Yorkers crowded the sidewalks and swarmed into the streets, shouting and hugging the soldiers and each other indiscriminately. At the docks, where a transport was waiting to take the regiment to Annapolis, men and boys climbed into the rigging of nearby ships and to the tops of pier sheds to watch the spectacle. So far, there was nothing but glory to war, and the men of the Sixty-Ninth, unaccustomed to being treated like heroes in New York, enjoyed the experience and responded with a swagger. Thanks to the resourcefulness of those who smuggled whiskey aboard, they also enjoyed their short voyage down the coast, though they were momentarily sobered by the disappearance of two men over the side and one down the hatch.

At Annapolis, the duty of the Sixty-Ninth was to guard against sabotage the railroad from Annapolis to the junction with the Baltimore-Washington line, a duty it performed under hardships which seemed nearly unendurable at the time, but later became familiar enough. The men had no protection but their blankets against a week of nearly constant rain, and Halpine, apparently serving as civilian commissary while awaiting a commission as second lieutenant, was able to find them little but salt pork to eat.[1]

The night of their arrival, Halpine volunteered to take dispatches through the unfriendly countryside to Washington. Halfway, at Collington, he was seized as a spy by secessionists, the more ardent of whom threatened to hang him on the spot. But he was rescued by an officer of the Maryland militia, who, failing to find the documents hidden in his boots, accepted his credentials as a newspaperman, and put him on the stage for Washington.[2]

Early in May, the regiment moved into the capital, taking up quarters first at the Catholic college in Georgetown, and, after May 24, across the Potomac, at Arlington Heights, Virginia. By this time, Halpine's commission had arrived, and he was kept busy writing orders, giving passes, questioning prisoners, and performing the other duties of an assistant adjutant for the Sixty-Ninth's commanding officer, Colonel Michael Corcoran, the holder in peacetime of a minor government office by Halpine's appointment. But on May 29, he transferred from the state militia to the United States Volunteer Forces, in order to accept an appointment as *aide-de-camp* to Colonel David Hunter, commander of a brigade composed of three New York regiments, including the Sixty-Ninth. The transfer, he assured Margaret in a letter, did not obligate him to serve more than the original three months, and since Hunter made his headquarters with the Sixty-Ninth, he would not even be separated from the men he knew so well. Of course Margaret was worried about his health with the hard-drinking soldiers, so he said that he was "straight" and meant to keep so.[3]

He also sent her a copy of the orders appointing him to Hunter's staff, but told her not to give it to the newspapers, "as I have a *horror* of appearing to court prominence." And it was true. Halpine was a publicist, but not a self-publicist. As a staff member of the New York *Times,* for which he had been writing editorials since the election—but not those "of a Republican tendency," he explained—he was necessarily anonymous. But the authorship of even his feature articles and Special Correspondence to both the *Times* and the *Leader,* which he sent from the camps around Washington, were disguised by pseudonyms ("Nobody" was one of particular significance), or bore only the initials "H" or "C. G. H." Prominence was something he desperately wanted, more desperately, even, than wealth, but he wanted to become famous in connection with some great achievement which would give him an honored place in history and make his children proud of him. He might have his opportunity in the battle for which the army was preparing. In the meantime, he would bide his time and refrain from calling attention to his every advance in rank and responsibility.

On Arlington Heights, the men of Hunter's brigade began immediately to dig trenches and erect the fortifications which became known first as Fort Corcoran, and then as Fort Lincoln. They were as little prepared for digging in the hot Virginia sun as they were for fighting, and Halpine wrote stories about their need for light clothing in the hope that the people of New York would supply it if the army could not. He also hoped that publicity would stop the contractors who were supplying uniforms which fell apart after a week's wear, but was discouraged to find that the major newspapers were reluctant to publish such reports. In letters to the *Leader* in June, he explained why: "The jobbers and indiscriminate rascals who are now making their booty out of the Public Emergency are both dexterous and ceaseless in suggesting that any criticism of the manner in which affairs are being conducted 'can only tend to aid and comfort the enemy.' " Some editors therefore remained silent. But not Halpine and Clancy, who believed that silence would only permit the further deterioration of conditions, and hoped that "a candid and public exposition of the dangers threatening the commonwealth may serve as the first step towards procuring an efficient remedy."

On June 25 the New York *Times* did publish one of Halpine's less serious and more easily remedied complaints—the easy availability of visitor's passes to the military camps on the Virginia side of the Potomac. The best Washington hotels had stacks of passes already signed to hand out to guests, and in the restaurants, diners could purchase them from waiters for twenty-five cents. The result was an unending and disruptive procession of idly curious civilian visitors, and an utterly indefensible risk to military security.

For the visitors, and even for the officers and men in their camps around Washington, the rebellion was not yet a war. Alarms and skirmishes, quick marches and long waits, tedious watches and arduous duties, heat, rain, bad food, illnesses, and discomforts there were aplenty, but they were all simply part of a memorable adventure, and nobody knew about the nightmare which lay ahead. Morale was therefore high; soldiers sang as they marched in and out of their camps, and officers galloped from place to place with a happy sense of their own importance. Halpine found the life agreeable. "I feel, strange to say," he wrote to Margaret, "that the camp here has become my home; and when returning from Washn the first view caught of the great starry flag floating over Fort Corcoran & the white tents on the hill behind the Fort, gives me all the thrill a man feels when getting within sight of home after a brief sojourn in some detested country."

Working with David Hunter was also agreeable. A "very elegant and courtly gentleman," Hunter was born in New Jersey in 1802, the son of a distinguished Presbyterian clergyman, and the grandson, on his mother's side, of a signer of the Declaration of Independence, Richard Stockton. Graduated from West Point in 1822, Hunter served in the West as an officer of infantry and dragoons. While stationed at Fort Dearborn in the 1830's, he married Martha Kinzie, invested in real estate in the growing village of Chicago, and finally resigned from the army to go into business with his wife's brother. But he rejoined the army in 1842 as a paymaster, for which those who wished later to disparage his ability as a field commander ridiculed him, and served as such during the Mexican War. He met Halpine in 1861, probably through Stephen A. Douglas, his good friend.

On duty in Kansas at the time of the election of 1860 and the secession crisis after it, Hunter wrote to Lincoln to warn him of a rumored assassination plot and to make suggestions for the defense of Washington. As a result of his concern, and no doubt partly because of his Chicago connections, Hunter was invited to accompany the President-elect to the capital. In Buffalo, he earned Lincoln's gratitude when he dislocated his shoulder protecting him against the press of a crowd. After the inauguration, he was assigned the duty of guarding the White House, lived for six weeks in the East Room, and, as a member of the Lincoln household, became acquainted with the President's private secretaries, John G. Nicolay and John Hay, to whom he introduced Halpine.[4]

Hunter was a strict man while on duty, and he kept his officers busy. But he was friendly and polite in an old-fashioned way, enjoyed telling his aide about his adventures fighting Indians and Mexicans, and listened with flattering attention to Halpine's stories of the famous men he knew. Mrs. Hunter lived in Washington, and though the colonel spent most of his nights with his men across the river, he and Halpine often rode into the city for an early breakfast, Halpine carrying a bouquet of roses from Robert E. Lee's estate. He was soon completely at home with the Hunters. Mrs. Hunter worked his name into his saddle blanket; her adopted daughter, Mrs. Stewart, made him a haversack, and he was even given his own room in the house. Hunter often admired a picture of Margaret and the children—there were three girls now, and one boy—and wished he had children of his own.

"He has taken a strange affection for me," Halpine wrote Margaret, "having no son himself; and I feel towards him the most sincere affection."

As the weeks passed and pressure increased from Greeley's *Tribune* and other papers to end the rebellion by simply marching to Richmond and seizing the traitors, it became certain that a battle was imminent. When it came, Hunter, promoted to brigadier general early in July, would play an important role in it, and Halpine therefore wrote to Margaret what to do in case "anything should happen." He wanted her to forgive him for being harsh with her when his system was "deranged," told her he had never loved anyone else ("though I have erred and wandered away more often than it is now pleasant to think of . . ."), and, in the event of his death, advised her to consult with Thurlow Weed and John Clancy, to sell everything, and to return to Ireland. To his children, he sent individual kisses. "Syble, kiss this. I have kissed it. X," and the same for Lucie, Lonnie, and Baby, "(when you are old enough). Kiss this. I have kissed it, X, and am happy." And he was happy. He felt sure that within a short time he would win that which was more important to him than anything else in life—honor and respect. He would either be in a soldier's honorable grave, or he would enjoy a hero's glory, "utterly wiping out anything that may have been unfortunate in the past."

But he was wrong. Destiny passed him by in the summer of 1861, as it would more than once again in the future. When his three-month enlistment expired in mid-July, he returned to New York, and thus missed the battle of Bull Run, in which the casualties suffered by the Sixty-Ninth were heavy, and Hunter himself was wounded.

In August, Lincoln promoted Hunter to the rank of major general of volunteers, and in September asked him to go to St. Louis, where the Union commander, John C. Fremont, was seriously embarrassing the administration by making policy decisions beyond his authority, and antagonizing regular army officers. "He needs to have, by his side," Lincoln told Hunter, "a man of large experience. Will you not, for me, take that place?" [5] Hunter was a man of experience, and he was more tactful and considerate in his personal relations than Fremont, but it was ironic that Lincoln should have selected him as a steadying influence, for within a few months he repeated in another theater the same action for which Lincoln was most critical of Fremont: the freeing of slaves on his own initiative. But Fremont did not want Hunter by his side, and so sent him on to Rolla, Missouri, in charge of a division consisting of only two regiments scattered over Missouri and

Kansas, and neither remotely ready to take the field. So far as Hunter could discover, all the regular army artillery, infantry, and cavalry remained directly under Fremont's command. "I shall remain a zero," he wrote in late September to Halpine, still at his *Leader* desk but not too far away to understand, "until we get another commander."

Early in October, having sold back to Clancy his stock in the *Leader* and put his affairs in order for a prolonged absence, Halpine made his emotional goodbyes to his family and joined Hunter in Missouri as assistant adjutant general, with the rank of major. By this time, Fremont had concentrated his army and was leading it on a much-heralded campaign in southwest Missouri. Halpine took with him a letter of introduction to Fremont from Thurlow Weed, and in presenting it received a taste of the Fremont arrogance. Escorted by two of the German officers with whom Fremont surrounded himself, he found Fremont standing before the door of his tent. One of the Germans took Halpine's letter and deferentially approached his commander with it. Taking it, Fremont tossed it backwards into the tent without even looking at it, gave Halpine a single supercilious glance, and, in the manner of royalty condescending to engage in ordinary conversation, began to exchange pleasantries with the officer. Outraged at the insult, Halpine did an about-face and returned to his quarters. Later, Fremont was apparently impressed by the letter—"one of the warmest & most heartily generous introductions man ever carried to man," Halpine told Weed in thanking him for it—and invited Halpine to call upon him. But Halpine refused, pleading the pressure of his duties.

Like others before him, Halpine soon found Fremont guilty of incompetence, as well as rudeness. One cavalry regiment in Hunter's division had neither swords nor pistols, not a single round of ammunition for its carbines, and two batteries of six-pound cannon had only enough ammunition to fire their guns a few times each. Supply problems were, of course, difficult in Missouri, but Halpine believed that they existed primarily because of private venality, and even treason. "The whole line of railroad between Sedalia & St. Louis," he wrote to Weed on October 17 in one of the most serious charges against Fremont ever to reach Washington,

> is in the hands of a set of irresponsible, non-commissioned German thieves & California rapscallions, who, to the best of my most solemn belief (and my duties have compelled me to investigate this matter closely), are now daily transmitting to [the commander

of the Missouri State Guard, Sterling] Price & the Secession Army *more than half of the army stores forwarded from St Louis to the federal army.* It is now a *rule* that we never receive at the depot quite a full half of the goods invoiced from the St. Louis arsenal.

The man in charge of transportation held no commission, had given no bond, and was responsible to no authority but Fremont, and no improvement could be expected until a new commander was appointed. It was almost impossible to see Fremont, and his staff of German officers, who had little or no personal interest in the war for the Union, treat complaints and requests for redress with contempt.[6]

To Greeley, also, Halpine wrote of Fremont's incompetence. The General, he said on October 10, was as unable to control his army as he was to equip it. Although the area through which it was marching was overwhelmingly friendly to the Union, the undisciplined soldiers were infuriating the people with indiscriminate burning and pillaging. "For God's sake believe me," he told Greeley. "Let us encounter a reverse in front and not a man can ever return to tell the tale; for we shall have left behind us a beggared, maddened, frenzied population, with nothing to lose but life & nothing to hope for but revenge." In a postscript he added, "Speak a good word for Gen. Hunter whenever you can." [7]

A week later, when most of Fremont's army had reached Warsaw, the prospect of encountering a reverse further south seemed remote, because by then Halpine had come to believe—and said so in his letter to Weed—that Fremont did not intend to go any further, and never had intended to. He had neither transportation nor supplies for a battle, and he knew it. He had made his march simply to prevent his own removal by making it seem that he was close to a battle which would crush the rebellion in Missouri and Arkansas and vindicate his months as head of the Department of the West. All of the telegrams and stories to the effect that a battle was imminent, Halpine told Weed, were "simple unadulterated lies."

For many weeks, angry letters about Fremont and demands for his replacement had been piling up on Lincoln's desk, and a long and devastating report by the adjutant general, Lorenzo Thomas, just back from a fact-finding trip to Missouri, was submitted on October 21.[8] By the time Halpine's letter arrived, Weed had read Thomas' report. Even so, he said he was shocked by the "atrocities" which his friend described. "Write often as you can," Weed told him on October 24. "I send your letters (in confidence) to the Secretary of State. Take good care of yourself, my Dear Friend."

The charges that Fremont was arrogant, incompetent, and if not corrupt, then tolerant of corruption were hardly new, but it is possible that Halpine's letter to Weed, with its startling allegation that Fremont never intended to fight, troubled the President most of all. It may have been in his mind, it may even have been at his hand (for it is still among his papers) when he wrote the order of October 24 removing Fremont from command. The order was sent to a brigadier general in St. Louis with instructions that it be promptly delivered unless, when reached by the messenger, Fremont had fought, or was about to fight, a battle. In that case, the order was to be held for further instructions.

When reached by the messenger, Fremont was at Springfield, well past the point where Halpine had said he would stop, but still some seventy miles away from the enemy. The messenger therefore delivered the order, despite Fremont's insistence that he was on the eve of a great victory.[9]

Fremont's successor was none other than David Hunter, who, acting upon a suggestion from Lincoln, broke off the pursuit of Price and returned to the railroad terminals at Sedalia and Rolla to retrain and re-equip the demoralized forces of the Department of the West. But Hunter's command, announced as temporary in the order which gave it to him, lasted only a week. On November 9, a general reorganization of the western military departments resulted in the creation of the Department of Kansas, comprising Kansas, the Indian territory west of Arkansas, and the territories of Nebraska, Colorado, and Dakota, with headquarters at Fort Leavenworth; Hunter was named its commander.[10]

In Kansas, too, Hunter was faced with the problem of turning a mob into an army. The regiments of Kansas infantry and cavalry recruited by the flamboyant Jayhawker and United States Senator James H. Lane, and known as Lane's Brigade, were in worse condition than any of Fremont's troops, and differed little from the gangs of border ruffians from Missouri with whom some of them had fought in the 1850's. As Halpine described them, their camps were vast pig-pens without any semblance of order, cleanliness, or discipline, in which the officers and men mingled, ate, and slept together. Furloughs and leaves of absence were passed out generously, but were taken whether granted or not. Drill was almost entirely abandoned, and the soldiers, a "ragged, half-armed, diseased, and mutinous rabble," took votes to see if unwelcome orders should be obeyed. Vast amounts of public property had disappeared from the department, and horses and other supplies had been purchased with government funds at exorbitant prices.[11]

Reforming and disciplining the Kansas regiments so far removed from the active military theaters was an unpleasant duty for Hunter, who wanted desperately to lead a large and powerful army against the enemies of his country, but he had been assured by men close to Lincoln that the assignment would be a short one. For that reason, Halpine had anticipated it with eagerness. The prospect of a short tour of duty in the American West excited his sense of adventure, and he wrote happily to Margaret in October and November of his chance to hunt buffalo and of a skirmish with pro-southern Indians. He liked the bigness and vigor of life in the West, and even spoke of moving to Kansas someday. "I have tasted nothing stronger than coffee since leaving New York," he told his wife, no doubt with characteristically western exaggeration, "nor will I until the war is over—probably in eight or ten years." He was also pleased to be back with David Hunter, who he never doubted would one day play a major role in the suppression of the rebellion, and who, in the meantime, knew how to whip volunteers into shape without ceasing to be kind and polite—at least to his staff. When God made Hunter, said Halpine, "He took the world's finest clay & broke the die after the cast was perfect."

Hunter's patience, however, was less than perfect as the weeks passed and the promised reassignment did not arrive. Feeling that he had been tricked by Lincoln's friends into accepting virtual banishment, he began to complain about the difficulties he faced. And when Brigadier General Don Carlos Buell was given a command of 100,000 men in Kentucky, while he himself, one of the highest-ranking major generals in the army, commanded only 3,000 men, he lost his temper and wrote directly to the President. "I am very deeply mortified, humiliated, insulted, and disgraced," he exclaimed.

"I am constrained to say it is difficult to answer so ugly a letter in good temper," wrote Lincoln in reply, and then proved himself equal to the challenge. Hunter had been neither wronged nor forgotten, and would someday have a larger command. "I have been, and am sincerely your friend"; the President concluded, "and if, as such, I dare to make a suggestion, I would say you are adopting the best possible way to ruin yourself. 'Act well your part, there all the honor lies.' He who does *something* at the head of one Regiment, will eclipse him who does *nothing* at the head of a hundred." [12]

There was almost a chance to do something in Kansas, after all. During the fall months of 1861, Jim Lane, who had received a brigadier general's commission from Lincoln but who still held on to his senate seat, conferred with the President and the Secretary of War about a plan to lead the Lane Brigade, reenforced with other troops, on a major campaign into north Texas. By the time such a campaign had become a serious possibility, Hunter was commander of the Department of Kansas, and General-in-Chief George B. McClellan assured him he would be allowed to organize and lead the expedition himself. Hunter was delighted, and immediately forwarded his estimate that 30,000 men would be needed, plus a large transportation train to carry supplies on a march of 440 miles.[13]

But Lane, who had gone out to Kansas, was unwilling to see another man lead the expedition he had come to think of as his own, and quarrelled bitterly with Hunter. At last Lincoln himself was forced to intervene, deciding the dispute in Hunter's favor.[14] Lane thereupon attempted to sabotage the expedition by pulling congressional strings. "I have been with the man you name," Representative John Covode of Pennsylvania replied to him by telegraph from Washington. "Hunter will not get the money or men he requires. His command cannot go forward." [15]

Hunter's command might have gone forward anyway, even though Lincoln, favoring "a snug, sober column," reduced its size to between 10,000 and 15,000 men, and rejected Hunter's request to permit the recruitment of Indians.[16] But other campaigns had higher priorities, and Hunter's men were drained off to the support of General Samuel Curtis at Pea Ridge, Arkansas, and General Ulysses S. Grant at Fort Donelson, Tennessee. The rapidity with which Hunter sent reenforcements to Fort Donelson helped make the Union victory there possible, and won him Grant's lasting gratitude.[17]

Early the next month, March, 1862, Hunter went to Washington to testify on Fremont before the Joint Committee on the Conduct of the War, and to try to get himself a new command. Halpine thought that he and an aide, Colonel J. W. Shaffer ("Lincoln's bosom friend & mine"), might visit New York, and was anxious for his home and children to look their best. The house, a modest one on Hammond Street, should be "perfect in its arrangements," he told Margaret, for Shaffer would probably stay in the spare room.

For a short time after Hunter's departure, Halpine was in charge of the Department of Kansas, an area, he wrote home boastfully, larger than all of Europe. Then he, too, left the West, stopping for a day in St. Louis and a long conference with General Henry W. Halleck, who offered him a staff position if he should ever become separated from Hunter.

Looking back on his months in the western theater of war, Halpine saw them as a time of preparation for his services to a general who was about to move from the wings onto the spotlighted military stage. For Hunter had been made commander of the Department of the South, with headquarters at Hilton Head, South Carolina, and given orders to strike against the Confederate ports of Charleston, Savannah, and Mobile. As his adjutant, Halpine would be by his side and share in the glory. "I now do not fear any part of my work," he wrote Margaret, who needed constant reassurances about his drinking, "and am thoroughly competent to the discharge of every duty."

CHAPTER 4

Getting High

THE VOYAGE to Hilton Head at the end of March, 1862, was broken by a short stopover at Fort Monroe, Virginia, one of the few United States forts in the seceded states which never fell to the Confederacy. Halpine examined it carefully, forming the impressions which were later incorporated into a famous book, and watched with fascination the arrival of sixteen steamships, each carrying 1,000 men and towing two or more large schooners full of horses and artillery, part of McClellan's command assembling for the peninsular campaign. He also paid a visit to that "eighth wonder of the world," the *Monitor,* just three weeks after its historical battle with the *Merrimac,* and still showing the marks of it. Its officers escorted him through it, and to his delight made the turret revolve when he was inside. "The possibilities of human power," he declared in a letter to Margaret, "have reached their highest development, thus far, in this magnificent little vessel." A year later, he was not so enthusiastic.

Lying close against the coast between Charleston and Savannah, Hilton Head Island was a flat and sandy triangle, its northern shore curving inward in a gentle arc, half-facing Port Royal Bay and half the Atlantic. Here were located the warehouses, ships, stables, barracks, and tents of what was the major United States military and naval base on the South Atlantic coast. A long wharf was built out into deep water to provide berths for the ships which regularly brought in supplies and equipment for the blockading fleet, and the headquarters building of the Department of the South, a long frame bungalow, was located nearby facing the beach. Next to it was Fort Welles (called Fort Walker before the Union conquest in November, 1861), with its earthworks and guns guarding the approaches from the sea. Despite the presence of the men and equipment of war, there was an unmilitary, tropical resort atmosphere to the base, with its seaward-looking verandas, its bright sun, and its salty breezes.[1]

But it was stimulating simply to be wearing a United States uniform in South Carolina in the spring of 1862, with plans for an attack on Fort Pulaski, guarding Savannah, and, if that proved successful, a similar attack on Fort Sumter. It required only a little imagination to see one's self hoisting the American flag over Charleston, the first rebel city to pull it down, and many men at Hilton Head must have written to their wives, as Halpine did to Margaret, that that was what they hoped to do.

On March 31 Hunter formally assumed command of the Department of the South, which nominally consisted of the states of South Carolina, Georgia, and Florida, but which in reality was confined to a few of the multitude of coastal islands, and installed his adjutant in a room connecting with his own. Morale at headquarters was high, for Hunter continued to be fatherly and considerate, and hinted that Halpine would not have long to wait for a promotion. The food—fish, oysters, fresh fruit, and poultry brought in by the island blacks—was a decided improvement over regular army rations, and a private tub was available for morning and evening baths. There was also an abundance of cheap servants among the Negroes, whom Halpine now saw in large numbers for the first time, and towards whom he felt the usual prejudices. "The contrabands are numerous," he wrote, "and ought all to be drowned. I have the least bad of many to look after my horse; but he is as black as the ace of spades, belongs to the 'Armstrong' family in odor & requires about 2 white orderlies to watch him."

The bombardment of Fort Pulaski from Tybee Island at the mouth of the Savannah River began on April 10. After thirty hours, a portion of the walls was breached and a storming party was making ready when the rebels struck their flag. The leader of the first party to reach the Fort was its real conqueror, Quincy A. Gillmore of the Army Engineers, who, under great difficulties, had placed rifled cannon beyond the reach of the Fort's smooth bore guns and mortars, and personally directed their fire. When the white flag was raised, Halpine, who had been watching the bombardment with Hunter, commandeered a flat-bottom boat lying on the beach, and calling for volunteer oarsmen, rowed across choppy waters to the long causeway outside the Fort. There he was met by the former editor of the Savannah *Republican,* whom he had first seen at the Charleston convention in 1860. They shook hands with strained politeness. After inspecting the Fort, parading the garrison, and ordering the Confederate soldiers to stack arms, the officers of both sides assembled in the quarters of the commandant, where one of the few Old World surrenders of the Civil War was acted out by flickering candle light. As the representative of the victorious commanding general, Halpine stood beside a table as each rebel officer in turn laid his sword upon it, stated his name and rank, and uttered an appropriate remark. When they were through, Halpine, who knew the old traditions and probably stage-managed the entire scene, declared that it was a painful duty to receive the swords of men who had shown by their bravery that they deserved so well to wear them. Then the United States officers, carrying the swords they had won, left the room and returned to their lines. But they were back for dinner and for subdued, but not unfriendly, conversation.[2]

It was a dramatic scene, and Halpine soon had a chance to tell about it, for in mid-April he left the Department of the South for temporary duty with General Halleck, who was organizing the new Department of Mississippi, including Hunter's old Department of Kansas, and may have wanted his help on administrative details. But he spent more time in New York in bed than in an office in St. Louis, for he was suffering from an intestinal infection picked up in the Carolina islands, and from a severe inflammation of the eyes, caused or aggravated by the glare of the sun on the Hilton Head beaches. He was under a doctor's care for a month, and his eyes were so sensitive to light that most of the time was spent in a darkened room. By June 19, he was back in South Carolina with David Hunter, promoted to chief of staff, but still at the rank of major.[3]

The duties of chief of staff were demanding only upon occasion, when special reports and orders had to be written and there was more than the usual amount of correspondence. As a rule, there was plenty of free time, and Halpine wrote home about good sailing, pleasant rides, and a newly acquired taste for turtle eggs and soup. His eyes recovered sufficiently for him to ask Margaret to send him volumes of Irish poems and ballads, the works of Poe and the Brownings, and a dozen copies of his own *Lyrics by the Letter H.*, still available from the publisher's.

There were also economic enterprises to keep him occupied. The needs of the thousands of men in Hunter's command were supplied by sutlers operating under military authorization and control. As chief of staff, Halpine was empowered to issue trading permits. Already experienced in commissary affairs, he was determined to see that both the government and the soldiers received a fair return for their money, but he was by no means reluctant to make a profit for himself and his friends in the process. Indeed, he believed that he and his Irish friend, John Savage, who had also made a career in New York journalism and Democratic politics and was still pursuing it, could supply the soldiers with light clothing, boots, shoes, fans, and pipes, and make a profit of 50 percent. But, judging from the continuing references in his letters to Margaret to unpaid bills and the need for strict household economy, the big money never came in. Perhaps it was because of the selling agents Savage sent down, like the one Halpine said was "a brute who cannot understand any of the necessities of my position, or the duties of his own." Savage should try to find men "having some approach to the exteriors & manners of gentlemen."

Lots of money was made at Hilton Head in the illegal sale of whiskey, sometimes marketed by ingenious merchants in innocent-looking cans labeled "fruit" or "oysters." The consumers were no less ingenious. On one occasion, the chief commissary officer stored some barrels of apple jack captured from the rebels on the first floor of a warehouse. The soldiers learned about it, of course, and drilled holes through the flooring and into the barrels, gulping the liquor as it flowed out, and catching it in containers for sale to comrades. Well understanding the men's desire for such beverages, Halpine was happy to issue an order, upon the authority of the chief surgeon, for a "prophylactic dose" of a gill of whiskey and ten grains of quinine for each man twice a day. It was, he said, the most popular order he ever wrote.[4]

If the Union army at Hilton Head had more to fear from malaria and other diseases than from its enemies locked up in nearby Charleston and Savannah, the Confederates did not have to worry very much about their Yankee enemies, scattered for 200 miles along the coast from South Carolina to Florida. With only 16,000 men in his entire command, Hunter was far from being able to undertake offensive actions and even had to abandon some of the coastal region he already controlled. Furthermore, McClellan's need for soldiers in Virginia made it unlikely that Hunter could expect any reenforcements within the foreseeable future. Faced with a shortage of men out West, Hunter had asked for permission to recruit Indians, and been denied it. Faced with a similar shortage down South, he once again turned to the unutilized local supply of manpower, and this time he knew enough not to ask permission.

The War Department's directive on the use of slaves as soldiers was self-contradictory, or could be made to seem to be. Back in October, 1861, when the combined army-navy invasion of Port Royal Sound was being planned, Secretary of War Simon Cameron had authorized the army commander to make use of any persons, "whether fugitives from labor or not," who offered their services. "You will employ such persons," the Secretary declared, "in such services as they may be fitted for —either as ordinary employes, or, if special circumstances seem to require it, in any other capacity, with such organization (in squads, com-

panies, or otherwise) as you may deem most beneficial to the service."
If these words had any meaning, it was that after landing in South Carolina the army could, at its discretion, use slave volunteers as soldiers.
But Lincoln hesitated to arm the slaves and, apparently at his insistence,
the sense of Cameron's order was modified by the proviso that the order
did not authorize "a general arming of them [the slaves] for military
service." [5]

Had the landings at Port Royal been vigorously resisted by the
rebels, it is possible that the army would have seen the "special circumstances" which Secretary Cameron had said would justify the organization of slave volunteers into squads and companies, and overlooked the
modifying clause at the end of the Secretary's order. It almost certainly
would have done so had it believed that slave soldiers would make the
difference between victory and defeat. Hunter did not need the help of
Negroes to defend his island beachheads against Confederate counter-
attacks, but he did need their help in order to carry out the offensive
movements which were part of his mission in the Department of the
South. It is not surprising, therefore, that faced with a choice between
action which might lead to a brilliant victory and inaction which could
only prolong a stalemate, he should have decided to act on the positive
part of Cameron's order and to ignore the negative part.

The word went out to his district commanders early in May: The
commanding general wanted their help in the organization of Negro
volunteers into squads and companies, "and perhaps into a regiment,"
the volunteers to be paid, fed, clothed, and drilled exactly the same as
white soldiers. On May 9, he went much further, issuing a proclamation
freeing all of the slaves in his department.[6] More sweeping in its terms
than either Fremont's proclamation or Congress' recent Confiscation
Act (which had only freed the slaves of rebels), the proclamation
caused such a furor that the fact Hunter was turning Negroes into
soldiers passed almost unnoticed for several weeks. Perhaps he had
intended that it should.

Lincoln revoked Hunter's proclamation as he had Fremont's, with
a proclamation of his own. The future of slavery, he explained, was a
question which "I reserve to myself, and which I cannot feel justified in
leaving to the decision of commanders in the field." [7]

Hunter understood the border state and anti-Negro pressures which
prompted Lincoln's action, and believed that his proclamation had not
displeased the President in the least. Indeed, he wrote, "I believe he re-
joiced in my action." For it gave Lincoln, who never rebuked Hunter
for it, either publicly or privately, another opportunity to promote his

plan for the gradual, compensated abolition of slavery. The lesson was clear: if the slave states refused to accept the economic help of the national government now, they might soon lose their slave property without any compensation. "You cannot, if you would," Lincoln said to the slaveowners, "be blind to the signs of the times." [8]

When there was no immediate response among the coastal island Negroes to Hunter's call for volunteers, the General concluded that stronger measures were required. He ordered his district commanders to send him, under guard, every able-bodied Negro capable of bearing arms within their commands. Out into the fields went the impressment parties looking for "volunteers," rounding them up as they worked, and often denying them even the chance to return to their houses for personal belongings. At gun point, they marched them off to rendezvous points, followed by their weeping women and children, who feared that enslavement in Cuba rather than military training at Hilton Head was their true destination. Some of the men sought to escape and were brutally punished, and others pleaded with their Yankee emancipators to be returned to their former masters. "The plea of military necessity has been stretched to cover up many a mistake and some acts of criminal injustice, but never, in my judgment," wrote one white observer of an incident on a plantation on Saint Helena Island, "did major general fall into a sadder blunder and rarely has humanity been outraged by an act of more unfeeling barbarity." Many such complaints were sent back to Washington by Edward L. Pierce, an agent of the United States Treasury, and his troop of missionaries, teachers, humanitarians, and adventurers who were engaged in an experimental work project with the masterless slaves of the Port Royal region.[9]

In its way, Hunter's "able-bodied" order was indeed as inhumane as the practices of slavery which Hunter so strongly disapproved. And yet the order also reflected the professional soldier's impatience with the civilian mind. On many occasions, Halpine was appalled at the way professional army men treated white volunteers, and in a postwar essay recommended that regular army officers, indispensable in high command positions, ought to have as little direct contact with volunteer soldiers as possible. The West Pointer, declared Halpine, tended to despise the men as an armed rabble. He forgot, or failed to make allowance for the fact that "just a few months ago the man in a private's or sergeant's uniform was a farmer, clerk, independent mechanic, or professional man —wholly unacquainted with the usages or discipline of military life." He saw only a man in uniform, and was "too apt to treat every breach or omission of strict technical duty or observance as a wanton and willful outrage deliberately committed. . . . Such being his view of the case, he resolves to 'teach the rascal better'; and forthwith, often amidst a storm of curses and, not infrequently, of cuffs and kicks, the volunteer private finds himself manacled or tied up by the hands in the Guard House." Halpine marveled that men so savagely oppressed should so tamely submit. "They clench their teeth, grow very pale; their eyes glisten with mingled anger and wonder—often tears, with the younger and more enthusiastic of them—and they march off silently to receive punishment for their unknown fault." The men could never understand, Halpine concluded, that in the eyes of the professional army officers their acts of enlistment, often prompted by the highest and most patriotic motives, "degraded them to a level little, if at all above that of convicted felons." [10]

If white men who volunteered for military service were treated like convicted felons, it is hardly surprising that black men who did not volunteer should have been. Hunter's dealings with the Negroes of Port Royal must be seen in relation to the rigors of military caste and discipline, as well as in relation to the racist assumptions which existed at the time.

By mid-June, 1862, when Halpine returned from his temporary duty with Halleck and his convalescence in New York, Hunter had some eight hundred Negroes wearing the uniform of the Union Army, and looking on parade, according to one reporter, "decidedly dark." [11]

By this time, too, rumors about Hunter's slave regiment had replaced his proclamation of freedom as a subject of controversy in the offices and drawing rooms of Washington. In the House of Representatives, an angry member from Kentucky, Charles A. Wickliffe, asked the Secretary of War to report whether or not Hunter had raised a regiment of fugitive slaves and, if he had, whether the War Department had authorized it.[12]

Cameron's successor, Edwin M. Stanton, forwarded the request for information to Hunter, who received it as he and Halpine were about to set out on an evening ride of the Hilton Head picket lines. It was an important moment for the General. He could not deny that he had organized the regiment of Negro soldiers, and he could not rest his case exclusively on the positive part of Cameron's 1861 order, for if political necessities required it, the War Department could easily disavow him on grounds that he had clearly violated the provisions of the negative part. If it did, how would he get the men he needed to undertake offensive operations? Carefully considering the problem, he recognized he had to present his argument in such a way as to win the support of men still undecided about the desirability of recruiting Negro soldiers, thus making it possible politically for the War Department to sanction what he had done. During the course of their ride, Hunter told Halpine the kind of answer he wanted to send to Stanton, and the two men worked through most of a stormy night composing it.[13]

Had he formed a regiment of fugitive slaves? No, indeed, Hunter informed the Secretary of War in absolute terms: "No regiment of 'fugitive slaves' has been, or is being, organized in this department. There is, however"—and here one can imagine a particularly loud thunderclap of laughter emanating from the bungalow headquarters of the Department of the South—"a fine regiment of loyal persons whose late masters are 'fugitive rebels,' " men who were fleeing from the national flag and leaving their loyal servants behind to shift for themselves. Far from trying to evade their masters, these loyal persons were training with commendable zeal to go in pursuit of them! For legal authority to organize his regiment of "loyal persons" for use against "fugitive rebels," Hunter of course cited Cameron's order. Had he been given time, he continued, returning to the more solid ground of pragmatic advantage, he could have organized five or six regiments. The experiment had been "a complete and even marvelous success." The Negroes were attentive, enthusiastic, amenable to military discipline, and eager for action. They would prove invaluable auxiliaries to the United States Army, fully equal to the colored regiments used so successfully by the British in the West Indies.[14]

The text of Hunter's letter was read in the House of Representatives on July 2, and caused a commotion. The arming of a slave population was an act of barbarism unthinkable to all civilized men, declared Representative Robert Mallory, of Kentucky, scandalized that Hunter's explanation had been "received with loud applause and boisterous manifestations of approbation by the Republican members of the House. I never witnessed a scene more deeply mortifying. I shall not lose the memory of it while I live. It was a scene, in my opinion, disgraceful to the American Congress." Congressman Wickcliffe of course agreed. The use of slaves as soldiers, he said, would "stamp this war with infamy," and provide civilized governments with the excuse needed to intervene. Among the members of the House who defended Hunter's regiment was Thaddeus Stevens, who argued that the only way to win the war was to appeal to the entire slave population, "asking them to come from their masters, to take the weapons which we furnish, and to join us in their war of freedom against traitors and rebels." As a starter, Stevens would train 100,000 Negro soldiers! [15]

The happy distinction between "fugitive slaves" and "fugitive masters"—Halpine's inspiration, one feels sure, rather than Hunter's—burst upon the public, wrote Halpine, like a "politico-military champagne cocktail," dispelling some of the public gloom accompanying McClellan's defeat on the peninsula before Richmond, and winning friends for the use of Negro soldiers. But despite the desire of Secretary Stanton and other members of the cabinet, Lincoln refused to allow the War Department to recognize Hunter's regiment or to authorize others.[16]

As late as 4 August 1862, Hunter was still hopeful that his regiment would be accepted, and more than ever convinced that the needs of his department required it. He had stopped formal recruiting, but his agents were still rounding up able-bodied "volunteers" and taking them to central depots, from which it would be easy to turn them into soldiers if he received permission to do so. He could raise six Negro regiments in two months, he told Stanton, and many more if he were allowed to extend his recruiting to the Georgia coast. The slaves would flock to his camps, he declared, ignoring the fact that they had not done so at Hilton Head, and this would hurt their masters badly. It was his experience, he wrote, that slave owners "would rather lose one of their children than a good negro." [17] But the War Department continued to deny him authorization, and finally he gave up. On August 10, he discharged his Negro soldiers, and sent them back to their homes, their three months of enforced service unrecognized by the United States government, and unpaid for. Hunter then asked for and received a sixty-day leave of absence, and disappointed and angry, went home himself—to Washington.

The failure of the War Department to support Hunter amounted to a public expression of a lack of confidence in him personally, for by the time he disbanded his regiment the Lincoln administration had already decided to adopt the policies he advocated—the emancipation of slaves, and the enlistment of Negro soldiers—and two weeks later the War Department granted to Brigadier General Rufus B. Saxton the authority which Hunter had so long sought for himself. It authorized Saxton "to arm, uniform, equip, and receive into the service of the United States," up to 5,000 Negro soldiers. It was clear that Lincoln and Stanton believed that Saxton, who had been sent to the Department of the South in June as a result of the protests received about Hunter's treatment of "volunteers," was suited to the task of recruiting and training Negroes, and that Hunter was not.[18]

Saxton found some difficulty in raising Negro soldiers in South Carolina, because the men who had been impressed into Hunter's regiment and served for so long without pay were naturally reluctant to trust the United States again. It was also so easy for Negroes at Hilton Head to get jobs with the Quartermaster or Engineers, or with officers as personal servants, that military service lacked the appeal it might otherwise have held for them. Yet, by November over five hundred men had signed up, and Saxton was even able to send a company of them on a raiding expedition down the Georgia coast. Later in the month, Thomas Wentworth Higginson became the colonel of this regiment, the First South Carolina, and under his leadership it became just the kind of fighting force which Hunter had envisioned.[19]

The repudiation of David Hunter and the sudden, if temporary, end to his hopes of conducting a major military operation against the rebels was both a personal and a professional disappointment for Halpine. The General, for whom he felt such close affection and to whose career in the army he had linked his own, was in disfavor with superior authorities, and consequently his old dream of redemption through an act of conspicuous heroism faded away. The fact that Hunter's policies were being adopted by the government at the same time that Hunter himself was being rebuked added a sense of frustration and persecution to disappointment. Hunter had been treated badly, Halpine believed, but at least he thought he knew who was responsible. It was those people with the Treasury Department, those "blackcoated, white-chokered, cotton-speculating, long-faced, philanthropy-preaching fanatics" who had criticized Hunter's recruiting methods. He also thought that some prominent speculators, with ambitious plans for dishonest profits, were involved.[20]

During the hot summer days when Hunter's fate was being debated in Washington, the unpleasant realities of life at Hilton Head became more obtrusive and objectionable. Increasingly, Halpine's letters home complained of the fleas, jiggers, and sand flies, and he suffered from diarrhea and other camp diseases. More serious was the recurring trouble with his eyes. Already strained by writing and reading, his eyes were so sensitive to the bright glare of the sun on the white beach that his headaches became unbearable, and sometimes his eyes were so badly inflamed that he could scarcely see. Frequently he had to be read to by his clerks, and to dictate his correspondence to them. His morale was as bad as his health, for he failed to receive the promotion he had so confidently expected.

Back in April, while participating in the last-minute preparations for the attack on Fort Pulaski, Halpine had told Margaret that he expected the Fort to fall after a hard fight, "and then hurrah for my shoulder straps with silver eagles." The Fort did indeed fall, with Halpine himself accepting its surrender, but no promotion followed. Hunter presented him with one of the surrendered swords, instead! Later, when he became Hunter's chief of staff, he told Margaret that the position could not fail to bring a colonelcy. "I believe I am in for a long strong spell of going up in the world," he wrote her, "to be attained, strange as it may seem, by never 'getting high.' " At the end of July, he was still hopeful, writing Margaret that if she came down for a visit—Mrs. Hunter was now at Hilton Head and had offered to share her beach house with the Halpines—it would improve his chances. If she came, Margaret should spend $50 on light muslin clothing and a broad-brimmed hat, and "Be as nice & neat as ever you can be." She could even spend $75, if necessary.

The fact that Halpine believed his wife could help him get his promotion suggests the extent to which his confidence of Hunter's favor had eroded during the past few months. And with reason. Since January, five officers on Hunter's staff had been promoted to the rank of colonel, while he, the chief of staff, remained a major! Hunter claimed that he had not asked for the promotion of any of them, and to reassure Halpine wrote a letter in his behalf to Secretary Stanton. "Maj. Halpine," he declared, "is intelligent, talented, industrious & perfectly devoted to his duties." [21] From a General with a reputation for not over-praising his subordinates, it was a satisfactorily flattering letter, though hardly unrestrained, and Halpine was so pleased with it as a way to save face that he told Margaret he wanted a copy of it "framed & glazed as part of the family archives of the New Halpine Family founded in America."

Halpine also sent a copy of Hunter's letter to Thurlow Weed, asking Weed to speak about him to both Halleck, now in Washington as Lincoln's chief military adviser, and Stanton.[22] In addition, he applied some not very subtle pressure on Lincoln's secretary, John Hay, whose brother Charles was a junior officer on Hunter's staff. Charles was well, Halpine wrote, and discharged his duties faithfully. Hunter was only awaiting some favorable occasion to make a tangible show of his appreciation. So far as his own promotion was concerned, Halpine thought Hay might be able to hasten a "favorable occasion" by seeking recommendations from Weed and Horace Greeley for presentation to the Commander-in-Chief himself. Weed and Greeley were divided on almost every subject, Halpine continued, but they were "united in being my warm and zealous friends." [23] But even with such top-level support, he received no promotion, and when, at the time of Hunter's departure, he left Hilton Head for duty in Washington on the staff of General-in-Chief Halleck, he went as a major.

As Halpine said in his letter to John Hay, he had done as much and as responsible work as any of Hunter's officers who had received their colonelcies. Since he was also a special favorite of the commanding

General, his failure to be promoted must have had something to do with the condition of his health. His eyes gave him much trouble, and so did various intestinal disorders, and he probably also suffered those periodic attacks of brain fever which had so long bedeviled him. The glaring sun on the flat, white beach was blamed for his inflamed eyes and splitting headaches, but overdrinking could also have caused and complicated them, and it is probable that Hunter believed much of Halpine's suffering came out of a bottle. Heavy drinking was common in the army, and Hunter could hardly have been shocked by it, though he was only a moderate drinker himself. But he might easily have concluded that an aide whose drinking was a probable factor in his recurrent incapacity for duty should not be promoted. If Halpine did not go up in rank as he had told Margaret he expected to, perhaps it was because he was "getting high" too often, after all.

In Washington as an aide to General Halleck, Halpine moved in the highest military and political circles, and had frequent contacts with Lincoln, both at the White House and, in September, when Lee undertook his first invasion of Maryland, at Halleck's home, where the President spent several anxious evenings. After the war, Halpine remembered being impressed by Lincoln's homely honesty, his humor and kindliness, and by the force, shrewdness, and originality of his character, although he wrote nothing quite so favorable before the assassination. Nevertheless, he was conscious of the privilege of being close to the President of the United States at such a moment in history, and proudly wrote home in October of the time he was picked up at his rooms by Lincoln's own carriage, and driven out to a conference at the Soldiers' Home. He must have been even more pleased when Lincoln borrowed *Lyrics by the Letter H.* from the Library of Congress.[24]

Halpine's descriptions of his various conversations with Lincoln at the White House have become familiar parts of the vast Lincoln literature, though his name is seldom connected with them. One time while entering the President's office with John Hay, Halpine saw Lincoln bowing an elderly woman out the door, and heard him tell her, "I am really very sorry, madam; very sorry. But your own good sense must tell you that I am not here to collect small debts. You must appeal to the courts in regular order." When she had left, Lincoln sat down, crossed his legs, and, locking his hands over his knee, began to laugh. "What odd kinds of people come in to see me," he said. "She may have come in here a loyal woman, but I'll be bound she has gone away believing that the worst pictures of me in the Richmond press only lack truth in not being half black and bad enough." Halpine expressed surprise that such a visitor should be allowed to take up the President's time. At Halleck's, he said, every visitor was filtered through a sieve of assistant adjutants, so that only those with legitimate business ever reached the General. "Ah, yes!" Lincoln replied seriously. "Such things do very well for you military people, with your arbitrary rule, and in your camps." But the presidency, he said, was a civil office, and heavy as was the tax on his time, he considered his hours of conversation with ordinary people well spent. "I tell you, Major," he said, "that I call these receptions my public-opinion baths, . . . and though they may not be pleasant in all their particulars, the effect as a whole is renovating and invigorating."

The conversation then turned to the ease with which an assassin could approach Lincoln. Halpine declared that on many occasions he had entered the White House as late as nine or ten o'clock at night, and walked upstairs to the rooms of Lincoln's secretaries without being challenged or seen by anyone, and he knew from innumerable letters in Halleck's office that among Lincoln's enemies were a great many unstable individuals. Lincoln heard him out with a smile, his hands still holding his knee, and his body rocking slowly back and forth. He was not afraid of political assassins, he said, because Vice-President Hannibal Hamlin would be no more satisfactory than he to the Confederates. And as for the maniacs, well, there was no protection against them, anyway. After signing the papers which Halpine had brought, Lincoln arose with a sigh and went back to his public-opinion bath.

On one other occasion Halpine heard Lincoln mention the possibility of being killed. The President complained that the clatter of the sabres and spurs of the armed guard which escorted him and Mrs. Lincoln to and from the Soldiers' Home was so loud that they could hardly hear themselves talk, and the cavalrymen looked so young and inexperienced that he really feared the accidental discharge of one of their carbines or revolvers more than he did any deliberate attempt on his life.

Although these conversations were not recorded until after the war, Halpine had been much impressed by them, and believed his memory was of "more than average tenacity." He described them, he said, exactly as he would testify to them under oath.[25]

Halpine's visits to the White House led to friendships with all of Lincoln's secretaries. One of the lesser known of them, William O. Stoddard, remembered the evenings he had spent in the northeast room upstairs, sitting in " 'Andrew Jackson's chair'—the queer, old leather-bottomed Mexican," with his feet on the table, listening to the arguments between Nicolay, Hay, Halpine, and others who stopped by.[26] And they must have been memorable evenings, for Lincoln's secretaries were his ardent champions, and Halpine, the most opinionated and witty of men, was a Douglas Democrat whose opinion of the Republican President was not flattering, especially after the way Lincoln had treated Hunter. So close to the top echelon of power in the United States, but bearing no personal responsibility for its failures, the young men (Halpine and Nicolay were in their early thirties, Hay and Stoddard in their twenties) diagnosed the nation's ills and prescribed the proper remedies with the ebullient confidence of youth. It is easy to imagine the raised voices, the vigorous gestures, the derisive laugh at an opponent's argument, the good masculine fellowship resulting from the easy exchange of strong and informed views. With John Hay, who shared his interest in poetry and pretty girls, Halpine became especially close.

Equally memorable were the evenings spent in Washington restaurants with a cultivated and ever-changing group of actors and writers, and such of the capital's political and military leaders who enjoyed their company. After dinner there were wine and cards, but conversation and impromptu performances—speeches, recitations, songs—were the real entertainment. John W. Forney, the Philadelphia newspaperman who was secretary of the United States Senate during the war, wished they could have been taken down phonographically. "But," he wrote a few years later in a long sentence which does more than shorthand to keep alive the spirit of the evenings,

> when William E. Burton came to Washington to play, and after the curtain fell would join one of these assemblies, and give us his raciest things spontaneously, when Charles Oakford, of Philadelphia— clever, genial, and ever-ready Oakford—rolled out Drake's "Ode to the American Flag," with a voice so rich and mellow; when Murdhoch moved us to tears with Janvier's "Sleeping Sentinel," or stilled us with the sweet drowsiness of Buchanan Read's "Drifting"; when John Hay recited one of his fine creations or FitzJames O'Brien or Charles G. Halpine thrilled us with a song of war or of love, when Jack Savage sung us "The Temptation of St. Anthony," or rare Forrest dropped the tragedian and played for us the mimic and the comedian, or Jefferson sung his "Cuckoo song"; or Nesmith of Oregon left the Senate to set our table in a roar, we had no thought of phonography, and no time that was not crowded with ecstasy.[27]

Among the things which Halpine tried to accomplish during his assignment in Washington was the improvement of relations between the army and the press. Many military commanders, especially the professionals, treated newspapermen with hostility and even contempt, failing to appreciate that journalists could be of great service to them as recruiting agents and as authors of stories planted to mislead the enemy. He advocated the establishment of a special bureau within the War Department to supervise the press and furnish it with such war news as could be safely printed, thus uniting the military and publicity forces of the Union, and suggested that he himself might be appointed director. As a matter of fact, he was already performing some of the functions he had in mind, since one of his duties in Halleck's office was passing on to the Associated Press those portions of the dispatches from the field which could be safely published.[28]

Unfortunately, Halpine's clearing house for news was not established, and misunderstandings between the War Department and the press, many of them easily preventable, continued. Once Halleck became furious over a story appearing in the New York *Tribune,* which he believed compromised military security. Halpine checked with Greeley, and learned that the story had been taken from Richmond and Petersburg, Virginia, newspapers! [29] War Department officials were extremely sensitive to what they read in the papers. In November, 1862, Stanton invited Charles A. Dana, Managing Editor of the *Tribune,* to become assistant secretary of war. Dana told Halpine and Halpine published the news, thus offending Stanton, who had wanted to release the story himself. The appointment was temporarily withdrawn.[30]

In addition to his duties in Halleck's office—in October he asked Weed to call on him there and thus increase his stature in the General's eye—Halpine wrote Washington correspondence for the New York *Times,* for Weed's Albany *Evening Journal* and for Forney's Philadelphia *Press,* and for a time he even edited a party journal in Washington, the *National Republican.* The position paid nothing, but it was useful to him in other ways.

The fact that Halpine combined the duties of staff officer and journalist and was intimate with John Hay has suggested to one historian that he was a kind of official propagandist for the war. "From the [references to Halpine in the] Hay diary," wrote Tyler Dennett, "it would appear that throughout the Civil War it was not uncommon to place journalists in important military and political positions, whence they could write for the papers with a view to directing public opinion." [31] In Halpine's case, however, there does not seem to have been at this time any deliberate effort on the part of the administration to shape public opinion; far from being encouraged to write for the papers, Halpine had had to persuade Halleck to give him permission to do so. It seems likely that Halpine resumed his career in journalism because, as a reporter so close to news centers and news makers, he could not help it. Furthermore, he wanted the money. "I am making money like winking," he wrote to Margaret, suggesting how easily he turned out copy, and he estimated that his Washington correspondence would bring in an extra $2,000 a year. If Margaret would only be patient, someday she would be as rich as the lady with three cows!

Although Halpine was happy to be able to practice his profession, he still did not receive his promotion, and his disgust with the army was *"unspeakable."* Twice the Secretary of War had told him he would promote him if he could, but that some kind of technicality prevented him. If he were not promoted "very soon," he told Margaret in October, he would resign his commission and move West.

Hunter, too, was disgusted with the army and the Administration and tempted to resign. At a private dinner at the home of Secretary of the Treasury Salmon P. Chase, whose favorable attention he had attracted with his proclamation of emancipation and his Negro regiment, Hunter declared that he would like to "resume" his career as a journalist. He had been writing recently for the *Republican,* he told the publicity conscious Secretary, and all he needed in order to devote himself wholly to writing for the press was a position in New York. It was a tempting suggestion and not at all too subtle for a man with Chase's political ambitions and his control over patronage positions in New York. "I found him well read and extremely intelligent," Chase wrote after questioning him on politics. No doubt he found Hunter's explanation of Lincoln especially intelligent. Lincoln, declared the embittered General, was "a man irresolute but of honest intentions—born a poor white in a Slave State, and, of course among aristocrats—kind in spirit and not envious, but anxious for approval, especially of those to whom he has been accustomed to look up—hence solicitous of support of the Slaveholders in the Border States, and unwilling to offend them—without the large mind necessary to grasp great questions—uncertain of himself, and in many things ready to lean too much on others." [32]

Accompanying Hunter to the dinner, Halpine also made a good impression on Chase, and before the evening was over was offered a position as Chase's confidential secretary, in case he resigned from the army. It was a thrilling possibility for Halpine, warmed as he was by Chase's hospitality, by the beauty and charm of his daughter Kate, and by the faintly conspiratorial tone of the conversation. What if Chase should become president? To Margaret he wrote, "I sometimes stand almost paralyzed before the immensity of the movements in which I have become involved."

However inclined Hunter and Halpine might have been in October
to quit the army and go to work to make Chase the next president, they
put the idea out of their minds in November, when Hunter was told
he could once again take over command of the Department of the
South, and when Halpine at last received his promotion. Their return to
South Carolina was delayed for two months (during which Halpine was
incapacitated by another attack of his eye trouble) by a yellow fever
epidemic in the islands, but on 20 January 1863, they were back in
their familiar quarters on the beach at Hilton Head. Halpine was now
a lieutenant colonel and assistant adjutant general. But Brigadier
General Truman Seymour was chief of staff.

CHAPTER 5

The Butchered Bull

WHEN Halpine returned to Hilton Head in January, 1863, his mood was vastly different from what it had been the previous year, when his enthusiasm had been fired by dreams of raising the flag over Charleston or dying gallantly in the attempt. "Everything has dropped into its place as of old," he wrote Margaret, "as if I had never ceased to be Chief of Staff. . . . Hunter is as ever to me." But things were not really the same, for even though Hunter was still cordial, there was a certain reserve in his manner which made Halpine uneasy. He was afraid that his enemies had been seeking to prejudice the General against him.

His friends, too, were making it difficult for him with their unending requests for jobs and trading permits, some of them accompanied by promises of liberal commissions. He wanted to help them, and four months in Washington, where he had seen many men making fortunes, had not abated his desire for wealth. But he was determined to be careful. "A theft from the altar would not be more horrible in my sight," he said earnestly, "than the use of official station to join the harpy crew who batten on the plunder of our country." Yet he saw nothing wrong in sending his stockbroker advance information about military activities which might affect the stock market. But for all his desire and opportunity, he failed to make money during the war. "A fortune for you, Charley," wrote his old friend Shillaber, who knew how badly he wanted one, "would be no idle pile accumulated for a selfish ease in age, but a jolly life you would lead of it, with your friends about you. Avast, though, your glorious geniality stands in the way of your fortune, for men have to be mean, and groveling, and pinching, and coveting, and watchful, and doubting and grasping, and deceiving, and hum-bugging, before they can be rich, and your big soul is too high up to come down to the place for money making." [1] Perhaps so, but Halpine knew he had to have money to live as he wanted to.

After only a few days of squinting against the sun on the beach, his eye trouble flared up again. But the recurrent headaches were more easily endured than his constant fear of failure. So far as the public was concerned, he brooded, he was a nobody, a carefree staff officer who wore fine clothes, dined in gay company, and was close as a son to a fatherly general. Much as he loved and trusted Hunter, he was frustrated as his adjutant; there seemed to be nothing he could do in such a position to distinguish himself, and he feared that in the future, far from being able to look back upon his military career with pride, he would have to explain and defend it. He wanted action, danger, and he believed that no hell which the guns of Charleston were capable of making could be worse than the inner torment he was suffering.

As one of the few officers in headquarters who would assume responsibility, he complained in letters to Margaret during February and March that he was badly overworked. A steady stream of orderlies entered his office, their arms piled high with letters, requisitions, charges, returns, reports, requests—all demanding attention, all demanding decisions. His eyes ached with the strain, and for a while became numb. His fingers twitched nervously, and his temper flared. He became angry with the officers who crowded his desk to ask for orders, decisions, explanations, each believing his case to be unique and more urgent than anyone else's, each sure that Halpine could help him if he only would. In all but name, he was still Hunter's chief of staff, but the name, the rank, the prestige, were of extreme importance to him, and what comfort was there in Hunter's assurance that he was chief of staff "by divine spirit?" Why did he not hold the office in fact? That Hunter loved and appreciated him he did not doubt, but the General was a touchy patron, and was sometimes better at showing disapproval than appreciation.

But Halpine's moods of despondency, miserable as he was while they lasted, alternated with periods of light-hearted conviviality and good humor. One day an Ohio lady called at headquarters to complain to General Hunter that some of his soldiers had killed the only bull on the plantation where she was supervising the work of Negroes, under General Saxton's direction. Since Hunter was not present, Halpine asked her to put her complaint in writing. But the lady was in a hurry, and asked Halpine to do it for her. With the smile of comic inspiration on his face, Halpine sat down and composed "The Butchered Bull."

> Dear General H., my heart is full
> Lamenting for my butchered bull;

The only bull our islands had,
  And all my widowed cows are sad.

With briny tears and drooping tails,
  And loud boo-hoos and bovine wails,
My kine lament with wifely zeal
  Their perished hopes of future veal.

Sad is the wail of human wife
  To see her partner snatched from life;
But he, the husband of a score,
  For him the grief is more and more!

Henceforth no hope of golden cream—
  Even milk in tea becomes a dream;
Whey, bonnyclabber, cheese, and curds,
  Are now, ah, me! mere idle words.

The cruel soldiers, fierce and full
  Of reckless wrath, have shot my bull;
The stateliest bull—let scoffers laugh—
  That e'er was Father called by calf.

A bull as noble, firm and fair,
  As that which aided Jove to bear
Europe from the flowery glade
  Where she, amidst her maidens played.

So, General dear, accept my vows,
  And oh! take pity on my cows,
With whom, bereft of wifely ties,
  All tender hearts must sympathize.

Quick to the North your order send
  (By Smith's congenial spirit penned),
And order them, in language full,
  At once to send me down a bull:

If possible, a youthful beast,
  With warm affections yet unplaced,
Who to my widowed cows may prove
  A husband of undying love.[2]

It was the first verse he had written in many months, and his spirits were raised by the laughter it caused. Somebody in the office—perhaps

Major E. W. Smith, another assistant adjutant, referred to in the next-to-last verse—printed copies of it, and soon the joke spread Halpine's reputation as a wit through the islands.

A few weeks later, Fletcher Harper of the publishing firm, Charles Nordhoff of the New York *Evening Post,* and Mrs. Henry J. Raymond and an attractive young companion, Mary Brooks, arrived for a visit. Few white women besides the wives of some of the officers and the school teachers (many of them no longer marriageable), sent down to teach the Negro children, were seen by the men on Hilton Head Island. Miss Brooks, therefore, was especially welcome, and Hunter, expansive in his role as host, ordered Halpine to appoint her an acting *aide-de-camp.* Within a few minutes, Halpine obeyed with a poem, "Special Orders A, Number 1, Headquarters, Department of the South." One regrets that he did not take a little longer, for the poem needs reworking. Yet, its spontaneity was what so delighted the whole party. Mary Brooks was to be provided with a very fetching uniform by the quartermaster and to receive the rank of an honorary captain of cavalry, provided she agreed to report each morning to Colonel Halpine, "And hold herself ready, on all fit occasions,/To give him of flirting his full army rations."

It was a pleasantry which set a happy tone for the whole visit. John Hay, stopping off at Hilton Head in April on his way to Florida, arrived while the joke was still fresh, and wrote Nicolay about it, and Charles Nordhoff published it, along with "The Butchered Bull," in *Harper's Monthly.* Indeed, everyone thought it fun except Captain Mary's parents, and Halpine had to write a letter of apology.[3]

The major campaign being planned within the Department of the South during the Spring of 1863 was an attack on Charleston. The harbor at Charleston had been all but closed by the naval blockade, but the capture of the city itself, so closely associated with the extremism which had brought on the war, would give a significant boost to northern morale and a serious blow to southern. Furthermore, Gustavus V. Fox, the dynamic assistant secretary of the navy who had conceived and helped to plan the successful and easy conquests of Port Royal in November, 1861, and of New Orleans in April, 1862, believed that Charleston could be taken quickly and cheaply. An eyewitness to the *Monitor's* victory over the *Merrimac,* Fox had been so impressed with the little vessel that he believed it could "go all over the harbor [at Charleston] and return with impunity. She is absolutely impregnable." Having ordered ten additional monitors, Fox promised the commander of the South Atlantic Blockading Squadron, Rear Admiral Samuel F.

Du Pont, that they would "laugh" at the forts guarding the city, and by threatening Charleston itself, force its surrender.[4] As at Port Royal and New Orleans, the navy would win the victory; the army would be needed only for occupation duty.

Under the circumstances, there was bound to be a certain amount of jealousy on the part of the army, and not all of it was unfounded. "I feel that my duties are twofold," Fox once told Du Pont; "first, to beat our southern friends; second, to beat the army." [5] But on the surface, relations between Hunter and Du Pont and their staffs were polite, and Halpine became friends with C. R. P. Rodgers, the fleet commander, and several of the monitor captains. He exchanged dinners and went riding with them, and in February he was aboard the monitor *Patapsco* during the bombardment of a Confederate installation along the Broad River. "Nothing can be more glorious than the sense of invincibility one feels in these iron monsters," he exclaimed to Margaret, "and I long for the peppering of the Forts, and the rattling of the idle shot against the immovable and impenetrable walls of the turret, as for a new and most delightful sensation." He was convinced that nothing could damage a monitor above the water, and that the danger from underwater torpedoes was less than the danger from internal accidents, especially fire, which could spread below decks and into the magazine by means of the grains of powder scattered through the ship. Like Fox, he did not doubt that the monitors would take Charleston in a matter of days.

Although it was to be a naval operation, there was excitement enough for the men of Hunter's command, for it seemed unlikely to many army officers that Charleston could be taken without a fight. As adjutant, Halpine wrote an order rallying the spirits of the soldiers, and then sat down to write another last letter to Margaret. An unabashedly sentimental man in a sentimental age, he asked that she keep his letters as reminders of him, and sent a father's farewell advice to his four daughters and his son. It was comforting for him to realize that if he were killed he would die a hero, and he said of Nicholas, now six, "In all that he need ever know of my life, he will have nothing to be ashamed of."

On April 3, Hunter loaded about 10,000 of his men aboard transports and took them thirty-five miles up the coast to the North Edisto River, just south of Charleston. There, surrounded by gunboats, mortar schooners, miscellaneous support vessels, and the little monitors from whom so much was expected, they landed on nearby Folly Island, and waited for Du Pont to attack. Late in the afternoon of April 7, he did. From the transport *Ben de Ford,* Halpine and Hunter watched through glasses the procession of monitors steaming single-file into the mouth of Charleston harbor. The first in line, the *Weehawken,* little more than a distant black speck on the surface of the water, seemed especially gallant as it moved into range of the big guns of Fort Sumter.

But gallantry was not enough. The little ships were hopelessly outmatched, and they could neither reduce Fort Sumter and the other forts nor remove the obstructions placed in the harbor channel to keep them away from the city. Five of them were seriously damaged by rebel fire, and one, the *Keokuk,* sank of its wounds the next day. From his flagship, Du Pont called them back, consulted with their shaken commanders, and decided not to try again. To do so, he reported to Secretary of the Navy Gideon Welles, would convert "a failure into a disaster." The navy could not take Charleston by itself, after all.[6]

In the Navy Department, Du Pont's failure was itself considered a disaster, Fox and Welles quickly claiming that the Admiral had given up too soon. In the White House, there was the sickening suspicion that Du Pont was another McClellan who would not fight unless specifically ordered to. But should he be ordered to? The administration equivocated.[7]

Sometime during the middle of April, John G. Nicolay wrote a letter to one of Hunter's aides. Presumably an indirect attempt by Lincoln to elicit an unofficial army view of Du Pont's performance, the letter criticized the Admiral for calling off the attack when so few casualties had been suffered. Halpine wrote the reply, and his letter, which he sent to the *Tribune,* was an authoritative and influential defense of Du Pont.[8]

The fight against the Charleston forts had not been a conventional fight, Halpine reminded Nicolay, and the vigor with which it had been pressed could not be measured by the amount of bloodshed. It had been an experiment to see if a city could be captured by machinery alone. As soon as it was clear that the machines were inadequate to the job, common sense required that they be withdrawn; no good purpose could have been served by exposing them any longer. The monitors matched a total of thirty-two guns in cramped and unstable quarters against over three hundred guns with every advantage of space and stability. Fort Sumter was the rebel stronghold most feared because of its central position, but even if it had fallen, the battle would have been far from won. The other batteries and forts protecting the city were made of earth, not bricks and mortar, and were practically impregnable to the monitors' guns.

Another reason Du Pont had been correct in calling off the attack was that in plain view behind their forts were three enemy ironclads. None of them was a match for a healthy monitor, but any could have captured a disabled one if given the opportunity. If the rebels had captured just one monitor, it would have placed the entire blockading fleet in jeopardy, and raised once again the possibility of foreign intervention. Should such a risk have been taken for nothing?

Halpine's defense of Du Pont entailed an attack on the monitors, about which he had previously been so enthusiastic. Suppose that at some time in the future, he continued in his letter to Nicolay, enough monitors could be brought into position to reduce a land fortification. What else could they do? They swamped so easily they could not cross the ocean without a guarantee of calm weather, they were unfit for human beings to live in for any length of time, and they were useless as floating batteries to protect the nation's harbors, because they were no match in speed and fire power for the ironclad frigates being built by England and France. He concluded his letter with a poem ridiculing Gideon Welles as a fuddy-duddy and a reactionary, asleep to all criticism of the monitors, responsive to the exaggerated claims of their builders, dominated by Fox, and involved in a close study of the plans for Noah's ark.[9]

In addition to the fact that the poem could not have described Welles's interest in modernizing the Navy with less perspicacity, it is notable as the first public introduction of the mythical character who would make Halpine rich and famous, Private Miles O'Reilly. Private O'Reilly, Halpine explained, was a young soldier of "Italian extraction," who had found the anti-Welles poem inside a bottle on a beach near Charleston. Since several of the monitors were lying in the area, it was possible that the poem had been written by one of their officers, and Halpine, aware that most men were not as reluctant as Mary Brooks to see their names in print, suggested some of his special friends as likely suspects. Yet there were those who believed, he continued in the mock seriousness which always characterized his writings about Miles, that O'Reilly himself was the author, because he had a reputation within the Department of the South as a writer of comic songs and impromptu verses. In such a casual and off-hand way did the celebrated Miles O'Reilly make his debut.[10]

Hunter was of course consulted during the writing of Halpine's letter, and was thought by some to be its author. He knew the monitors had shortcomings to which Washington authorities were blind, and he did not believe that the navy by itself could destroy Fort Sumter and capture Charleston. But he did believe that the army could do it (or, at least, could have done it) with naval support. On the day after the attack of the monitors, Hunter's men were ready to move from Folly Island across Lighthouse Inlet to Morris Island; indeed, they were "almost in the act" of doing it. Aided by a cross-fire from the navy, Hunter was convinced that they could have driven the enemy from Cummings Point at the north end of Morris Island, and that Fort Sumter would have fallen within two days to a bombardment from that position. Fort Pulaski had been conquered from a similar location on Tybee Island with guns less powerful than those which could have been used against Fort Sumter. But Du Pont refused either to renew the attack against Sumter from the sea, or to support the army's move on Point Cummings. To Hunter's entreaties, he replied he "would not fire another shot," and for weeks he did not. Hunter kept some of his men on Folly Island, and on Seabrook Island nearby, but the enemy, perceiving at last its danger, fortified the shore of Morris Island so strongly that a crossing of Lighthouse Inlet would now require protracted operations and a serious loss of life. Hunter believed that Du Pont's distrust of the monitors was so great that he would do nothing with them all summer, and he therefore asked Lincoln to "liberate me from those orders to 'cooperate with the Navy' which now tie me down to share the admiral's inactivity." [11]

In the meantime, Hunter was preparing for offensive operations and replying to the attacks of his southern enemies, who saw in his earlier recruitment of Negro soldiers a conscious and deliberate effort to bring about what the South most feared—a massive slave rebellion. Public reaction against him in the Confederacy approached the hysterical, and the Confederate War Department proclaimed that he and all officers associated with him in the training and use of slaves for military purposes were to be considered outlaws. If captured, they were to be hanged as felons.[12]

Outraged though flattered to be singled-out for such a distinction, Hunter responded with a threatening letter (written by Halpine) to Jefferson Davis, who had once been an adjutant in Hunter's regiment of dragoons. Unless Davis revoked the outlaw proclamation within thirty days, the letter stated, Hunter would hang every rebel officer who came into his hands. Unlike many of Davis' former comrades-in-arms, Hunter did not view the movement of which Davis was the leader as "a mere error of judgment, . . . a thing to be regretted, . . . a slight political miscalculation." On the contrary, he considered it to be treason, "the sum of all felonies and crimes," and believed that it required the severest retribution. If unrevoked, the proclamation would untie his hands and permit him "to treat rebellion as it deserves, and give to the felony of treason, a felon's death." [13]

The letter was suppressed on orders from Lincoln, who was reluctant to step onto the retaliation escalator, and refused ever to treat rebel officers as other than prisoners of war.

After Du Pont's defeat in April, Hunter wrote once again to Jefferson Davis, this time to protest against the treatment of captured Negro soldiers (now in extensive use in the Union army), who were sometimes executed and sometimes sold back into slavery. For every such outrage which took place in his department, Hunter warned, he would execute the rebel prisoner of highest rank in his possession. "The United States flag," he said, "must protect all its defenders, white, black, or yellow." In addition, if Davis did not immediately revoke the still extant outlaw order, "I will at once cause the execution of every rebel officer and every rebel slaveholder in my possession."

The letter containing this fantastic threat was also suppressed, as Hunter and Halpine knew it would be. But sent to Stanton, it was preserved in the War Department's official records,[14] and reveals the kind of pressure from the field which led to the signing of a general order of retaliation by Lincoln in July, 1863.

If Hunter's advocacy and use of Negro soldiers aroused the implacable hatred of southerners it also aroused bitter feelings among northerners. Many people in the North shared the South's belief that the arming of a slave population was an uncivilized way to wage war, that it invited the commission of horrible crimes against women and children. White soldiers generally believed that blacks were inferior beings, and, finding the assumption confirmed by contact with slaves, felt themselves insulted when the Negroes were urged to put on the army uniform. Economic considerations were also involved in race prejudices, especially among workers who feared that emancipated southern Negroes would further depress the wages paid in northern cities. The Irishmen of the Sixty-Ninth New York were so strongly opposed to accepting any help at all from southern slaves, Halpine had reported in the New York *Times* at the beginning of the war, that they would rather see the Union fall than be saved by Negroes.

By the end of 1862, however, resistance to the use of Negro soldiers began to decline, and General Saxton, picking up recruiting and training activities in South Carolina where Hunter had been forced to stop them, found it easier than he expected to persuade white men to serve as officers in the new Negro regiments.[15] The announcement by Lincoln in September of the emancipation policy was one factor in the change; after January 1, 1863, the Negroes would be free men, not slaves, and there was therefore less objection to their wearing the uniform. Lincoln justified the Emancipation Proclamation as a military necessity, and it was chiefly as a military necessity that whites began to accept and favor the organization of Negro regiments. "Were I a soldier," Shillaber wrote Halpine, in his 28 February 1863 letter expressing what became a dominant point of view, "I should feel right happy to let Sambo take his trick at the trigger." The point was an obvious one: colored regiments were better than none.

But obvious and logical points are sometimes difficult to see, particularly when vision is obscured by an emotion like race prejudice. In order to be wholly approved by the people, the utilization of Negro soldiers had to be presented not only as a necessary policy, but as a desirable one. The advantages to whites had to be immediate and real, and they had to be expressed in terms which even the most bigoted would accept. Perhaps inspired by Shillaber's comment, Halpine wrote a poem which did it all, and did it most effectively because his defense of black soldiers was put in the form of a joke which everybody (except blacks) could appreciate, and written to a familiar melody ("The Low Backed Car") which nearly everybody could sing. The humor in "Sambo's Right To Be Kilt" was cruel and cold-blooded, but that was the secret of its success. Halpine's reasoning could persuade whites to accept blacks as soldiers without in the least disturbing their fundamental prejudices against Negroes.

> Some tell us 'tis a burnin' shame
>   To make the naygers fight;
> And that the thrade of bein' kilt
>   Belongs but to the white:
> But as for me, upon my sowl!
>   So liberal are we here,
> I'll let Sambo be murthered instead of myself,
>   On every day in the year.
>
> > On every day in the year, boys,
> >   And in every hour of the day;
> > The right to be kilt I'll divide wid him,
> >   And divil a word I'll say.
>
> In battle's wild commotion
>   I shouldn't at all object
> If Sambo's body should stop a ball

That was comin' for me direct;
And the prod of a Southern bagnet,
So ginerous are we here,
I'll resign, and let Sambo take it
On every day in the year.

On every day in the year, boys,
And wid none o' your nasty pride,
All my right in a Southern bagnet prod,
Wid Sambo I'll divide!

The men who object to Sambo
Should take his place and fight;
And it's better to have a nayger's hue
Than a liver that's wake and white.
Though Sambo's black as the ace of spades,
His finger a thrigger can pull,
And his eye runs sthraight on the barrel-sights
From undher its thatch of wool.

So hear me all, boys darlin',
Don't think I'm tippin' you chaff,
The right to be kilt we'll divide wid him,
And give him the largest half.[16]

The white soldiers at Hilton Head picked up their adjutant's newest song immediately, and were apparently quickly influenced by it. Their prejudices against Negro troops, Hunter informed Stanton at the end of April, "are rapidly softening or fading out." [17] But it was not until the next year that "Sambo's Right To Be Kilt" was presented to the public at large.

Hunter was eager to lead his soldiers, black and white, into battle. The South was "a mere hollow shell," he told Lincoln, and he was sure he could crack it open by marching 10,000 troops into the heavily slave-populated counties of Georgia, avoiding military strongholds, but destroying railroads, food, and supplies, and spreading panic among the whites by arming the slaves with pikes, "the simplest and most effective" weapons which could be placed in their hands. The rebels would either sue for peace, or be forced to withdraw their slaves into the interior, thus leaving empty their most productive coastal counties. Later, when he feared that war-weariness in the North might force the administration to make a compromise peace which would preserve the institution of slavery, he proposed an expedition he thought would end the rebellion quickly. He asked permission to march an army from Brunswick, Georgia, through the heart of the Deep South to New Orleans, arming the slaves as he went and destroying the property of slaveholders. "A passage of this kind," he declared, "would create such a commotion among the negroes that they themselves could be left to do the rest of the work." [18]

But until his orders to assist the navy in its operations against Charleston were changed, Hunter could do little but engage in small-scale hit and run raids along the coast and a short distance up the rivers. One such raid, involving two Negro regiments—the Second South Carolina, commanded by a former Kansas Jayhawker, Colonel James Montgomery, and the newly arrived Fifty-Fourth Massachusetts, commanded by Colonel Robert Gould Shaw—took place at Darien, Georgia, on June 11. After searching the undefended town for stores of value, Montgomery announced that he was going to burn it to the ground. "Southerners must be made to feel that this is a real war," he said. When Shaw protested, Montgomery declared he was acting on orders from Hunter, and that as outlaws under the Confederate proclamation he and Shaw were not bound by the regular rules of war, anyway. And so the town was burned.[19]

Heartsick at the senseless destruction and afraid that it would reflect against Negro soldiers everywhere, Shaw wrote to Halpine to learn if Montgomery really had acted under orders from Hunter.[20] Halpine's reply has not survived, but it would have been natural for him to quote Hunter's orders to Montgomery dated June 9, two days before the raid. According to these orders, Montgomery was to welcome and protect all Negroes who sought his lines, to arm the able-bodied as soldiers, and to seize or destroy horses, mules, cattle, grain, and other food useful to the enemy. But, the orders continued, "you will avoid any devastation which does not strike immediately at the resources or material" of the enemy, and "all household furniture, libraries, churches, and hospitals you will of course spare." There were times, Hunter conceded, when the needs of self-defense against an unscrupulous foe demanded more ruthless conduct, "but until such time shall have arrived, and until the proof, not merely of declarations or resolves but of acts, is unmistakable, it will be both right and wise to hold the troops under your command to the very strictest interpretation of the laws and usages of civilized warfare." [21] In burning the town of Darien just forty-eight hours later, Montgomery clearly violated his orders.

If Hunter had no direct responsibility for the destruction of Darien, he had to bear some responsibility for having kept Montgomery in command. No officer was more unfit to conduct operations in enemy country, Halpine believed. The fact was, Halpine wrote after the war, that Montgomery "was fighting out and avenging old Kansas feuds and quarrels of a personal nature with the slaveholders and the whole South in general, rather than fighting in any legitimate sense for the restoration of the Union." Among his grievances against the South, it was rumored, was the murder of his wife and other members of his family by pro-slavery ruffians in Kansas.

Hunter's new orders finally arrived, but much to his surprise they did not unleash him for a comprehensive series of attacks along the coast or for an expedition into the interior. Instead, they "temporarily" removed him from command of the Department of the South!

Taking effect on June 12, the day after Darien, the timing was extremely unfortunate for Hunter and those associated with him. As Hunter himself angrily wrote to Lincoln, "my removal . . . has been all but universally regarded as a censure on my conduct," [22] and as recently as 1959 a historian implied a connection between Hunter's removal and the Darien raid, though he should have known—as most of Hunter's contemporary enemies could not have—that the order changing the command of the Department was dated June 3, eight days before Darien.[23]

Hunter's removal had nothing whatsoever to do with the Darien raid nor, as the President himself declared, with anything else Hunter had done or failed to do. "Why then was I removed," asked the anguished General in a three-hour interview in the White House. "Well now, Gen. Hunter," Lincoln replied, "I will tell you all about how that happened." Horace Greeley had told him that General Gillmore, the conqueror of Fort Pulaski, would be able to take Fort Sumter. After talking it over with Gillmore, and with Fox, Halleck, and Stanton, Lincoln decided to give him a chance. He ordered Halleck to draw up the order, but Halleck believed that Gillmore would not be able to act effectively in a subordinate position, and that there would be trouble if he were given authority independent of Hunter. "So," the President concluded, "you were relieved temporarily to give Gillmore a chance to do the job."

Was it not insulting, Hunter asked, to relieve an officer when there was a job to do, and then send him back when the work was completed? "O Gen. Hunter, this is an engineering job, purely engineering."

"Well, Mr. Lincoln, do you relieve all your Generals when there are engineering jobs to be done? I had an engineer with me, who is infinitely Gillmore's superior as acknowledged by the whole Army."

"Well, Gen. Hunter, how was I to know that?"

"You should have taken it for granted, Mr. Lincoln, that I had a competent engineer with me."

The conversation then turned to the war in general, and Lincoln observed how reluctant he had been to replace Major General Joseph Hooker as commander of the Army of the Potomac after his single failure at Chancellorsville. "Why then, Mr. Lincoln," Hunter interrupted, "do you give me up, at the instance of that vagabond Greeley, when you acknowledge I have not failed? etc. etc. etc. etc." [24]

To Greeley, Hunter sent a bitter and sarcastic note congratulating him for his part in the new "On to Charleston" movement, and hoping it would be as successful as the "On to Richmond" movement Greeley had led in 1861.[25] He got his wish, although of course he did not really want to. After fighting hard for Morris Island, Gillmore placed his batteries on Cummings Point, and succeeded in reducing Fort Sumter to rubble. But times had changed since the easy surrender of Fort Pulaski, and the Confederates fought on, using the wreckage itself for protection and, even as the Fort was pounded down above them, becoming invulnerable to Gillmore's big guns. Charleston did not fall until late in February, 1865, when Sherman's army, conducting the kind of march which Hunter had advocated long before, outflanked it to the west.

Caught in the crossfire between Hunter and "General" Greeley, as Hunter called him, Halpine did not know whether to continue in the army or return to the profession of journalism in New York. He was now once again Hunter's chief of staff, or at least Hunter said he was in a pre-Darien letter to Lincoln asking that Halpine be promoted to brigadier general as "a personal favor." Greeley, too, was trying to help with the promotion, though he wrote Halpine on June 1 that he thought brigadiers were "just about the most useless, superabundant, insignificant and unpopular animals in the service. I think," he said, "if the country heard that Lincoln had just traded off 100 brigadiers for so many jackasses, designed for kicking off the blocks of the Rebels, there would be a general rejoicing, and a revival of confidence in our ultimate success." Perhaps so, but if Halpine stayed in the army, he wanted to be a general. On the other hand, he was known in military circles as a Hunter man, and if Hunter's future was as bleak as it now seemed to be, Halpine might as well resign and pursue fame and fortune as a civilian.

Meanwhile, his health again collapsed under the strain of frustration and indecision and the amount of liquor he consumed to escape from them. The sight in his right eye was practically gone, and it seemed certain that if he remained on the Carolina beaches he would lose vision also in his left, and so, supported by certificates from various army physicians, he returned to New York on sick leave. By the end of July his mind was made up. After consultation with Hunter, he asked to be relieved from active duty, effective retroactively to July 1, and on August 1 he accepted the position of civilian commissary-general of subsistence on the staff of the Governor of New York, Horatio Seymour.[26]

CHAPTER 6

Private Miles O'Reilly

IN MID-JULY, 1863, rejoicing in the North over the military victories at Gettysburg and Vicksburg was interrupted by bad news from New York. There, for four terrible days, mobs of thousands of rioters, mostly depressed Irishmen, roamed the streets looting, burning, and lynching innocent Negroes in protest at having to participate in a war they disliked. Isolated in the ghettoes, driven into degraded and underpaid labor, and excluded from the mainstream of American society by prejudice against their poverty, their religion, and the very limits that were forced upon them, the Irish were not moved by Lincoln's vision of the Union as the hope of world freedom. It had not meant freedom for them. Many of them associated the South's war for independence with Ireland's long struggle to be free of England, and did not fancy themselves in the role of Cromwell. Others were convinced that Republican abolitionists, anxious to exterminate them for their anti-Negro sentiments, deliberately placed the segregated Irish regiments in the front line of battle. The chances for survival, they believed, were better in the native-born regiments, which many of them joined as substitutes for drafted men upon payment of a few hundred dollars; the price of a Negro field hand in the South, they knew, was about $1,000.[1] Most of all, they resented being forced to fight to free the slaves, whose freedom might result in the further deterioration of their precarious economic position. When the draft was scheduled to go into effect in New York, therefore, they rioted.

The anti-draft riots have been called "the most brutal, tragic, and shameful episode in the entire history of New York City," [2] and many contemporaries felt just as strongly. The patrician diarist, George Templeton Strong, described the mob as a "Celtic beast with many heads," and contrasted the conduct of the New York Irish with that of the New Orleans Negroes. "Southern Cuffee," he exclaimed, "seems of higher social grade than Northern Paddy." According to Strong, feeling against the Irish in New York was stronger and more bitter than it had been at the height of the nativist movement ten years before. He himself believed there was only one way to deal with any future rioting, and that was with "heroic doses of lead and steel." [3]

Major General John A. Dix, who rushed to New York from his post at Fort Monroe, Virginia, to take over command of the Department of the East on July 18, agreed. A prominent and wealthy New York landowner, businessman, and gentleman-politician, with military experience dating back to the War of 1812, Dix had attracted much favorable publicity in the North as Secretary of the Treasury during the last months of the Buchanan administration, when he instructed a United States Treasury official in New Orleans, "If anyone attempts to haul down the American flag, shoot him on the spot." Now he had to deal with thousands of men in his own city who were hauling down the flag, defying the American government, and burning, not simply their draft cards as in a later unpopular war, but the building in which the draft was held! On his very first day on the job in New York, he ordered his troops to use live ammunition, not blank cartridges, and not only to disperse any future mob, but to pursue it and so deal with its members that they would never again assemble. He also requested and received the loan of thousands of United States soldiers, some of them recent veterans of Gettysburg, and so over-awed the Irish with his vigor and determination that in mid-August the draft was resumed without significant incident.[4]

But Dix knew that the permanent maintenance of order in New York required more than the forcible suppression of disorder. It required nothing less than changing the mood of the Irish community, convincing its leaders that it was their war after all, and converting hostility for the United States government to support. To go to work on this seemingly impossible assignment, Dix requested that Halpine be appointed to his staff as assistant adjutant general.

Acceptance of the position required an important personal sacrifice for the state's new civilian commissary-general, for the War Department ruled that having been relieved of active duty he was entitled only to his permanent rank of major, not his temporary rank of lieutenant colonel. He had been in civil life for such a short time that if he took the job it would look to his friends as if he had been demoted, as if he had failed in the army. But he agreed to join Dix anyway, because he recognized the importance of the assignment and believed that with his ready access to the city's news media and his personal contacts among the Irish he had a chance to perform it successfully. Besides, only a technicality was involved, and with his powerful friends to help him, he would soon be restored to his old rank. In September, he explained the matter in a detailed letter to the President himself, and was gratified to learn that Lincoln had signed a letter (drafted by Hay) to Secretary Stanton. "I believe Col. Halpine to be a most capable and deserving officer," said Lincoln, "and hope that his request [to be given his old rank] may be granted if it can be, consistently with the interests of the service." [5]

Lincoln and his staff were fully aware of Halpine's potential influence as a moulder of public opinion among the Irish in New York, and may indeed have recommended his appointment to Dix. Certainly John Hay did his best to convince his Democratic friend of the administration's good faith and good works, his letters to Halpine continuing the frank discussions begun during their evenings together at the White House and renewed whenever they saw each other. But now Halpine was working in direct contact with Lincoln's most militant opponents, so Hay's letters were no longer merely personal; everything he said in defense of the Lincoln administration might help to influence the Irish in its favor. Did New Yorkers believe that the conscription law was being administered by Republicans in a partisan manner? Hay assured Halpine that neither the President nor the Secretary of War ever interfered in such matters, and reminded him that in New York the draft was in the charge of a Democrat. Did critics believe that Lincoln was a weakling, and that his administration was divided against itself? Such charges looked silly to an insider. "Abraham Rex," said Hay in a letter dated August 14, "is the central figure continually. I wish you could see as I do, that he is devilish near an autocrat in this administration." Did some people believe that Lincoln's interference with the military was prolonging the war? "You must pardon me for saying that if the Tycoon had kept his finger from meddling with the war, we should now have had neither war nor government. . . . I believe he will fill a bigger place in history than he even dreams of himself."

Other men, too, were anxious for Halpine's help in publicizing their causes. Late in August, Halpine dined at the Astor House with his old navy friends, Du Pont and Rodgers. John L. Worden was also there, his eyes still delicate from injuries sustained from the *Merrimac's* direct hit on the *Monitor's* pilot house, and they were joined later in the evening by two more monitor captains, Percival Drayton and Daniel Ammen. The occasion was not a mere "ironclad revival," as Halpine described it for Margaret; the group was really looking for a way to rehabilitate the reputation of Admiral Du Pont.

Relieved of his command early in July and, like David Hunter, not given another, Du Pont and his captains believed that he was being unfairly treated by the Navy Department, that he was being made the scapegoat for the over-commitment to monitors of Secretary Welles and Assistant Secretary Fox. He was not allowed to defend himself by publicizing the weaknesses of the monitors, and, to make his position all the more frustrating, he was succeeded in command of the South Atlantic Blockading Squadron by a man who had had very little experience at sea, Rear Admiral John A. Dahlgren. As with Hunter, Du Pont's removal seemed to reflect upon his competence, even his courage, and the Admiral was just as angry with superior authorities as was the General. Halpine, a sympathetic friend who had witnessed the abortive attack on Fort Sumter and already written at least one article in Du Pont's defense, was now in a position to be of further assistance.

On September 3 he published in the *Herald* an unsigned article criticizing the monitors and attacking Gideon Welles. But it was a routine effort, no more persuasive than the well-publicized letter to Nicolay written the previous April. In Washington at Halleck's the very evening it went to press, he must have brooded about it, for he returned to his room at Willard's and tossed restlessly on his bed—a result of too much of Mrs. Halleck's tea, he told Du Pont. Suddenly the lines of a poem began to form themselves in his mind, and at dawn he wrote it down and sent a copy to the Admiral. It would appear in a few days in the *Herald*, he told Du Pont, as the work of a soldier in the Tenth Army Corps, the Department of the South.[6] The poem proved to be mere doggerel; the inspiration was in the manner of its presentation. Whether or not it did anything for Du Pont, it made Halpine famous.

On September 8, the *Herald* carried a story, supposedly written by the paper's South Carolina correspondent on Morris Island, about the arrest by the Provost Marshal of a certain Private Miles O'Reilly, of the Forty-Seventh New York, Tenth Army Corps, an "odd character" who had frequently entertained his fellows with songs and humorous verses. His offense was the composition and publication of a song advising Admiral Dahlgren to go home, and calling for the return of Admiral Du Pont and his gallant monitor captains.

> Give us back our own Du Pont!
> Ramon Rodgers, too, we want,
> Send the say-dogs to the front
>   Who have fought the fight before;
> John Rodgers, Dhrayton, Rhind,

Ammen—grim, but always kind—
Aye, and Worden, though half blind,
Let us have their lead once more!

For seven verses O'Reilly told the Navy Department what to do, with the result that he was seized by the military authorities for breach of discipline, and confined to prison on a diet of bread and water with a sixty-four-pound cannon ball attached to each leg to prevent any further poetic flights. After telling of O'Reilly's predicament, the *Herald*'s sympathetic correspondent added his own analysis of the controversy involving Du Pont. It was not fair, he declared, to charge that Du Pont had failed to press his attack against Fort Sumter vigorously enough, for he had sent the monitors to within a few hundred feet of the Fort, while Dahlgren was currently keeping them some 2,000 feet away. Even with Sumter in ruins, the fact was that Charleston was too well protected to be taken from the sea. Du Pont had not failed; he had been asked to do the impossible.[7]

Since reports of officers and men being arrested for various offenses against military law and custom were common in the newspapers, it was natural for many of the *Herald*'s readers to take the plight of Private Miles O'Reilly seriously. If Halpine was surprised to find his joke accepted as fact, he quickly recognized that he had a good thing going, and he determined to make as much out of it as he could. Public sympathy for a courageous Irish soldier who had gone to prison because of a simple poem defending an admiral might be translated into sympathy for the admiral. Even if it could not, it was bound to lead to a more favorable public view of the Irish, for there had not been many Irish heroes in the news in recent weeks.

Halpine's delight at the public interest in Miles O'Reilly was tempered by another strain in his relations with Thurlow Weed. Back in November, 1861, President Lincoln had sent Weed, along with recently retired General Winfield Scott, Archbishop John Hughes, and Bishop Charles McIlvaine, on a special mission to Europe. These four prominent leaders, who embarked at a time when Anglo-American relations were critical, were supposed to assist the regular American ministers in persuading England and France to remain neutral. Weed was in Paris in January, 1862, shortly before the Emperor was scheduled to address the French Chambers. It was feared that Napoleon's speech would include a denunciation of the United States blockade of southern ports, and, in particular, of the efforts to close permanently the harbor at Charleston by sinking ships loaded with stones in the channel.

Criticism of these actions might well be the prelude to intervention on the part of the French and English fleets, in the name of freedom of commerce. For the fact that the Emperor did not take the stand expected of him, Weed seems to have told Halpine that he himself was responsible.

As Weed told the story, he had arranged an interview with the Emperor's half-brother, the Duke de Morny, during which he cleverly steered the conversation away from the opera and other noncontroversial topics to the subject of French foreign policy, which the Duke wished to avoid. Very subtly, Weed manipulated the conversation to the point where he could inform the Duke of precedents for the actions of the United States government in European and even in French history. Apparently unaware of these precedents, the Duke was visibly shaken, for it would not do for France to denounce the United States for doing what it itself had done. Thanking Weed profusely for the information, Morny hastened away to warn the Emperor, who proceeded to eliminate the much-feared passage from his address, thus preventing a crisis and perhaps even war between France and the United States.

Impressed with the drama of the story, Halpine spent an idle Sunday morning writing it up, and showed his manuscript to Henry J. Raymond, who promptly printed it in the New York *Times* on 8 September 1863. Weed was furious at what he considered a breach of confidence, and in three letters written in two days to "My injured friend," Halpine apologized abjectly. He had embellished the story with too many details, he admitted, but this was a mere literary vanity and he had planned to revise the final copy. But Raymond had published without giving him a chance to examine the proofs. "Guilty of a blunder so unpardonable," he wrote, "I fear you never again can feel at ease with me. . . . I have never in my life felt more utterly dejected. I know not how to sign myself, so only put my initials." [8]

It does not seem possible that it was Halpine's literary details which so embarrassed Weed. The incident itself must have been untrue, or exaggerated out of all relation to the facts, thus humiliating Weed before John Bigelow, the American minister to France, and others who knew the truth. [9]

Halpine's story, published in the *Times* under the signature "Ex-diplomat," was reprinted after Weed's death in Thurlow Weed Barnes's *Memoir* of his grandfather, and has therefore been assumed to be Weed's own work, or at least a version of the incident he approved. In *Diplomat in Carpet Slippers,* Jay Monaghan repeats the story, but notes inaccuracies in the historical precedents Weed was supposed to have cited for Morny, and concludes, "Perhaps the rest of his account was out of place, too." [10] Indeed it was.

Early in October readers of the *Herald* were shocked to read in another dispatch from the paper's correspondent in the Department of the South that Private Miles O'Reilly was still languishing in prison on Morris Island. Indeed, he was worse off than before the *Herald*'s revelation of his plight and its publication of his poem in behalf of Admiral Du Pont. What could have been treated as a mere impropriety and forgiven after token punishment so long as knowledge of it remained confined to the department was now known throughout the nation, and authorities therefore had no choice but to let the Private pay the full penalty of his impudence. To pardon him now would threaten discipline throughout the services, and encourage other privates to tell their betters how to run the war! Indignant readers were assured, however, that Miles was being treated humanely, and that he was regularly visited by the chaplain, surgeons, and other officers, all mentioned by name. The Private's greatest worry was that the commanding officer of the Forty-Seventh was on leave in New York City, and might not be present at the court martial to testify to his generally good conduct.

Perhaps because of the absence of his colonel, Miles had written a petition for a pardon direct to the Secretary of War. It was in verse, naturally, and designed for singing to the tune of "The Fine Old English Gentleman."

> I'll sing to you a navy song
>   Made by a soldier's pate,
> Of a galliant, grim ould Admiral,
>   Whom iron jobbers hate. . . .

In a long recitative, which, according to the *Herald*'s correspondent, he sang in a particularly impressive manner, Miles promised both Stanton and Welles that, if pardoned, he would do everything he could for them,

> (Votin' airly and votin' often for yez both,
> or for aither of you, if yez ever chance to be
> candydates in any dishtrick or county where I
> can get widin ten rods of the ballot box,)

> An' now my name I thrace—
> Miles O'Reilly, who wrote of the Admiral,
>   And is havin' a hard ould time!

Of course the Secretary of War could not be expected to give serious consideration to Miles's appeal, but the correspondent suggested that if

President Lincoln's attention could be called to the case, his well-known appreciation of a joke might cause him to take mercy on the wretched soldier. The correspondent concluded his article with still another defense of Du Pont and criticism of the Navy Department. The point of the whole controversy, he declared, was to show that the monitors were not what the navy needed, and that Du Pont's reputation was suffering unjustly. Miles O'Reilly was being punished for telling the truth.[11]

Except for the burlesque poem to Stanton, there was even less reason for readers to question the legitimacy of this report than of the first. It was written dead-pan and published as straight news, and most people accepted it unquestioningly, as they did most other things they saw in their papers. Even Lincoln, who had been embarrassed by military arrests before, seems to have been fooled. "The Pres. was completely gulled," exclaimed Halpine (who may have heard of it from Hay) to Du Pont, "and believed every word of the story." [12] If so, he soon learned the truth, for in the next installment of the story he read that, even though Miles had not gone to sleep on sentry duty, he had pardoned him.

The President intervened in the case, so Halpine wrote, partly because he recognized that the offending poem had been meant as an innocent joke, and partly because someone showed him a copy of another O'Reilly poem—a poem which had been of the "utmost value" in reconciling soldiers in the Department of the South to the recruitment and use of Negro soldiers. The poem was, of course, "Sambo's Right To Be Kilt." Placing it in this context not only allowed Halpine to expose it to a very large civilian audience, but to speak a few words in defense of David Hunter, whom he believed to have been as unfairly treated by his critics as Du Pont by his. When Hunter organized his black regiment, said Halpine, he had no intention of initiating any new political or social policy; he had acted out of military considerations exclusively, and without any thought whatsoever of "humanitarian proletarianism." He had simply seen that every black regiment in the field would take the place of a white regiment. "Every ball stopped by a black man would save the life of a white soldier." [13]

Lincoln liked "Sambo's Right To Be Kilt," Halpine's story continued, and told John Hay that it reminded him of what the deacon in Menard County said when a prostitute dropped a half-eagle into the collection plate. No matter how she got it, said the pragmatic deacon, the money was good and would do good. "I have no doubt, Hay," the President continued, "that O'Reilly, in whom you seem to take such an interest, might be a great deal better man than he is. But that song of his is both good and will do good." So Lincoln pardoned Miles O'Reilly and ordered him sent North on the next steamer for eventual assignment, it was reported, to the White House, where he would be given the duty of rendering the President's stories into song.[14]

"Sambo's Right To Be Kilt" did in fact "do good." Immediately popular, it was extensively reprinted, and later, along with other of Halpine's popular war songs, was printed in sheet music form (with a dedication to David Hunter). A hit among prejudiced whites everywhere, it was most influential among the bitterest foes of the Lincoln administration, the New York Irish, whom it helped to reconcile to the policy they most strongly opposed—the involvement of the Negro in the war. In a single poem, Halpine accomplished his major mission on the staff of General Dix. If Negro help was the decisive factor in the Union's ultimate triumph, as Lincoln believed it was, then "Sambo's Right To Be Kilt," for all its cruelty, must be considered a contribution to the victory.

The climax in the Miles O'Reilly affair occurred at a fantastic banquet held in honor of the Private on October 23, 1863, in New York's fashionable Delmonico's restaurant. The fiction provided Halpine with a chance to satirize testimonial dinners, to make fun of some prominent officials and give favorable publicity to others, to score points in behalf of Admiral Du Pont, clean local government, and other subjects of interest to him, and, above all, to celebrate the Union cause and to publicize the support the Irish were giving it. By this time, testimonial dinners for generals and political leaders had become established features of fashionable social life, the public sharing their glamor vicariously by reading lengthy stories about them in the press. Menus, room and table decorations, the distinction of the guests present, the formal regrets of those absent, toasts, speeches, and entertainment were all described in elaborate detail. During October, two especially sumptuous banquets were held at the Astor House for the Admiral and officers of the Russian fleet, then visiting in New York harbor. But even these were scarcely equal in magnificence to the dinner which Halpine gave for his humble private.

Mindful of the publicity recently received by the Astor House, Delmonico was determined to reestablish the preeminence of his restaurant for elegance and good food. In honor of Miles O'Reilly, he decorated his walls with national and regimental battle flags (by no means hiding that of the Irish Brigade); his tables sparkled with gold and silver dishes containing treasures of exotic tropical fruit and dazzling palaces of flavored gelatin and charlotte russe; his windows were decorated with flowers and sprigs of evergreen, and the air was cooled and made musical by fountains playing in crystal basins.

The guest list was as brilliant as the banquet room. It included many of Halpine's closest friends from the army and navy, the New York bar, the city government, the press, politics, and the world of business and finance. Among those unable to attend who sent their written regrets was the President, who telegraphed that he had to remain in Washington to keep an eye on his cabinet, but that he was reminded of a story which he would tell some other time. Another was identified only as a "Distinguished Naval Officer," but his name, omitted "for reasons connected with the Navy Department," was easily guessed by those who had followed the fortunes and misfortunes of Miles O'Reilly. "I think," wrote this unmysterious individual, "that Private O'Reilly . . . has given us honest and manly songs—songs of the kind we much need." Ulysses S. Grant wired from Chattanooga that the invitation had reached him just as he was preparing to move upon the enemy's works, and the irascible Count Gurowski, who found so much to condemn in official Washington, felt the banquet to be beneath him socially. "I, who have bearded a Russian Emperor," he wrote, "am not to bow in homage abject to any of the great asses who are in this country heroes made." Gideon Welles could not attend because he was busy with his study of naval science. He had already progressed as far as the Spanish Armada, and hoped before the end of the war to reach Robert Fulton. Much to the chagrin of those in charge, it was soon discovered that nobody had thought to invite the guest of honor, so a special committee was selected on the spot to find him and escort him to the banquet.

While waiting for Miles, the guests heard a stirring speech denouncing those Democrats, a great many of them New Yorkers, who were more critical of the members of the Lincoln administration than they were of the leaders of the Confederacy. There was room for disagreement over specific administration policies—emancipation, the draft, suspension of the writ of habeas corpus—but these were only minor questions compared to the importance of winning the war. Such were the sentiments put by Halpine into the mouth of James T. Brady, a much respected leader of the New York bar who had been the candidate of the Breckenridge Democrats for Governor in 1860, but who was now loyally supporting the war. Like Halpine an immigrant from Ireland, Brady declared that all refugees from that wronged and degraded land should fight to the end to preserve their adopted land. "We need a country," he declared, as if he were speaking directly to the anti-draft rioters, "we must have a country."

Generous quantities of food and drink, toasts, songs, and speeches less serious than Brady's were served up by a great assortment of individuals. Increasingly noisy and impatient calls for the still-absent Miles O'Reilly also varied the pace of the evening and kept interest in Halpine's story alive. Peace Democrats were ridiculed by having Benjamin Wood, editor of the New York *News* and brother of Fernando, speak in favor of peace at any price. "All he wished," he was reported as having said, "was that we should withdraw our armies from every square foot of soil south of Mason and Dixon's line, divide our navy in two, giving the South half, accept the Montgomery constitution, and confer on Mr. Jeff. Davis the Loyal Union League nomination for the next Presidency." Wood's speech continued, but his words were lost in a chorus of groans, hisses, hootings, and cries of "Put him out," and "Scotch the Copperhead."

Finally, it became clear that Miles O'Reilly never would appear at his own banquet, and so the guests, shouting their low opinions of the Committee on Arrangements, staggered to their feet and made their way unsteadily to the door. The banquet was over.[15]

But Miles O'Reilly, just six weeks after the announcement of his imprisonment, was a hero, the subject of conversation everywhere. Was he a real person? Had he really been imprisoned for writing a poem in favor of Admiral Du Pont? Was it true that Lincoln had pardoned him? Had there been a banquet in his honor, and, if so, was it possible that no one had asked him to attend? Insiders were soon on to the hoax, but then there was another mystery to solve. Who was the author? New York newspapermen learned his identity before government officials, but by the time of the story of the Miles O'Reilly banquet most people in Washington knew that the heroic private was Charles G. Halpine. Among the public at large, O'Reilly's fame was always greater than Halpine's, whose name in print was often followed by the identifying parenthesis ("Miles O'Reilly").

The public took to Miles with good-humored affection. There was something refreshing about this brash, happy-go-lucky Irishman who made fun of admirals, attempted to bribe the Secretaries of War and Navy with promises of his political support, and in a poem of thanks for his pardon, addressed the President of the United States as an equal.

> Long life to you, Misther Lincoln!
> May you die both late an' aisy;
> An' whin you lie wid the top of aich toe
> Turned up to the roots of a daisy,

May this be your epitaph, nately writ—
"Though thraitors abused him vilely,
He was honest an' kindly, he loved a joke,
An' he pardoned Miles O'Reilly!" [16]

Big-talking generals were no novelty, but how many privates were so brazen? Yet there was an endearing innocence to his presumption. He did not see that the army and American society had relegated him to the lowest social position but one, and so he artlessly practiced the democratic equalitarianism he heard so much talk about. The liberties he took with convention were inoffensive because he was, after all, just a child in a soldier's uniform (Halpine often referred to him as "The Boy"), big-hearted, well meaning, and courageous in his loyalties. Whatever, if anything, Halpine at first intended him to be, by the time of the second installment of his story, Miles had evolved into the Lovable Irishman, luckless but happy, unlettered but wise, boastful but innocent and affectionate, the product of Halpine's eagerness to cancel out the unfavorable images of the 1850's and the New York riots.

Public figures quickly recognized the importance of Miles O'Reilly to their careers. The Boy dealt, after all, with real issues and real individuals. At the Miles O'Reilly Banquet alone, 113 different men were mentioned, their names merely dropped, or woven skillfully into the narrative in connection with some office, policy, or event. Naturally, they were concerned about how they were presented. Most references, including the original criticism of Admiral Dahlgren, were friendly, but once the sketches and songs multiplied and became something of a national institution, any reference was considered preferable to none. To appear in a Miles O'Reilly story was a sign that one counted, had influence, was a man to be reckoned with—all of which meant that Charles G. Halpine counted, had influence, was a man to be reckoned with. And he loved it.

Among the Irish, Miles O'Reilly quickly attained heroic stature. The patriotic private not only restored their self-respect by publicizing the support they were giving to the government, he helped to develop a sense of participation in the great struggle for national survival. Thanks to Miles, it was their war, after all, and their nation.

Since many of the corrupt city officials were not supporters of the war, Halpine was able to combine his responsibilities as a war propagandist with a renewal of his old campaign for honest government. After national patriotism, the major theme of the Miles O'Reilly Banquet was the need for political reform in New York, and on both subjects Halpine spoke through the person of James T. Brady. Part of a citizen's duty to his country, declared Brady in the banquet's principal address, was to help drain the swamp of local government of the toads, reptiles, and vermin which flourished in it through their control of the official party organizations. The coalition between Republicans of easy virtue and Democrats of no virtue at all had debased government in New York to the point that to be called a politician was the equivalent of being called a rogue. The first step toward reform was the election of a truly independent judiciary, and Brady urged Miles's friends to vote for his slate of candidates for Superior Court judgeships in the November elections.

In still another effort to influence the elections, Halpine wrote an allegory about the bipartisan machine which ruled and looted New York. He attempted to demonstrate the extent of the machine's control by describing its private model of the city, which was complete to the smallest detail and designed to reflect the machine's interests. The shanties and saloons, for example, were over-sized, dwarfing the churches and schools near which they stood. The biggest building of all was the City Hall, whose cupola reached for the clouds and whose base spread nearly from river to river and threatened to absorb half the island. Tammany Hall, Mozart Hall, Republican party headquarters, the police station, the comptroller's office, and the tenement houses scattered throughout the city were built on the same exaggerated scale. Close examination revealed that a complex network of wires radiated in all directions from City Hall. The wires, powerful and numerous and dripping gold, led to the site of every building erected under city contract, to every city railroad under construction, to every ferry franchise, to every pier and dock, and, indeed, to the Russian banquets and all the others. A cable consisting of four thick and seventeen thin strands (representing the city's senators and assemblymen in Albany), connected the whole mechanism to the state capitol, a model of which stood in overgrown grandeur on a pedestal behind the city hall. Such was the apparatus by which the representatives of both parties who constituted the machine planned and executed their systematic looting of the city.[17]

Halpine was pleased with his story (which was given the title "The Miles O'Reilly Caucus" by James Gordon Bennett, though it had nothing to do with Miles), and believed that if the *Herald* had published it a day or two before the election it might have influenced the results. But by "treachery" in the *Herald* office, it was held off until election morning, November 3, too late for maximum effect. He told Hay the piece would give him some further insights into the iniquities of New York politics, "with which, down in So. Ca. and elsewhere, I used to horrify your unsophisticated ears." [18]

Statewide the election was a Unionist victory, but in New York City, where it could fabricate voting returns as needed, the machine continued its domination, losing a single judicial seat. What else could be expected, Halpine asked Hay in his post-election letter, when Tammany and Mozart were "in conjunction with the regular Republican (Thurlow Weed) machine?" It was a private question, but after the Miles O'Reilly Caucus, Weed, who was so powerful in Albany, could not have been ignorant of the fact that Halpine linked him directly to the corrupt city government. The friendship between the two men, previously strained on several occasions, was never entirely broken, but it must have ceased now to be close. Other New York leaders were less tolerant. "My 'Miles O'Reilly-isms,'" Halpine told Hay, "can never be forgotten and never forgiven." To his commanding officer, General Dix, he wrote that he had even heard some of his enemies were trying to get him transferred to duty in New Mexico! [19]

Presidential politics were never far from Halpine's thoughts, and it was only natural for him to consider the possibility that Dix might receive the presidential or vice-presidential nomination of a Unionist coalition of Republicans and War Democrats. Horace Greeley liked him, and Dix's work in New York after the riots associated him with administration policy and could not fail to recommend him to Republicans. He was, furthermore, a general, even something of a hero, and he was well known as a man of experience and integrity. He had a chance and therefore, Halpine advised him, should keep his speeches short, pithy, and "nationally democratic."

To some New York Republicans, Dix's prospects for a position on the Unionist ticket in 1864 seemed sufficiently good to cause alarm, for if he did receive a nomination, he would transfer the seat of power in the Unionist coalition from the Republicans to the Democrats. Thus, they tried to sidetrack him into running for mayor of New York. But there were others who for different reasons wanted Dix to run for mayor in the December, 1863, city elections. A group of reform-minded New Yorkers thought that he might be able to beat the machine, and they offered him their support. Finding him reluctant to run, they sent William B. Astor and Robert B. Roosevelt to Washington with a petition asking Lincoln to request Dix to make the race. The petition bore twenty-one of the most distinguished signatures in New York, including those of John Jacob Astor, Jr., Peter Cooper, and Alexander Stewart. In response, Lincoln spoke of his appreciation of Dix's services, but beyond declaring that nothing would please him more if Dix were elected mayor, declined to interfere.[20]

But Dix had already decided not to run, and Halpine, so recently impressed by the ability of the city machine to steal an election, called the efforts of Astor, Roosevelt, and "those other Fifth Avenue noodles," ridiculous. He feared Dix might be defeated for mayor; if he were, he would no longer be available for higher office, and his usefulness in his present position would be lessened. At the very least, Dix should run for governor, an office he could win easily, thus helping the Unionist candidates for president and vice-president—unless he were one of them himself.

Other presidential election possibilities were considered in the next installment of the adventures of Miles O'Reilly, The Boy's visit to the White House to thank the President for pardoning him. Since no story about an interview with Lincoln would be complete without an anecdote, Halpine wrote to John Hay for something recent and authentic. Hay replied:

My Dear Miles   Nov 22 [1863]

Ever since I got your letter I have been skulking in the shadow of the Tycoon, setting all sorts of dextrous traps for a joke, telling good stories myself to draw him out and suborning Nicolay to aid in the foul conspiracy. But not a joke has flashed from the Tycoonial thundercloud. He is as dumb as an oyster. Once or twice a gleam of hope has lit up my soul as he would begin 'That puts me in mind of Tom Skeeters out in Bourbon County[,]' but the story of Skeeters would come out unfit for family reading; and the dawning promise of a reminiscence of Menard County would turn to ashes as it developed a ferble [?] personality [which] would move rage & not laughter if repeated. . . .

I give you my word of honor if he says a good thing within a week to faithfully report it to you. . . .

After all, my dear Miles, you had better . . . get up your own jokes than ask anything authentic from me. They will fit in more neatly than the crude originals.

> God Bless you Miles my darlint,
>   May you die both late and aisy,
> And when you lie wid the top [of] aich toe
>   Turned up to the roots of a daisy,
> May this be your epitaph nately writ
>   Though the *World* abused ye vilely:
> "A broth of a boy at a fight or a faist
>   Was Private Miles O'Reilly."

Halpine took Hay's advice and went ahead and made up his own Lincoln anecdote, assuring Hay it was so true to the President's style he'd think "the Tycoon himself is in correspondence with me." [21] The *Herald* published the story on November 28. Like the other Miles O'Reilly hoaxes, it was presented as a straight news event, and it took an alert and wary reader to realize that it was not. Under such provocative headings as "MILES O'REILLY AT THE WHITE HOUSE. MR. LINCOLN, THE CABINET AND THE FOREIGN DIPLOMATIC BODY. DEEPLY INTERESTING CEREMONIAL. SONGS TO SUIT EVERYBODY. MR. LINCOLN TELLS HIS BEST STORY," the hoax took up nearly a page, was reprinted, and fooled thousands of readers, including some historians who assumed that Halpine made the visit to the White House even if they knew Miles had not.[22]

The story began with the first published description of Miles O'Reilly, "a brawny, large-boned, rather good-looking young Milesian, with curly reddish hair, grey eyes, one of which has a blemish upon it, high cheek bones, a cocked nose, square lower jaws, and the usual strong type of Irish forehead—the perceptive bumps, immediately above the eyes, being extremely prominent." His face was "good-humored" and "radiantly expressive," and it beamed "with a candor and unreserve equal to that of a mealy potato which has burst its skin or jacket by too rapid boiling." Miles was about six feet three inches tall, he was broad-chested and barrel-bodied, and his fists were hard and heavy.

Inside the White House, Miles stood rigidly at attention while his escort, the popular Irish general, Thomas Francis Meagher, introduced him to the President, the cabinet, and half the diplomats of Washington. It was, of course, an opportunity for a speech about the gallantry of Irish soldiers. The blood the Irish were shedding for the Union, declared Meagher, was changing them from exiles in a foreign land to the peers of the proudest and best Americans. They were earning their right to the equality and fraternity of citizenship.

Before even acknowledging the presence of the awe-struck young Private, still standing at attention, Lincoln began to tell the story which Halpine thought so true to the President's style. It was the story about the Widow Zollicoffer's slave, down in Bourbon County. One day while making cranberry jam, the good widow was called away to a neighbor's. "Sam, you rascal," she said, "you'll be eating my jam when I'm away." Sam denied it, but as a precaution she ran her finger along his lips, pretending she was applying a coating of chalk so that she could tell if he had eaten anything. When she returned, Sam's lips really were thickly chalked, and she had all the evidence against him she needed. It was much the same, said Lincoln, with the presidency. Half the cabinet and most of the generals in the army professed not to be interested in it, but their lips were thickly chalked.

Amidst the laughter which followed, Lincoln shook hands with O'Reilly and took him up to the other distinguished guests, who were anxious to hear his opinion about the presidential election. Miles, who had a bad stammer at tense moments ("the words bubbled up so quick to his tongue that they choked and killed each other—like an audience crowding out through the narrow doors of a theatre"), was unable to answer until taken into Nicolay's office and given a jug of water "with no more whiskey in it than President Pierce took at the opening of the Crystal Palace." He returned in a moment wiping his mouth on his sleeve and, responding immediately to the treatment, declared that only one man in the country who wore a black coat could be elected president. He might not be, but he was the only civilian who could be. On the other hand, there were a number of men in blue coats and brass buttons who might make it, and he briefly examined the chances of Grant, Dix, Halleck, and McClellan.

And so the story progressed from topic to topic. In a song which became one of the public's favorites, "The Song of the Soldiers" (to the tune of "Jamie's on the Stormy Sea"), Miles stressed the solidarity of the men in the ranks, regardless of their places of birth:

> By communion of the banner—
> Battle-scarred but victor banner,
> By the baptism of the banner,
>   Brothers of one church are we!
> Creed nor faction can divide us,
> Race nor language can divide us,
> Still, whatever fate betide us,
>   Children of the flag are we!

At the request of the President, who insisted he wanted a frank evaluation of the public's attitude toward his administration, another song described the various cabinet members. The first was Secretary of War Stanton, who had ruled that the rank of major given to Halpine when he joined Dix's staff was "conformably to regulations."

> Stanton's beard is thick and long,
>   And rough and tough his portly figure;
> But his heart is brave and strong
>   With fierce vitality and vigor.

> Work that might a dozen men
> Tire to death, he knocks off gaily,
> And blundering badly now and then,
> Does true and noble service daily.
> Oh, my Edwin, dread and dear,
> Dispensing fount of pay and rations,
> Private Miles upon you smiles,
> "Conformably to Regulations."

In the same song, Seward was criticized for cringing before England, Chase for issuing so much paper money, and Welles for learning his lessons from Noah. Corruption in New York was treated in "The Lament of St. Tammany," in which the machine mourned the loss of the judgeship in the recent election, and England was attacked for its violations of neutrality. Miles expressed his admiration for Lord Palmerston, however, who, at the age of eighty, had just been named as corespondent in the divorce of an Irish woman.

> There's somethin' quare in Irish air
> And a diet of pitaties,
> That makes us all so prone to fall
> To whiskkey and the ladies. . . .

The story ended when Lincoln, fearing an international incident, changed the subject by telling another story, bade goodbye to his official guests, and invited General Meagher and Private O'Reilly to join him and his family at their Thanksgiving turkey.[23]

Two weeks passed before he heard any reaction from Washington, and Halpine began to fear that he had offended Lincoln. "Once, when a little shaver," he told Dix, "I came home from school crying. 'What were you whipped for Charlie,' asked my father. 'Please, Papa, I was too funny,' was my answer, and perhaps I may have been 'too funny' again." [24]

But he had not been. "The President was immensely amused with Miles's last," wrote Hay at last in December. "He is too sick to read and not well enough to object to anything. So I had him at my mercy and read him into a fever." The White House was not reluctant to agree that only one black coat could be elected president, and Hay was newly confident "that he will be." Complimenting his friend on the poem to Palmerston and "The Song of the Soldiers," Hay told him, "You are a scoundrel to do so little of these things."

CHAPTER 7

The Bogus Proclamation

THE PUBLISHER George W. Carleton caused a literary sensation in 1862 when he brought out *Artemus Ward. His Book*. Early in 1864, he followed it with another best seller: *Miles O'Reilly. His Book* (as it was called on its cover) or *The Life and Adventures of Miles O'Reilly* (as it was listed on its title page). It was an immediate success, selling 3,000 copies the first day, exhausting the first printing by March 1, and receiving enthusiastic reviews in newspapers all over the country.[1] The more attention Halpine could get from his journalist friends the better, Carleton advised him.[2] Indeed, the stories were more effective and more entertaining in book form than they had been as serials in the *Herald,* where they were sometimes cut and sometimes obscured by the bulk of news from the battle fronts. Royalty checks appeared, and Halpine suddenly discovered that he was famous, his poems and songs in demand by national magazine and music publishers, his name known everywhere.

The success of Miles O'Reilly was more than just a personal satisfaction to Halpine, more than the simple gratification of his ambition. It represented, as well, a reprieve from the sentence of failure which he had so often pronounced against himself, and a temporary acquittal from the harsh judgments he believed the elders who took an interest in his career had levied against him—that he was a bright young man who could amount to something if he only stopped drinking and settled down. Now, in the inner circles of journalism, politics, and the military, where he had so long served as an apprentice and where his various patrons ruled, he was a celebrity and a power in his own right; he could feel (at least for the time being) that the promise of his youth would be fulfilled, after all, that his gifts would not go to waste.

His sense of fulfillment and emancipation was made especially pleasurable by the fact that he was stationed in New York, where the achievement of a national reputation could be most fully savored, and living at home, where he was surrounded by adoring women and children. In addition to his family, his household included for the winter the two daughters of a Chicago lawyer, James H. Collins, who was acquainted with Lincoln and was probably a friend of Hunter's. As described for John Hay's benefit, the younger girl, Posie, was particularly succulent, "with masses of brown hair, teeth that glisten like pulled almonds, pure Grecian features, a bust that in its outline gives guarantee of future joy to generations yet unborn, and a soul . . . pure, spotless and sweetly simple." Halpine was so anxious to please her that he made of Lincoln what he promised would be his only request—an appointment to West Point for her brother. Young Collins was dutifully placed on the President's waiting list, but he never received the appointment.[3]

The only thing which marred Halpine's happiness was the fact that despite all of his efforts to be restored to his old rank, despite the help of his powerful friends and the letter to the Secretary of War from the President himself, he who had once been a lieutenant colonel with a chance of becoming a brigadier general was still only a major. After so many months, it was both tiresome and mortifying to have to explain to friends and acquaintances that he had not been demoted, that he was a major, in Stanton's phrase, "conformably to regulations." Military authorities could find a way around regulations if they wanted to. Why had they not? Perhaps they would if he could show that while in South Carolina he had played an important role in the capture of the rebel ironclad, *Atlanta.* Surely, Halpine thought, such a service deserved recognition and reward.

Six months before, on June 17, 1863, the *Atlanta,* a steamer converted into an ironclad monster very much like the famed *Merrimac* in appearance, had moved down the Wilmington River and approached Wassaw Sound, Georgia. Considered by the Confederates to be the best of their ironclads, the *Atlanta* expected to dispose of any United States warships in its way and proceed to open water, breaking the blockade, and two boats of spectators from Savannah had followed close behind to watch the spectacle. But waiting for *Atlanta* at the mouth of the river were the monitors *Weehawken* and *Nahant.* In an unequal fifteen-minute battle, *Weehawken* struck her with four out of five shots, disabled her temporarily, and drove her aground. She surrendered with her crew of 145 officers and men, and with the Stars and Stripes at her masthead, was taken to Port Royal for repairs. It was a major victory for the United States, and Halpine claimed that he had played an essential part in it.

It was he, so he asserted, who was responsible for the fact that the

monitors were waiting for *Atlanta*. He had learned of the ironclad's preparations from three Confederate deserters brought into his headquarters
from the Savannah area, and he had "at once" forwarded the information to Captain Rodgers, who immediately requested an army transport
to tow the monitors into position. Had it not been for his interrogation of
the prisoners and his quick action afterwards, *Atlanta*'s plans might well
have succeeded. Yet Admiral Du Pont, in the official report which was
published at the end of 1863, had failed to give him any credit whatsoever.

Irritated that the man he and Miles O'Reilly had been trying so
earnestly to help had passed up an opportunity to help him by acknowledging his contribution to the victory, Halpine wrote to Rodgers
to complain. In two letters written on consecutive days, Rodgers
apologized for what he was sure was a simple oversight. Du Pont would
be especially regretful about the omission when he learned that he
could have helped Halpine get his promotion, and he was sure, said
Rodgers, that "our noble old Admiral" would do his best to make it
up to him.

A few days later, Du Pont tried.

Colonel: January 8, 1864

A friend has called my attention to an omission in my official
report of June 17 to the Navy Department, to be found in public
documents recently published.

I omitted in that letter to state the source of the information
which had led me to believe that the rebel ironclad *Atlanta* was
preparing for a raid, and about moving. This most important fact
was sent off by you to the fleet captain, Commander C. R. P.
Rodgers, after you had closely interrogated certain deserters just
in from Savannah. I acted instantly on your letter. . . .

How I committed the oversight not to mention officially this
opportune public service so valuable to me as the commanding
naval officer on the coast, I can only account for by great pressure
of business and great haste, in order to avail myself of a depart-
ing mail.

I seize this opportunity, not only to rectify this omission, but
to state also how often I had occasion to recognize your intelligent
and efficient zeal in conducting the duties and business of your
important position in the Department of the South whenever the
military and naval services were blended or had official relations

and intercourse. Taking the greatest pleasure in making these statements,

I am, colonel, very respectfully, your obedient servant,

S. F. Du Pont
Rear-Admiral, U.S. Navy [4]

Halpine was delighted. Du Pont's letter would be of decisive importance in his campaign to attain the rank he was entitled to, he told the Admiral in thanking him for it. And he had always believed the omission to have been a mere oversight.[5] He then sent copies of the document to General Halleck and to the much-abused Secretary Welles, who assured him it would become part of the Navy Department's official records.[6]

But memories play tricks, and Halpine's, reenforced by ambition and a sense of injustice, perhaps tricked him. The service he performed in alerting the navy to the danger from *Atlanta* occurred on March 13, 1863, over three months before the ironclad's capture. Upon receiving the intelligence Halpine obtained from the deserters, Du Pont might well have taken immediate steps to increase surveillance of *Atlanta,* but he did not send *Weehawken* and *Nahant* to Wassaw Sound until June 10, one week before the battle. When he did so, it was on the strength of information dated June 2, to the effect that *Atlanta* would be ready for action "in about two weeks." [7] In his official report, Du Pont had failed to mention Halpine for the simple reason that Halpine's information had not really been a factor in the victory.

In recalling the incident in January, 1864, both Rodgers and Du Pont no doubt remembered that Halpine had indeed passed on intelligence of some kind about the *Atlanta,* and their memories may have tricked them, as well, into thinking they had acted on the basis of it. If so, failure to give Halpine credit certainly did demand a handsome letter of apology, and an attempt to set the record straight. More likely, however, they simply decided to play along with their old friend who had been doing so much to help them, and whose book of Miles O'Reilly stories would give national publicity to their side of the controversy with the Navy Department over the monitors.

In addition to seeking and receiving official credit for a role in the capture of *Atlanta,* Halpine talked over the problem of his rank with United States Senator Edwin D. Morgan of New York. At Morgan's suggestion, he put his whole case in a long letter outlining his military career and recounting his efforts as a publicist to win support for the

government and the war.[8] He also gathered together a group of
testimonial letters from prominent friends and gave them to John Hay
for presentation to the President.[9] Horace Greeley wrote directly to
Lincoln. "I trust," said the powerful editor, "you already know my
excellent friend Major Charles G. Halpine, Asst. Adj. General (better
known as 'Private Miles O'Reilly') who has done more than any other
man to popularize and strengthen the War with the Irish Democracy of
this city. I assure you that few men have deserved more than he, and
that any favor you can do him will be very favorably received in this
city." [10]

But if it was true that Halpine had done "more than any other
man" to popularize the war in the city where it had been most unpopular, if few men really deserved more from the government than he, why
was it necessary for him to wage such a campaign for a mere lieutenant-
colonelcy? Why must he humiliate himself in efforts to persuade the
administration he had served so well to remove the stigma of an
apparent demotion? Why did so many men with lesser responsibilities,
lesser influence, lesser friends, fly past him in the race for eagles and
stars? Charles G. Halpine knew the answer better than any man; the
trouble was he couldn't do anything about it.

In January, 1864, Halpine went to Washington to serve on a committee, along with Major General Ethan Allen Hitchcock and Brigadier
General Edward R. S. Canby, to collate and revise the Rules and
Articles of War. From the first, politicians and businessmen crowded his
room at Willard's. "I never was so well received before," he wrote to
Margaret, "and have half the town running after me." To his publisher
he sent word that "All Washn. is 'Miles O'Reilly' mad. The applications
for my autographs for Sanitary Fairs etc etc are overwhelming; & to a
modest man it is not pleasant to find himself suddenly stared at by a ball
room full of company. Everybody seems to know me as Miles." Admiral
Du Pont, in Washington and grateful to be back on good terms with
Halpine, was elated; he believed *The Life and Adventures of Private
Miles O'Reilly* would stir up such a storm that Secretary Welles would
be forced out of office. Halpine was surprised at his reception, and confessed to John Savage early in February that if he had guessed how
important Miles O'Reilly would be, he would have taken more time and
"made a better thing of it."

Among his visitors was Salmon P. Chase, who came by his room one
Sunday evening and stayed for four hours ("What do you think of that?"
Halpine asked Margaret) talking about the subject closest to his heart
—his chances of becoming president. He must have been both optimistic

and persuasive, for Halpine, forgetting Miles O'Reilly's prediction that the only black coat which could be elected was Lincoln's, told Sidney Howard Gay, managing editor of Greeley's *Tribune* that Chase's presidential stock was booming and "I am thinking of going with it for a 'comer.' " [11] But within a few days, well before the publication of the Pomeroy Circular, which is usually credited with ending the Chase boom, Halpine had come to believe the ambitious Secretary couldn't make it. Lincoln, too, was finished, he thought, or would be within a month. Maybe Halleck had a chance. Like most people in Washington, Halpine saw a possible candidate wherever he looked, and only hoped he would be looking in the right direction when the nominations were made.

While working on the Rules and Articles of War and doing his best to get his promotion, it was embarrassing for Halpine to have to acknowledge authorship of "The Flaunting Lie," the poem he had written attacking the flag for its association with the return to slavery of Anthony Burns, back in 1854. The poem was revived early in 1864 when Horace Greeley, one of its greatest admirers, published it anonymously in his history, *The American Conflict,* as an example of public reaction to enforcement of the Fugitive Slave Act. Copperhead newspapers, long angry at being denounced for disloyalty by Greeley, now seized the opportunity to challenge Greeley's own loyalty by reprinting "The Flaunting Lie" out of context and attributing it to him. To protect his old friend, it was of course necessary for Halpine to admit authorship, and to show that the poem was not really an attack on the flag, but on its desecration in the Burns case. Yet the timing was unfortunate. At the moment he was doing everything in his power to demonstrate his services to the flag, he had to explain away the fact that he had once called it a "polluted rag." As he put it to Gay, "That which I greatly feared has come upon me." He was, at least for the moment, a controversial figure whom it might be difficult for the administration to promote.

Among the friends Halpine saw in Washington was David Hunter. Still without a command, but encouraged by Stanton to believe he would soon receive an important one, Hunter had been dutifully serving on various War Department boards and commissions, and making official inspection and fact-finding trips. He was at Chattanooga with Grant for three weeks late in the fall of 1863. Grant shared his room with him, lent him his favorite horse, allowed him to read his In and Out dispatches, and told him of his plans. "So you see," Hunter had written Halpine, "I had a good opportunity of judging the man. And I must say I am very much pleased with him—he writes his own dispatches and orders, and does his own thinking. He is quiet, modest and frank; does not swear or drink; listens to the opinions of all, and then promptly decides for himself, and is ever ready to avail himself of the errors of his enemy." [12]

In February, Stanton asked Hunter to accept command of United States military forces on the Pacific coast, and offered a brigadiership for Halpine as his chief of staff. But Hunter, who hoped to be given a corps of the Army of the Potomac, if not the army itself, refused. It was a great disappointment for Halpine, for whom the position represented the vindication and recognition he so desperately wanted, and who rather liked the idea of moving to California. Possibly he even tried behind Hunter's back to get him to accept the Pacific command. Contacting United States Senator John Conness of California about something or other, he received Conness' promise that he would talk to Stanton. And later, in March, Halpine heard from Hunter that the administration still wanted him to go to California, and that Senator Conness had spoken in his favor to Lincoln.[13]

Halpine returned to New York on February 11. A few days later, the revised copy of the Rules and Articles of War, on which he had spent many tedious hours, was sent to the Adjutant General's office, filed, and never heard of again.[14] Perhaps Halpine had a premonition of the futility of the work, of his efforts to be promoted, of the chance to go to California, for despite the thrill he had felt at being treated as a person of consequence in Washington, he was very discouraged when he arrived back at his office in the Department of the East. Facing a large pile of accumulated paper work, he concluded a note to Nicolay: with "weariness of the burden we call life—I am thine, Usedupedly [and] everlastingly." [15]

In addition to his efforts to win support for the war among the Irish, a major portion of Halpine's time on Dix's staff was spent in the investigation and exposure of ruthless and corrupt recruiting practices in New York. The Conscription Act of March 3, 1863, provided for the establishment of quotas of men to be furnished for military service by the various Congressional Districts, and the drafting of men to fill the quotas when there was a deficiency of volunteers. Since the draft was tremendously unpopular—nowhere more so than in New York—all levels of government sought to avoid having to resort to it by offering generous bounties to encourage enlistments. The availability of these large sums of money, in turn, attracted corrupt "bounty brokers," who rounded up ignorant and credulous volunteers for nominal payments, took them to

wealthy districts where bounties were high, and pocketed the difference.
Sometimes the most cruel frauds were practiced against boys below
eighteen years of age, who were drugged or made drunk, and, with the
connivance of dishonest officials, signed up and robbed of their bounties
before they knew what had happened. Old men and men physically unfit
for service were also signed up and cheated, and some men volunteered
under threats of physical violence if they refused.[16]

Brigadier General Francis B. Spinola, on recruiting duty in New
York, at first denied that such crimes were committed within his juris-
diction. But he later admitted to Halpine that they were, and described
in detail the corrupt arrangements between brokers, county officials, and
military officers. If he himself had committed any errors, he insisted, they
were only the result of his eagerness to fill up a brigade and return to
action against the enemy. As the result of Halpine's investigations, Spinola was court-martialed for "conniving with bounty brokers to defraud
and swindle recruits," and sentenced to dismissal from the army.[17] Halpine was also responsible for the arrest and imprisonment of the worst
offenders among the bounty brokers, and in mid-April General Dix was
able to announce that the whole system of fraudulent recruiting had been
virtually broken up.[18]

By the spring, Halpine was reconciled to remaining a major—"conformably to regulations"—so long as he stayed on staff duty in New
York. Since the challenging part of his work with the Department of the
East had been completed, he therefore decided that if he were not
promptly reassigned at his old rank to a field command, he would resign
from the army. The kind of field assignment he wanted and felt qualified
to perform depended upon David Hunter, and after all the months which
had passed since Hilton Head, he was not sure Hunter still wanted and
needed him. So he wrote and asked, and the General's reply was all that
his sensitive ego could have asked. "I am in wonder at your last letter,"
wrote Hunter. "You talk of my not needing your services; you might as
well talk of my not needing my right arm, my right leg, my eyes, my
tongue, or my ears. Has an extraordinary fit of modesty come over you,
or are you getting somewhat crazed[?] I should judge the latter . . .
but you know I have always insisted you were flighty, and if it were not
for your best of wives there is no knowing what would become of you."
At a recent dinner at the White House, Stanton had agreed that Hunter
had never really had a chance to show what he could do with an army,
and once again told him that his time would come. "I am an old man,"
Hunter continued, "but I tell you what [that] if they give me a command

I intend to make it fly." So Halpine should not become discouraged. Sooner or later they would get their fighting command. In the meantime, Hunter declared, "you must keep yourself clear for action." [19]

But Halpine did not keep himself clear for action. He was drinking so heavily that in March he was unable to perform his duties at department headquarters, and Dix obligingly sent him on a trip to New England. Ostensibly, the trip was undertaken to inspect recruiting depots for scandals like those uncovered in New York, but in reality it was to enable Halpine to take the water cure at Wesselhoeft's, a health resort in Brattleboro, Vermont.[20] Only twice before in his life, he confessed to Margaret in a letter from the sanitorium, had he been in such bad condition as the day he left New York. In fact, that day he had not been able to go any further than Hartford, Connecticut. "And yet," he added, "from the very first night I was under treatment, I slept as you, dear, might sleep, if you were not kept awake by anxiety for your poor worthless husband."

In New York, Halpine's doctors had considered his craving for drink a physical disease, and had futilely prescribed a variety of medicines in their treatment of it. At Wesselhoeft's, the treatment consisted of putting nothing but pure cold water in his stomach. From the simple old German who lighted his fire and bathed him, Halpine derived a new understanding of his dipsomania, and believed he could overcome it in the future, "should the mad appetite ever return." It all depended upon being with someone who cared enough for him to do what he said. He wanted Margaret to come up for a few days, and then they would go back together to a new life in New York.

It was to be a new life as a civilian. For as he tramped the Vermont roads, breathing the cold, clean air and succumbing, as he always did, to the countryside, he made up his mind not to wait any longer for General Hunter, but to resign his commission on April 20, the third anniversary of the commencement of his career with the Sixty-Ninth Regiment. He thought he was entitled to a small pension for the loss of vision in his right eye, and believed he could obtain a political office which would provide the security of a fixed income. Then he would be free to write, to express himself on a large number of political and military questions, and to enjoy as a writer the success which was denied him in the army.

His mind made up and his health restored, Halpine returned to New York early in April. Securing affidavits from his personal physician and from a surgeon in the Department of the East that he had lost the sight of one eye in the Army and that continued service threatened the other, he sent his letter of resignation, with Dix's endorsement, to the War Department. He concluded the letter, he told Samuel L. M. Barlow, who understood the sarcasm, with professions of "undying affection for Stanton, Halleck & all others in authority." [21]

A prominent New York lawyer, Democrat, and man-about-town, Barlow was one of the owners of the New York *World,* a leading anti-Lincoln newspaper. Like many other northern Democrats, he believed that the Republican policy of freeing and elevating southern Negroes was prolonging the war by stiffening southern resistance and that some scheme to postpone emancipation would find widespread support in both North and South and provide the basis for peace and reunion.[22] Since Lincoln refused to modify or withdraw his Emancipation Proclamation, the only way to end the war was to elect a Democrat to the presidency in 1864. To help persuade the electorate, Barlow approached Halpine, whose readiness to think and say the worst about a Republican president was reenforced by his personal bitterness.

Halpine agreed to write for the *World,* but he was anxious that his association with Barlow, and with the *World*'s angry young editor, Manton Marble, remain a secret until after the War Department had accepted his resignation. "At present," he told Barlow, in a passage which reveals the corrosiveness of his resentment, "I want you to know that I am for the reelection of Abraham Lincoln, whom I regard as the ablest, honestest and handsomest man in the world—his figure tall, comely and delightfully graceful; . . . his mind a vast reservoir of wisdom & classical acquirements. . . . These are my present views. What they will be after my resignation is accepted—who can tell? There might possibly be a change."

A few days later, when the War Department, instead of accepting his resignation, offered him a sixty-day leave and sent him a complimentary letter, it came as no surprise; it was the kind of treatment he had come to expect. Besides, he still hoped that his friends in Washington could bring about his discharge by the time of his third anniversary, and if they could not he had decided to arrange for a court-martial which would force a decision in his favor. His medical certificates, he assured Barlow, entitled him to return to civilian life.

Like Halpine's own, the third anniversary of the wartime service of the Sixty-Ninth New York occurred in April. To commemorate it, Halpine wrote a poem, "April 20, 1864"—or as it came to be known in sheet music form, "The Swords Were Thirty-Seven"—describing a reunion of the surviving officers of an unspecified regiment. Of the original thirty-seven who had raised their swords after Fort Sumter, only eleven remained.

> There were two limped in on crutches,
>   And two had each but a hand
> To pour the wine and raise the cup,
>   As we toasted "Our flag and land!"
>
> And the room seemed filled with whispers
>   As we looked at the vacant seats,
> And, with choking throats, we pushed aside
>   The rich but untasted meats;
> Then in silence we brimmed our glasses,
>   As we rose up—just eleven,
> And bowed as we drank, to the loved and the dead
>   Who had made us thirty-seven!

With a dramatic and emotional illustration, the poem occupied the entire front page of *Harper's Weekly* for 30 April 1864, further spreading the fame of Miles O'Reilly, and subtly linking the Irish with military heroism and sacrifice. No doubt it also suggested to some readers the need for electing a president who could end the slaughter.

If his friendship with John Hay, the cordiality of his contacts with Lincoln, and the stimulating hours he had spent in the White House caused Halpine any uneasiness as the presidential campaign opened, if a not-quite-suppressed suspicion that he might be blaming the administration for his own failings occasionally flashed across his consciousness, all doubts were removed when he received orders originating with the President himself to arrest his new *World* friends, Barlow and Marble, for treason against the United States.

On the morning of May 18, 1864, the *World* and the *Journal of Commerce,* another New York newspaper hostile to the administration, published over Lincoln's name a proclamation calculated to turn war-weariness in the North into defeatism. Grant's blood-soaked campaign in Virginia was "virtually closed," the proclamation announced, and because of the disastrous ending to the recent Red River campaign and the continued failure to capture Charleston, the President was setting aside May 26 as a day of fasting and prayer, and calling for 400,000 additional soldiers. Suspicious because he had received no official confirmation of the proclamation and because it did not appear in any of the other morning papers, Dix wired to Washington to learn if it was genuine. It was not, and Dix received a telegram from Lincoln himself ordering him to arrest and imprison the editors and proprietors of the offending newspapers, and to take possession of their offices. The false proclamation, the telegram declared, "is of a treasonable nature, designed to give aid and comfort to the enemies of the United States." [23] Dix relayed Lincoln's order to two of his officers, including Halpine, and in the name of the President gave them written instructions to take the guilty parties, whose names he left blank for the officers themselves to fill in, to prison in Fort Lafayette, in New York harbor. Choosing to deal with his own friends himself, Halpine wrote the names of Barlow and Marble, and that of one Nathan D. Bangs, on the face of his orders, and then proceeded to do his distasteful duty.[24]

Surprised by the immediacy and force of the administration's action, the author of the hoax promptly confessed. He was Joseph Howard, Jr., the newspaperman whose 1861 fiction of how Lincoln had sneaked into Washington in disguise Halpine had helped to spread in his poem, "The Night Ride of Ancient Abe." At that time, Howard was simply belittling the President-elect; this time, he was apparently planning to profit from the financial alarm his proclamation was bound to cause on Wall Street, for he and at least one collaborator had been buying gold, which they planned to sell as its price shot up.[25]

As soon as it became clear that there was no more serious conspiracy behind the Bogus Proclamation (as it came to be called), and that the officials of the *World* and *Journal of Commerce* had only been the victims of a hoax, Stanton modified Lincoln's order and permitted their release from custody. So rapidly had the telegrams sped back and forth between New York and Washington, that the newspapermen were not even detained overnight, although their offices remained closed for several days.[26]

During the time in which the publication of the two papers was suspended, other newspapers in New York rallied to their defense. The *Tribune, Express, Herald,* and *Sun* all informed Lincoln that the hoax had been perpetuated by an "ingenious rogue" who might have fooled any of them. Since the proclamation had been written on exactly the kind of paper used by the Associated Press when it distributed bulletins to its members, and since it was delivered in properly sealed envelopes just as the morning editions went to press (when there was no time for checking), it was fortunate that only two papers had been deceived.[27]

Manton Marble's protest was more vigorous. He called Lincoln's action "outrageous," "oppressive," "unjust," "arbitrary," and "unconstitutional," and asked the President an embarrassing question. "Had the *Tribune* and the *Times* published the forgery, . . . would you, sir, have suppressed . . . [them] as you have suppressed the *World* and *Journal of Commerce?* You know you would not." [28]

Indeed, the suspension of the two opposition newspapers and the arrest of their editors did raise serious questions of civil liberty, and caused even many of the friends of the administration to wonder if once again it had not gone too far. For the Democrats, the issue promised substantial political rewards in the presidential campaign.

From condemnation of Lincoln's action, it was only a short step to the defense of Howard, who was held in prison until August. The charge that Howard had written the proclamation in order to profit from the panic it would cause on the stock market, Halpine asserted after the war, in the New York *Citizen,* 29 June 1867, was "pure poppycock, or something worse." Howard had been guilty only of a "very bad blunder in the way of a practical joke," and so Halpine rewarded him with a job.

At the very moment of his greatest disgust with the Lincoln administration, Halpine suddenly forgave it most of its sins. On May 15, 1864, Major General Franz Sigel, marching up the Shenandoah Valley of Virginia with a small federal army, was defeated and turned back at New Market by a Confederate force which included the celebrated battalion of boys from the Virginia Military Institute. As Sigel's successor in command of the Department of Western Virginia, Lincoln appointed David Hunter, and on the day after his arrest of Barlow and Marble, Halpine rushed to Washington to rejoin his old leader. He would be Hunter's adjutant, not his chief of staff as he had hoped, but it was of greater importance to him that at last his old brevet rank was restored, and that he could go off to war as a lieutenant colonel once again.

For Hunter even more than for Halpine, the war had so far meant frustration, unfulfilled expectations, and a bitter sense of injustice. Since his removal from command of the Department of the South, he had never ceased trying to get hold of another army, or thinking about what he would do with it when he did. He consulted a phrenologist, and was told that he himself was responsible for a large part of his failure. In Carolina, he had been too easy-going, too ready to respond to the persuasions of others, and he was now determined never to make that mistake again. "Should I ever have another command," he wrote to Halpine, 20 September 1863—at a time when they were both languishing at their desks —"I shall be as absolute as a Turk, and consult nobody on the face of the earth, except perhaps it may be you." For Hunter, the new assignment in the Shenandoah Valley represented the main—and the last— chance, and with grim resolution the old warrior reached out to grasp it.

CHAPTER 8

Hunter's Expedition

STRETCHING long and narrow between the Alleghenies and the Blue Ridge, from the Potomac River in the north to the headwaters of the James 150 miles to the southwest, lay the Shenandoah Valley, the major source of food for Lee's army. Although its lower, or northern, portion had been the scene of Stonewall Jackson's brilliant campaign in May and June, 1862, most of the Valley had escaped the destruction experienced by so much of the rest of Virginia. Its continued productivity was, indeed, a major factor in the ability of the battered Confederacy to prolong a losing war, and Grant, preparing to move south into the wilderness with 100,000 men, was determined to keep it from sustaining Lee any longer. He ordered Hunter to move up the Valley as far as Staunton, then cross the Blue Ridge through Rockfish Gap and descend upon the railroad centers of Charlottesville and Gordonsville. "If he can hold at bay a force equal to his own," Grant told Halleck, "he will be doing good service." A few days later, he modified his instructions, asking that Hunter push on to Lynchburg if he possibly could, destroying railroads and the James River Canal, and living off the countryside.[1]

The army with which Hunter was to undertake this formidable and important mission, so similar to the ones he had—over a year before— asked Lincoln for permission to make, was not only new to him, it was suffering from an acute case of demoralization. Spread out by regiments and divisions over all of West Virginia and western Maryland, its confidence in itself had been shattered by a very nearly continuous record of defeat in battle, under a series of inept generals. It had also been more than normally plundered by corrupt quartermasters. When Hunter assumed command, 1,500 of the 10,000 men he was to lead up the Valley were barefoot, and the regiments of infantry and cavalry commanded by Generals George Crook and William W. Averell, which were to move eastward from their camp in West Virginia and meet him at Staunton, were so miserably equipped it was "indispensably necessary"

107

to overburden his own train by carrying supplies to them. The quarter-masters were scoundrels, Halpine wrote in the diary he began to keep the day he learned of Hunter's expedition; they were just clerks whose knowledge of merchandise had put them in positions where they could make fortunes at the expense of the soldiers and the taxpayers.[2]

To help him lead his luckless new army—the Army of the Shenandoah—Hunter chose a personal staff which was not only close but familial. First of all, there was Halpine. Then came the Chief of Staff, a distant cousin who bore the General's own name, Colonel David Hunter Strother. A Virginia Yankee, Strother was a contributor to various national magazines, and wrote and illustrated in the 1850's a popular series of articles on life in the South under the pseudonym "Port Crayon," for *Harper's Monthly*. For his *aide-de-camp* Hunter chose another cousin, young Lieutenant Samuel W. Stockton, of whom he thought so highly that he asked Halleck to jump him to the rank of brigadier general.[3]

The morale of the army, and of its leaders, was not high as it readied itself for the big march. Halpine told Margaret that only half of the 10,000 men were first-class soldiers, and that many of their officers were worthless. Of the two division commanders, one was inexperienced, and a replacement who possessed "grit, zeal, activity, and courage" was requested for the other.[4] Less than two weeks before, the same army had undertaken a similar expedition, only to be turned back within fifty miles at a cost of a thousand casualties. The only replacements received since included a green and unreliable regiment of Ohio hundred-day men, so the army was actually weaker now than it had been. Furthermore, the Confederate force under General John C. Breckinridge which had stopped Sigel was not known for sure to have left the Valley; it might be waiting up the road in some entrenched position to cut the Army of the Shenandoah to pieces once again. Although Hunter quickly established himself as a disciplinarian, there was no reason to believe he would be any more successful than his predecessors. "We don't like his looks," wrote one soldier, suspiciously. The mood in camp was pessimistic, uneasy, distrustful, and as the men talked in small groups in their camp at Cedar Creek, near the north end of the Valley, or sat barefoot before their cooking fires, they realized uncomfortably that the surrounding hills were swarming with squads of guerrilla fighters led by the daring John Singleton Mosby, and that their every move was being observed through glasses.[5] Even Hunter was tense and bad-tempered, Halpine noted in his diary, and remained so for days.

The guerrillas were among the many problems facing Hunter's expedition. The narrow valley, its thickly wooded sides broken by innumerable passes, was ideally suited to sudden raids against the Union supply trains; even stray bands of bushwackers were capable of hurting the army as its columns stretched out during the march. When one train was fired upon from a house in Newtown (now Stephens City), therefore, Hunter reacted quickly. He ordered the house from which the shot was fired to be burned to the ground, and announced in a circular spread through the lower Valley towns that if any other wagon trains or escorts were fired upon, he would burn every rebel house within a radius of five miles.[6] Previous commanders had treated rebel sympathizers so tenderly, Halpine explained, "that they seem to think we are only in the valley by their toleration." Hunter would show them that it was United States soil.

A total of three houses were burned in Newtown, one of them a guerrilla depot full of supplies. Convinced now that Hunter's threat was not an idle one, the townspeople there and elsewhere hastened to assure Hunter that the guerrillas were not local men but from all parts of the South, and some sought to protect themselves by telling him which of their neighbors gave them food and shelter. Newtown must have received an especially bad report, for on May 30 Hunter ordered the entire village destroyed, an order which, however, he allowed to remain unexecuted.[7]

It is easy to romanticize the "Gray Ghosts" who swooped down from the mountains in daring raids against Union guards and wagons, but guerrillas are never popular with their conventional army opponents, who naturally prefer to stand up and fight, and they were anything but romantic heroes to Halpine. As he described them in a postwar essay, they were, on the contrary, "about the filthiest, drunkennest, meanest, most ill-looking, ragged, mutinous, diseased, undisciplined, lousy, and utterly cowardly gang of horse and chicken-thieves, highway robbers, grand and petty larcenists, that the Lord . . . ever permitted to disgrace the noble calling of the soldier. . . . They were terrible, indeed, to the stampeded muleteers, sutlers, and camp-followers of some unprotected train; but still more terrible to the wretched residents of their own section in the regions through which they operated." [8]

While waiting for the train bringing in shoes and other supplies needed for the march, Halpine was able to ride about and to talk with the people. In the home of one rebel family in Woodstock, a girl sang him the popular Confederate songs, including "that glorious 'Stonewall Jackson's Way.' (Posie should learn it for me)," he wrote home at the end of May. Fond as always of talking about feminine beauty, Halpine teased Margaret (or was it her young house guest, Posie Collins?) by describing the girl from her wavy brown hair to her full bosom. "I was

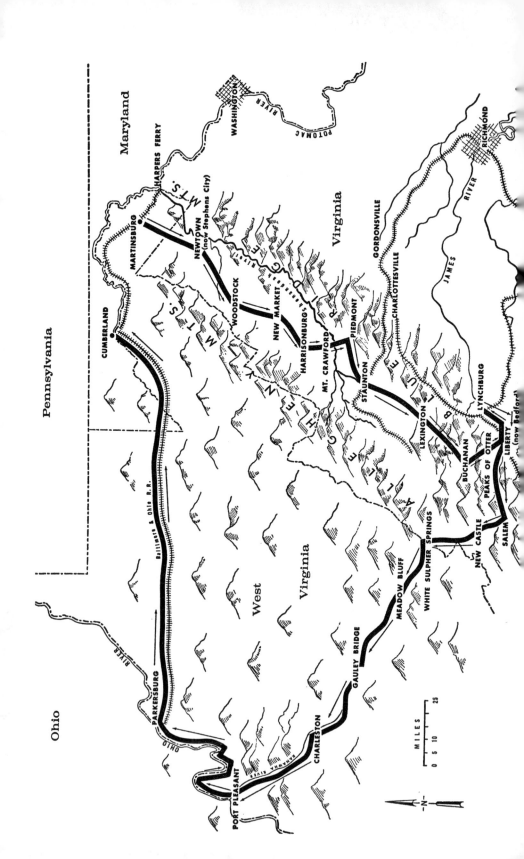

madly in love with her for half an hour," he declared, "and have not yet quite got over it." Though she struggled when he kissed her, he boasted he could convert her to the Union in a day or two. That night there was another concert, this one of northern songs played by Massachusetts and New York military bands. It was an occasion to write about in his diary, the lights glimmering through the trees, the river falling hoarsely against the rocks, the music echoing from the hills, the realization that one was on the eve of a great adventure.

There was no more time for the idle pleasures of camp life, for the shoes arrived the next day, and before dawn on May 29 the Army of the Shenandoah began its famous expedition up the Valley. Marching in three columns, one on the pike and one on each side of it, the army planned to move quickly. Each regiment had only a single wagon for the carrying of spare ammunition and mess equipment, and the soldiers carried only the clothes on their backs, with 100 rounds of ammunition, some bread, coffee, sugar, salt, and an extra pair of shoes and socks in their knapsacks. Nothing else. "We are contending against an enemy who is in earnest," stated Halpine's order to the troops, "and if we expect success, we too must be in earnest. We must be willing to make sacrifices, willing to suffer for a short time, that a glorious result may crown our efforts." [9]

As the army moved up into Confederate territory, it was greeted by hundreds of civilian refugees, some claiming to be loyal Unionists, some admittedly the wives and children of rebel deserters. Other people were unfriendly, and stood in their doorways in hostile silence as the columns passed through town. Occasionally, some bold-spirited person would call out an epithet; one woman shouted to the soldiers that men in blue uniforms had recently come back down the Valley road a lot faster than they had gone up it. She was right, of course. At the time of the retreat from New Market, Strother had joked that things were normal in the Department of Western Virginia—Averell was tearing up the railroad, and Sigel was tearing down the pike! [10]

On May 30 the army passed near the scene of Sigel's defeat. For some miles they had seen and smelled the rotting carcasses of dead horses; finally they were forced to see and smell the remains of their dead comrades. Although Confederate soldiers slain in the battle at New Market had been decently buried in a nearby churchyard, the Union dead had been just lightly covered with earth, much of which had washed away with the rain. Among the blackening arms and legs protruding horribly from thin covers of dirt, Halpine saw one man, dropped into a short, shallow grave, whose head and boots had been uncovered. "All the bodies were stripped of everything but shirts, except this one," he noted. "His legs were probably shattered so that they couldn't draw 'em off." Such a grisly sight would anger any group of men; upon Hunter and his apprehensive and undisciplined soldiers, the effect was especially strong, and perhaps helps to explain their conduct in the Valley.

Hunter was marching up the Valley to destroy factories, supplies, and transportation facilities useful to the rebel armies. The presence of guerrillas, who threatened him on all sides, made it necessary for him to deal roughly with sympathetic civilians, and because he was moving away from his base he had to feed his men off the land. It was not an expedition calculated to make friends in the countryside through which it passed. Still, at the outset he sought to minimize damage and inconvenience to noncombat property and individuals. In his very first general order to his army, he announced that no straggling or pillaging would be permitted, and that the seizure of meat and other food would be carefully regulated. Later, he directed Halpine to inform his commanders what the regulations were. Foraging parties commanded by "reliable and just" officers were to collect only such food and forage as was actually needed, and were to allow no waste, pillage, plunder, or oppression. Farmers who could prove their loyalty to the United States were to be paid for what was taken from them in certificates against the government. On the very day he studied the macabre scene near New Market, Hunter ordered Halpine to write a letter to one of the division commanders censuring him for insufficient control over foraging parties. Too many soldiers, Halpine's letter declared, "break away from their officers and straggle into houses, carrying off dresses, ornaments, books, money, and doing wanton injury to furniture." One group of men, finding six or eight barrels of flour in a house, helped themselves to what they wanted and spread the rest across a field. Such practices were dangerous to the army in a country infested with guerrillas, and were "in gross violation of the spirit of the order for levying supplies. . . . In sending out foraging parties no men should be allowed to enter any house except in company with a commissioned officer." The division commander, Halpine concluded, was expected to adopt "prompt and severe measures" to control his men.[11] Hunter's own measures were certainly prompt and severe. Non-commissioned officers guilty of plundering were broken to privates, and privates were made to carry fence rails while walking four-hour beats. Soldiers unused to such discipline did not take kindly to it, and inevitably there was grumbling against the new General. "The life of a soldier in the field is not a picnic," wrote one of the men.[12]

A few miles beyond New Market, Halpine discovered a Yankee soldier, shot through the breast two weeks before and left to die where he fell, who was being nursed back to health by the women of a secessionist family. For their humanity, Halpine gave them a pass safeguarding their property. It was in order to protect such people, as well as the loyal Unionists, that Hunter tried to check plundering. Furthermore, marching rapidly through unfriendly country and almost constantly liable to harassing fire from unseen snipers, he could not take his sick and wounded with him, but had to leave them along the road with whomever would care for them. Such men, tempting targets for bushwhackers, would be in near-hopeless danger if the countryside were aroused by unnecessary acts of plunder and destruction.

Yet every mile Hunter pushed up the Valley, his reasons for demanding good behavior from his unruly troops became less important. The further south he went, the fewer Unionists there were to protect, and the closer he came to the end of his advance, the less the need to leave men behind—returning, he could take them with him. In addition, the constant loss of scouts and pickets to guerrilla raids, and the sight of the corpses at New Market, must have helped to make him less sensitive to damages caused the people by his soldiers, and to reaffirm his long-standing conviction that rebels must be dealt with severely. Possibly he also feared that if he continued to try to protect Virginians against his own men, the rank and file would not fight for him in the battle which could not be very far ahead.

As far up the road as Harrisonburg, it was possible to see scars of three years of war—fences down at the campsites of earlier armies of both sides, creeks and gullies without bridges, blackened chimneys pointing where houses had been, and occasionally the weather-washed remains of trenches and earthworks. But no Union army had penetrated beyond, and the Valley had never looked lovelier or more peaceful than in early June, 1864. Hunter's temper remained bad, but without the responsibility of command, Halpine was relaxed and happy. "Am more glad than ever that Gen. decided to come," he scribbled in his diary. They marched twenty-two miles on June 2, the day they entered Harrisonburg, and Halpine believed he had ridden thirty. He was tired and saddle-sore, but exhilarated—the rebels had harmlessly fired some of Jackson's old six pounders as they approached the town—and full of the fellowship of men at arms. As he lay hot and exhausted in the tent of a friend, a soldier offered him a drink of water from his canteen. He took it eagerly, and passed it back with the words, "We have drunk from the same canteen." Later he entered the line in his diary with the note, "Another idea for a song." It became one of Miles O'Reilly's most popular, "The Canteen."

> There are bonds of all sorts in this world of ours,
> Fetters of friendship and ties of flowers,
>   And true-lovers' knots, I ween;
> The girl and the boy are bound by a kiss,
> But there's never a bond, old friend, like this—
>   We have drunk from the same canteen!
>
> It was sometimes water, and sometimes milk,
> And sometimes applejack, fine as silk,
>   But whatever the tipple has been,
> We shared it together, in bane or bliss,
> And I warm to you, friend, when I think of this—
>   We have drunk from the same canteen! [13]

At Harrisonburg, the soldier-writers Halpine and Strother planned to amuse themselves by editing the regular issue of the Rockingham (County) *Reporter* and distributing it among the soldiers and subscribers. Such a collaboration between Miles O'Reilly and Porte Crayon might have resulted in something memorable, but unfortunately an officer unaware of their plans broke up the type and press.

The expedition was about to lose its character of a country excursion anyway, for at Harrisonburg scouts reported that an enemy army had taken a strong position a few miles ahead at Mount Crawford, near where the road crossed the South Fork of the Shenandoah. The bridges were down, the rebels had planted sharpened harrows in the fords, and Confederate reenforcements were reported rushing in. "It is now certain," Halpine wrote in his diary the night of June 3, "that we shall begin to fight at about 10:00 A.M. tomorrow."

It was a prospect he faced with little confidence. Some of the men, following the example of the officer who destroyed the newspaper office, were looting the houses of Harrisonburg, and Hunter either could not control them or, on the eve of battle, decided not to try.[14] In addition to being undisciplined, many of the soldiers were either indifferent to victory or resigned to defeat. The cavalry was no better. "A squadron of good rebel horse could go back & forward thro' them," Halpine exclaimed, "unless they are much better than they look"—and it was clear that he did not think they were. Signal men reported the sound of guns twenty-five miles ahead at Staunton, indicating (erroneously, as it proved) the arrival there of Crook and Averell from their camp in West Virginia with 12,000 to 14,000 additional troops. But even the possibility of squeezing the enemy between two superior forces failed to inspire much faith in victory. Influenced, no doubt, by Hunter's belief that General FitzJohn Porter had been guilty of deliberately withholding assistance from John Pope at Second Bull Run, Halpine even wondered if Crook and Averell could really be depended upon. It was, he admitted, a cruel question. But it was a natural one under the circumstances.[15]

The fight which Halpine so confidently expected to begin the morning of June 4 was postponed a day when Hunter turned off the pike to the east, outflanking the enemy's position at Mount Crawford, and crossed the river at Port Republic. Because he lost five hours in building a pontoon bridge, the Confederates were able to fall back and take up a position near Piedmont on the new line of march.

The battle of Piedmont began on June 5 with a pre-dawn cavalry skirmish and at 6:30 A.M. with the firing of three pieces of Confederate artillery. The firing was lively, wrote Halpine, and it was plenty lively around Hunter's headquarters when one shell landed close enough to spatter the whole staff with flying dirt. Young Henry A. Du Pont, a cousin of the Admiral, who commanded Hunter's artillery, hurried his battery into position and drove off the rebel guns, opening the way for the infantry to move forward. With the flames and smoke from a nearby mill providing an apocalyptic background, Hunter formed his army into the line of battle. It was the time and place for an inspirational speech, and Hunter did his best. Standing directly before a Connecticut regiment which had been one of the first to panic at New Market, he told his nervous and wayward troops that they now had a chance to redeem their reputation. Strother thought it a good speech, direct and soldierly, but noted that the men "didn't seem much elated with the prospect and scarcely got up a decent cheer in response." [16] For the Army of the Shenandoah, the uncertain moment of truth had arrived.

Under cover of Du Pont's artillery, the infantry began to advance against the enemy, who had taken position in a natural horseshoe of wooded hills, with the town of Piedmont in the far curve. As they cautiously moved ahead, the men taking what cover they could behind the trees, the air came alive with the racking and whirring of muskets and artillery. It was no place for cowards, and this time the army proved that for all its faults it was not cowardly. Shortly before noon the enemy began to fall back, and in mid-afternoon the Union cavalry, sensing victory, cried "New Market, New Market!," and charged. By

6:40 P.M., it was all over. "The victory," wrote Halpine exultantly, "is magnificent," and he was right, even though the Confederates had numbered only about 6,000, including boys in their teens and men in their fifties. Confederate General William E. ("Grumble") Jones was killed, and so were approximately 200 rebel soldiers, some of whom were shot down as they fled into woods and corn fields, or drowned trying to escape across a creek. At least 500 more were wounded, and 1,000 were taken prisoner.[17]

Union casualties, less than 500 killed and wounded, according to Hunter's report, were by no means insignificant, but they were not enough to dampen the night's celebration. The luck of the Army of the Shenandoah had changed, and the men, heroes for once, drank the local liquors, and shouted and sang around their fires, while the bands played. Hunter restrained his own enthusiasm until in the privacy of a farmhouse, when he impulsively threw his arms around Halpine and Stockton, kissing their cheeks and slapping their backs. He had led a Union army to the first victory won by the United States in the upper Shenandoah Valley, and it now seemed more than possible that he would be able to accomplish his entire mission successfully. If he did, then Grant might be able to crush Lee and bring the war to a close, and in that case Hunter and all those with him would be among the nation's foremost heroes, their achievement noted throughout the world and celebrated in history. With his old dream of glory come intoxicatingly alive again, Halpine finally placed his blanket on the floor beside the General and went dizzily to sleep.

The next afternoon, with the bands playing "The Star Spangled Banner" and a large United States flag flying over the column, the Army of the Shenandoah marched into the railroad and manufacturing city of Staunton. The welcome was a surprisingly friendly one, many townspeople lining the streets, cheering and offering bouquets. Some of them were no doubt genuinely glad to see the old flag again, but all of them were decidedly apprehensive about their fate and anxious to appear conciliatory. Because of his uncertainty about the location of Crook and Averell, Hunter himself was "very cross" at this moment of triumph. But on June 7 his scouts made contact with theirs, and on June 8 they marched their armies, twelve additional regiments of infantry and eight of cavalry, into Staunton. "Nothing in the war has been prettier," exclaimed Halpine in his diary about the juncture of the two forces, "& we can laugh at anything less than one of Lee's Army Corps to reenforce the valley troops."

After paroling the 400 sick and wounded Confederate soldiers

found in Staunton, distributing captured commissary supplies and
ordnance among his own troops, and ordering the destruction of all the
railroad bridges, depots, workshops, and factories in the city and
vicinity, Hunter reported his success to Washington. "On the march and
in action," he declared, "the troops have behaved admirably. The
combined force, now in fine spirits and condition, will move day after
tomorrow to the accomplishment of its mission." [18]

It was true that the troops had behaved pretty well, if not admirably.
There had been some pillaging, inevitably, and Strother was repelled
by what he saw taking place in Staunton. On one street, he observed
a provost guard knocking holes in some barrels of apple brandy, which
flowed over the curb and into the street, along with "floating chips,
paper, horse dung, and dead rats. This luscious mixture," he noted with
disgust, "was greedily drunk by dozens of soldiers and vagabonds on
their hands and knees and their mouths in the gutter, while the more nice
were setting their canteens to catch it as it flowed over the curbs." He
also saw a "mixed mob" of soldiers and the local riffraff, black and
white, breaking into stores and shops, helping themselves to whatever
they fancied, and destroying much of what they did not.[19] But considering the fact that the army was deep in enemy territory on a mission of
destruction, its behavior was far from outrageous. Such horses, wheat,
and cattle as it needed for its own use were seized, but on the whole
both public and private property, including schools and an asylum where
public stores had been hidden, were respected and guarded against the
relatively small number of looters, many of whom were not United
States soldiers at all.[20]

Because of fires and wreckage downtown, Hunter set up his headquarters in an apple orchard, and Halpine, always easily made angry
with quartermasters, had to lose his temper and threaten legal
action in order to get a tent for use as an office. His paper work was
greatly increased by the arrival of Crook and Averell, and he worked
hard and long to keep up with it. But he had pleasant moments, as well.
He procured a fine new horse, wrote letters to James Gordon Bennett,
of the New York *Herald,* and to his close friend John Savage, and sent
to Margaret a piece of a coat said to have belonged to one rebel
he greatly admired, Stonewall Jackson. He quickly made friends with
the new officers, who knew him, so he said, "like a book," and who
called him Miles O'Reilly. He liked Averell in particular, describing him
as "a glorious fellow."

On June 10, the combined armies, consisting now of two divisions of
infantry and two of cavalry and totaling over 22,000 men, with thirty-

two cannon, renewed the southward march. The entry of the Army of Western Virginia, as it now called itself, into Lexington, thirty-five miles down the road, was delayed the following afternoon by a vigorous defense organized by a Confederate cavalry commander, Colonel John McCausland. From private houses and from the buildings of the Virginia Military Institute, located on a bluff above the river, a sharp and deadly fire of muskets and artillery was rained down upon them. Hunter might have destroyed the city with his own artillery, but instead he sent Averell upstream to find a ford and fall on McCausland on his flank and rear. When he perceived the move, McCausland withdrew from the city, and Hunter entered it.[21]

At Lexington Hunter committed an act for which, among others, he has been reviled by Virginians and the South: he burned the Virginia Military Institute and all the buildings connected with it except the home of the superintendent, which he used for his headquarters. "My heart revolts," exclaimed Halpine in his diary, when he heard of Hunter's intention. "My judgment does not concur. No seat of learning should be destroyed. If we subdue the rebellion, these places would be restored to the nation. If we fail, why this wanton waste? I can do nothing with Gen. Hunter." But after the war, he came to feel (or, at least, to say) that Hunter had been right. V.M.I. was state property, and its own commandant had warned that if McCausland used it as a military fortification in what was certain to be a vain attempt to defend the city, it would be destroyed. Halpine looked back upon the destruction "with feelings of inexpressible regret," but he was nevertheless "fully satisfied of the justice of the act." [22]

The burning of the Lexington home of John Letcher, former governor of Virginia, has been almost as strongly condemned as the burning of V.M.I. According to Halpine, Hunter had not intended to destroy it, had quartered some of his staff officers within it, and had even detailed a guard for its defense against the hostility of the West Virginia troops, who had a special dislike of the man who had once been their governor and was now their enemy. His intentions were changed, however, when some soldiers—from a West Virginia regiment—discovered in a printing office a half typeset manuscript in Letcher's hand urging the people of the area to "arise and slay the foul Yankee invader." Accepting the manuscript as genuine and interpreting it as an incitement to guerrilla warfare, Hunter burned the Letcher house as he had those of other Valley residents involved with the guerrillas. If Letcher himself had not fled, Halpine believed Hunter would have hanged him.[23]

As he sat on a hillside with Averell and Strother watching the fires,

Halpine was profoundly disturbed. "My God!" he wrote in his diary, "how I felt on seeing Gov. Letcher's family sitting out on the lawn on their trunks & furniture, while their house was on fire beside them. The old fool deserves it all; but it is hard on the women." He was afraid the V.M.I. fires might spread into the nearby residential neighborhood. "I wish it were over," he said. Hunter, whose moods had reflected the strain he was under from the beginning of the expedition, wished it were over, too. "His temper is curt & captious," wrote Halpine. "One may be with him & never out of his sight for three days, & if he happens to call at any moment that one is not there, it is as bad as if one had systematically neglected his duties for a week."

Later the same day, Halpine put on the best clothes he had with him and with Averell paid a visit to Stonewall Jackson's grave. Because of his admiration for Jackson—the "great Genius" of the war, he called him, as Lee was its "great Respectability"—and the anguish he felt over the burning of the institution at which Jackson had taught, it was really more than just a visit. It was a pilgrimage, an act of contrition. Respectfully, he placed roses on the simple mound of earth, and took away a few blades of grass. Sending them to Margaret, he asked that they be put in a locket. "They are worth more than pure gold," he told her.

Lynchburg, next to Richmond the most important railroad and industrial city in Virginia, lay just outside the east wall of the Shenandoah Valley, only some thirty-five miles from Lexington by the most direct route. The funnel through which the commerce of a vast inland area was directed to Lee's army, Grant had told Hunter it would be of "great value" to possess it for a single day.[24] The trouble was that since the city had direct rail communications with Richmond, it would be possible for Lee to send in within a short time as many troops as were necessary for its defense. Hunter's only chance for success, therefore, was to occupy it without a moment's loss, before the enemy could prevent him from doing so.

At Lexington, Hunter lost more than a moment. It was not, however, the burnings on June 12 which caused the loss, as his critics have taken pleasure in alleging,[25] but the absence of one cavalry division out on a raid and the arrival of a supply train from the base at Martinsburg, whose goods had to be distributed.[26] Unfortunately, the goods, consisting of more forage and clothing than desperately needed food and ammunition, proved not worth distributing. Another day was lost by the decision to approach Lynchburg from the southwest, through Buchanan and Liberty (now Bedford), rather than by the most direct route. Strother was among those who recommended the longer route, because it would enable Hunter to destroy additional miles of Virginia's Central Railroad, and, threatening all of western North Carolina, allow him to put his grip "upon the vitals of the Confederacy." [27] In addition, it seemed worthwhile to travel via Buchanan in order to destroy a branch of the Tredegar Iron Works located there, to attack Lynchburg from the southwest, where its defenses were weakest, and to keep open the readiest access to lines of retreat westward.

Even as the army climbed out of the Shenandoah Valley on June 15 and crossed the Blue Ridge between its highest peaks—the Peaks of Otter—and prepared itself for what might be one of the decisive actions of the war, it became necessary to plan for the retreat which, succeed or fail at Lynchburg, was only a few days away. An attempt to join Grant and the Army of the Potomac somewhere to the east was practically out of the question because it meant moving towards the enemy's strength and ran the risk of a head-on collision with a much larger army.[28] To withdraw northward down the Valley was also unfeasible, since the countryside had been nearly eaten out during the upward march, and especially because the guerrillas could be expected to operate with increasing daring against an army running low on ammunition and weakened by hunger and forced marches. There appeared to be, therefore, only one avenue of escape from the superior force which would sooner or later make its appearance at Lynchburg. Hunter's army would have to move westward to Salem, destroying the salt works there, and then turn either northwest into West Virginia or southwest into eastern Tennessee.

Hunter's error in delaying his departure from Lexington and in taking the long route to Lynchburg was compounded by the amount of time taken en route destroying the iron works, furnaces, and foundries at Buchanan, and several miles of Virginia and Eastern Tennessee Railroad at Liberty. These facilities were important to the Confederacy, but not so important as Lynchburg with its communications to the north and east, and Hunter should have allowed nothing to detain him from his primary objective. Still, it would have been difficult psychologically to pass through Buchanan and Liberty without destroying their major warmaking resources, and destruction was a task at which Hunter's men excelled. "The very moment our infantry struck a railroad," Halpine later recalled, "their fatigue, thirst, hunger, and sense of danger all seemed to fall from them with their dropping knapsacks; and they buckled down to the business of rendering that line of transportation of no further avail to the enemy for at least some months, with all the eager, joyous, and untiring energy of a flock of school-boys pelting snowballs at some detested usher." [29]

Early in the afternoon of June 17, the army reached the Confederate first line of defense outside Lynchburg, and in the evening broke through it. But, pausing to rescue some wounded soldiers from a burning forest, it did not resume its push into the city. With the same lack of urgency which had characterized the march from Lexington, Hunter and his advisers decided to wait until daylight. It was the last of a fatal series of delays.[30]

As the men threw themselves on the ground for a few hours' rest, they were confident, but hungry. "Tell them there is plenty of food in Lynchburg," said Hunter, and no one knew better than he how desperately they needed it. For if the army failed to break into the city and reprovision itself, it would have to make its long and dangerous retreat on empty stomachs.

No commander sensitive to his responsibilities and aware of the role of chance in the determination of victory and defeat can be entirely at ease within himself on the eve of battle. Hunter's self-confidence, built upon his easy and triumphant experience in the Valley and his conviction that he knew how to handle rebels, was substantial. Even so, it must have been shaken by the sounds from Lynchburg of screeching trains and cheering townspeople which repeatedly broke the quiet of the warm night, and indicated the arrival of reenforcements from Richmond. Since the main body of General Jubal Early's reenforcements did not arrive until the next afternoon, it is possible that some of the noisy activity in the railroad yards was only a clever ruse.[31] Yet it was not noise which drove Hunter away from Lynchburg.

When Halpine arose at 3:30 in the morning, he observed that it was the anniversary of Waterloo. But there would be no battle on this June 18, for Hunter's probes of Lynchburg's inner defenses in the morning, and his interrogations of rebel prisoners in the afternoon, convinced him that the city had indeed been reenforced, and that he could not take it, after all. He consulted with his division commanders, and at 4:00 P.M. told Halpine to order the army back down the road to Salem.[32]

Because there had been no serious fighting, neither the Confederate forces in Lynchburg nor many of Hunter's own men at first understood that the army was not simply withdrawing in order to regroup and renew the attack. Surprise and disappointment were common on both sides when it was realized that the Army of Western Virgina was in fact retreating headlong up the road it had just come down. All night long the army marched, and for two days it barely stopped to catch its breath as it passed its still-fresh campsite at a haunted house near Liberty, climbed the Blue Ridge through Buford's Gap, and at Salem entered the hilly country beyond the southern tip of the Shenandoah Valley.

But no sense of dejection or failure accompanied the flight, at least not among those officers close to Hunter. "The enemy did not pursue," wrote Halpine in his diary during one rest stop on June 18. "We beat them, but had neither food nor ammunition; & besides we had done all that was ordered of us." They had not been able to capture Lynchburg, or to destroy the James River Canal or the Virginia Central Railroad to the northeast, but they had indeed done almost everything asked of them in Grant's directives of May 20 and May 25. Not only had they reached Staunton and destroyed the branch of the railroad there, they had marched some eighty miles further south, and caused significant additional damage to Confederate transportation and industry. If Hunter could draw off and hold at bay a force equal to his own, Grant had told Halleck, "he will be doing good service." Well, Hunter had almost demolished one rebel army, and had drawn off from Richmond another one much superior to his own. At Lynchburg, the most extreme penetration of enemy country ever mentioned to him, he found himself perilously low on food and ammunition, and faced with an enemy he could not defeat, he had elected to lead his daring army to safety. He did so confident that he had performed, in Grant's phrase, "good service."

As soon as General Early discovered that Hunter had not simply retired in order to assume new offensive positions, he sent his cavalry in pursuit. It caught up with the Union army's rear guard at Liberty, where there was heavy skirmishing, and followed it across the Blue Ridge and on to Newcastle. There 200 rebel cavalrymen dashed down an unguarded side road, destroyed with hatchets the wheels of ten big guns which had become mixed-up with the wagon train, and dashed off again. Four of the guns were saved by being mounted on spare wheels, but six had to be spiked and left behind. It was the only major loss of matériel during the entire campaign, but the Richmond newspapers, from which it was learned about in Washington, played it up as a major Union defeat, and used it to substantiate their charge that Hunter's expedition was a failure and his retreat a disaster.[33]

At the little town of Newcastle, the last stop before entering the rugged Alleghenies, the hungry army gathered such food as it could find and moved on. Once in the mountains, it was free from pursuit by Confederate cavalry, but it was fleeing a still deadlier enemy, starvation. The nearest supply of food adequate to its needs—nearly a million rations left under guard by Crook and Averell when they went to meet Hunter at Staunton—was at Meadow Bluff, West Virginia. But Meadow Bluff was five days away—five days of forced marching through a wilderness of rising, falling, and twisting mountain roads over which, as Halpine described it, "our column trailed its weary length like a wounded, all but dying, serpent." [34] Driven before each regiment were still a few head of cattle, but these were soon gone, and then there was virtually nothing to eat, for there were few farms in the mountains to surrender their precious pigs and poultry. Soldiers slashed young trees along the road and tried to appease their hunger pains by chewing the inner bark. Cavalrymen, with a wider radius of movement, rode off in search of food for themselves and their mounts. Returning to the column, their horses greedily ate corn from nosebags, scattering kernels along the dusty road for the infantrymen to scramble for. Less fortunate horses and mules, too weak to pull and carry, or even to follow, were shot and their wagons burned.[35] Each day there were hundreds of stragglers, men whose strength simply gave out, who could go no further. Others, encouraged by the reminders of friends and mounted officers that Meadow Bluff was only three days away, only two, only one, found the strength to trudge on a little further. Some men, weak as they were, refused to throw away their knapsacks full of valuables and souvenirs taken from houses in the upper Valley, and Halpine came across one group of men, half-dead from hunger and fatigue but with a sustaining vision, who were carrying a billiard table. Diarrhea swept along the column. Halpine had a bad case of it, and traveled one night in an ambulance, well-dosed, no doubt, with his favorite medicine for physical and mental suffering.

The middle of the same night, June 24, the little army stumbled into the famous mountain resort of White Sulphur Springs. The great hotels and their many rows of villas and cottages, rented in happier times by fortunate Tidewater families escaping the summer heat, were empty now of guests, and had been for three years. Long before, their carpets and curtains had been impressed into Confederate service, and their tables and bureaus burned or put away; little but their iron bedsteads greeted the curious Yankee soldiers who crowded into their echoing halls to see, or imagine, what luxurious living was like. David Strother knew well. He had written about White Sulphur Springs in one of his Porte Crayon articles in *Harper's,* August, 1855, and had many anecdotes to tell of its days of glory and splendor as he and Halpine wandered about together. Other spas in the area, Sweet Sulphur Springs and Red Sulphur Springs, were also deserted because of the war, and Halpine wished he could say so much for Newport, Saratoga, and Lake George.

There was beauty at White Sulphur Springs, and good water, but not enough food for the stomachs of an army, so after a short rest the march was resumed. Some food was picked up at Lewisburg a few miles ahead, and some more at Bunger's Mill, but it was the plenty which awaited them at Meadow Bluff which pulled the weakening men along the road. On June 25, a week after leaving Lynchburg, they reached it. It was a day and night he would never forget, said Halpine. "How the horses broke down! How the men broke down!" The food was gone. Guerrilla activity had forced the guard to destroy part of it and move the rest to safety at Gauley Bridge, forty elongated miles ahead.[36]

Leaving the all but stupefied men behind, Hunter and his staff and an escort of cavalrymen pushed on to Gauley Bridge to hurry rations back. After a ride of thirty miles, they stopped at the house of "widow Jones," said to be an aunt of Ulysses S. Grant. Halpine found her a delightful old lady, "though excessively rebellious," and she served them a generous meal with "such gorgeous accompaniments as iron forks, a table-cloth, sweet milk in glasses, and tea—actual tea—in cups." They had not sat at such a table for weeks. The next day, June 27, they encountered two wagon trains carrying nearly 100,000 rations already on their way to the rescue, and the ordeal was over. "God be praised for the relief of the poor soldiers," wrote Halpine.

For the next three days the army rested near Gauley Bridge and waited for stragglers to catch up. It was a pleasant interval for Halpine. He enjoyed swims in the Kanawha River, good meals, and a chance to take off his boots at night. He enjoyed more than ever the company of the other officers, whom it was now possible to know under more relaxed conditions. The stolid, full-bearded Crook, he found, improved upon acquaintance, and Averell, with his guitar and repertoire of songs, was always an agreeable companion, even though he was worried that Hunter might hold him responsible for the loss of those six cannon. Closest of all was David Strother. The retreat had weakened Strother more than any other member of the staff, but with a little wine in him the old Porte Crayon blazed forth. So, presumably, did the old Miles O'Reilly, and one can imagine the two friends joyfully letting themselves go to Averell's accompaniment. Although he did not learn it until later, Halpine had something more than the safety of Hunter's army to celebrate. On June 29, his sixth child, and second son, was born. After the custom of the family, he was given a long name: Charles William Camac Hunter Halpine.

Although he was out of touch with Washington and had heard nothing from it since the arrival of the supply train at Lexington, Hunter took it for granted that with the Army of Western Virginia working its way out of the mountains many miles from the Shenandoah Valley, Early would take advantage of the opportunity to march into the northern Valley region. He therefore hastened to move his men back to the scene of action. On June 30 the army arrived at Charleston, West Virginia, where Halpine had some ice cream to prove that he was really back in civilization, and where, his health evidently restored, he saw several girls pretty enough to record the fact in his diary. Near Charleston, he visited some large salt works, all owned by rebels except one, whose loyalty was doubtful, telegraphed Margaret to tell her of his safe arrival, and worked over a large accumulation of routine mail from Washington and Martinsburg. On July 3, as much of the army as could be crowded aboard available boats embarked for Point Pleasant, at the confluence of the Kanawha and the Ohio, and on July 4 they traveled up the Ohio past Blennerhasset's Island, where Halpine heard for the first time of the Aaron Burr conspiracy of 1806, and arrived at Parkersburg. It was at Parkersburg that they first heard the bad news of Early's victorious sweep down through the lower Shenandoah.

The reports were vague and contradictory, but it was clear that the handful of Union troops left in the Valley had been unable to hold Early, and that the presence of Hunter and his army was urgently required. The trouble was that the army was spread thinly all the way back to Charleston, and it was very slow work getting it together at Parkersburg, where it could take the Baltimore and Ohio Railroad to Cumberland, Maryland. The rivers were so low that even boats with the shallowest drafts ran aground, making it repeatedly necessary for the men to disembark, march around the shallows, and then file back aboard. While he waited, there was little for Halpine to do but curse the return of his sickness, rejoice at the news of the birth of his son, and speculate about the effect upon his own career of the recent death of his old partner, John Clancy. "Poor fellow!" Halpine wrote of Clancy. "I am sorry for him, as, after a hard fight he had just begun to get his head well above water." But his death, he believed, "leaves me with a fairer course in N.Y. than heretofore," for now the most influential newspaperman-politician among the Irish in the city, was none other than Charles G. Halpine! "Clancy's death," he wrote Margaret, "is the political death of my enemies." He was more than ever anxious to get out of the army; all his personal interests required it.

By July 8, the army had reassembled at Parkersburg, and on that day it began to board the Baltimore and Ohio for the twelve-hour ride to Cumberland. As Hunter once again neared an active theater of war, the responsibilities began to pile up on his adjutant, and Halpine was busy till late at night hurrying the troops on to department headquarters at Martinsburg. There were alarming rumors that Early had moved all the way down the Shenandoah, crossed the Potomac, and invaded Maryland, and Halpine noted in his diary that Hunter, who knew that his enemies would blame him for having left the way open, was like "a chafed tiger" in his eagerness to arrive in time to help defend Washington and Baltimore. He did not make it; it was Grant who drove Early back into Virginia by rushing two divisions north from Petersburg.

History has not been kind to David Hunter's expedition, but that is largely because it has been written by his enemies, or from information supplied by them. From June 9, the day before he left Staunton, until June 28, the day after his arrival at Gauley Bridge, Hunter was unable to send any dispatches to Washington. In the capital, therefore, news of his progress, of the burning of V.M.I. and of John Letcher's home, of the destruction of private property all along his line of march, of his repulse at Lynchburg, and of his precipitous retreat up the Kanawha Valley, was all drawn from the southern press, a fact which prejudiced his case from the beginning. The people in Washington, furthermore, were all the more inclined to believe the worst of Hunter because his retreat had undeniably left the Shenandoah Valley wide open and enabled Early to march within sight of the Capitol dome, badly frightening the city if not actually endangering it.

The southern case against Hunter was a strong one, and no one stated it more forcefully than Jubal Early himself, who went down the Valley along Hunter's route. The scenes he described were heart-rending —the countryside stripped of food, many families left without anything at all to eat, furniture, bedding, and clothing hacked to pieces out of simple wantonness, houses burned to the ground by Hunter's order, and, at Lexington, "a most excellent christian gentleman" hanged for having killed a straggling Union soldier who was threatening the ladies of his house. "These are but some of the outrages committed by Hunter or his orders," Early exclaimed, "and I will not insult the memory of the ancient barbarians of the North by calling them 'acts of Vandalism.' If those old barbarians were savage and cruel, they at least had the manliness and daring of rude soldiers, with occasional traits of magnanimity. Hunter's deeds were those of a malignant and cowardly fanatic, who was better qualified to make war upon helpless women and children than upon armed soldiers." [37] The wife of one of Robert E. Lee's cousins, whose house and outbuildings in the northern Valley were burned, denounced Hunter with a bitterness which can only be described as pitiful. "Oh, Earth, behold the monster!" cried Mrs. Henrietta Lee. "Can I say, 'God forgive you?' No prayer can be offered for you. . . . The curses of thousands, the scorn of the manly and upright and the hatred of the true and honorable, will follow you and yours through all time, and brand your name *infamy*. INFAMY." [38]

Through the years, stories of Hunter's atrocities have lost nothing in the telling. In 1914, a Virginian who had been within sight and sound of the Army of the Shenandoah at the time of its march remembered that "Hunter destroyed everything in his path and left sections of the Valley along his route as bare as a desert." Strother's biographer, far more severe with Hunter than Strother himself was, calls Hunter the "Villain of the Valley," whose "wholesale depredations by torch and . . . occasional use of the hangman's noose were reflections" of his deep hatred for the South. "Poor Hunter!" exclaims another critic, "he seems to have had few friends, and it is almost cruel to recite his history." [39]

Among the friends he did have, however, was a man whose opinion ought to count for more than it has. "I am sorry to see such a disposition to condemn so brave an old soldier as General Hunter," wrote Ulysses S. Grant to Assistant Secretary of War Dana at a time when little was known of Hunter's expedition except what was presented in the southern press. "He is known to have advanced into the enemy's country toward their main army, inflicting a much greater damage upon them than they have inflicted upon us with double his force. . . . Hunter acted, too, in a country where we had no friends, whilst the enemy have only operated in territory where, to say the least, many of the inhabitants are their friends. . . . I fail to see yet that General Hunter has not acted with great promptness and great success." [40]

Aside from Grant, Halpine was virtually the only friend Hunter possessed who defended his record publicly. In articles published in 1865 in the New York *Citizen,* and reprinted and given much wider circulation in Miles O'Reilly's second book of essays, *Baked Meats of the Funeral* (1866), Halpine sketched Hunter's character and his achievements in the Valley in a way which could not contrast more with the unflattering portrait which emerged from the southern sources. Far from being a malignant and cowardly fanatic, Halpine called Hunter "the purest, gentlest, bravest, and most honest gentleman we have ever had the means of knowing. . . . Too fearless and sincere to be politic—too warm to be always wise—too innately noble and truthful to be what is called 'successful' in these miserable latter-days of intrigue and fraud." Hunter was "free from any vice, . . . incapable of any baseness, . . . [and] an absolutely pure gentleman." After his own father, said Halpine, Hunter was the "very noblest" man he had ever known. As to the alleged barbarities in the Valley, Halpine defended the destruction of the

Virginia Military Institute, treated the subject of pillaging and looting as if it were too inconsequential to be mentioned, and maintained that Hunter had ordered the burning of only five private houses, after proof in each case that their owners were involved with guerrillas. Over-all, the expedition had been a success. Success? It was, Halpine asserted, "one of the most brilliant and important successes of the entire war." [41]

Hunter was of course grateful for such flattering words, and once sent Halpine a clipping from the *Herald* to ask if he wrote it, for "I am anxious to find if there is any other man on the face of the earth inclined to do me justice." From time to time he even expressed his gratitude in cash. After reading in the *Citizen* Halpine's "spirited, graphic and strictly true account" of the formation of the first Negro regiment at Hilton Head, Hunter expressed his pleasure, and added, "I enclose you a check for Mrs. Halpine." A few months later he sent Halpine a check for $500 to be repaid "at convenience." [42]

As a professional publicist, a "literary Swiss," Halpine was by no means incapable of slanting his writing for money, but he did not do so in the case of David Hunter. There were times when he found Hunter difficult, but the sincerity of his admiration for him is proved by the frequency with which he stated it in his wartime letters to Margaret, and in other private letters written after the war.

If Halpine's uncritical veneration of Hunter grew out of the warmth of their personal relationship, the South's uncritical detestation of him was a product of the emotional ferocity of the Civil War. One would expect Hunter to be hated by the people against whom he waged war. If southerners hated him more than they hated Grant and Sherman and the real "Villain of the Valley," Philip Sheridan, it was because they considered him a traitor to the South and to his own family. Although he himself was born in New Jersey, his family was Virginian, and included among its members so distinguished a rebel leader as R. M. T. Hunter, a Confederate States Senator and once Confederate Secretary of State. There were Hunters, too, in the Shenandoah Valley, and one recent writer even claims that "Hunter seemed sadistically determined to inflict injuries upon his own relatives and those associated with them." [43]

Even more revolting, Hunter was the Union military leader most prominently associated in the South with the revolutionary change in the status of the Negro. Over six months before Lincoln's Emancipation Proclamation, he had not only freed slaves, but armed them and trained them to pursue and kill their former masters—so wicked a crime that he was officially proclaimed an outlaw. After the war, he supported the Radical Republican reconstruction program, and was an early advocate of Negro suffrage. Words were almost inadequate to describe the loathing such a man inspired.

But what Hunter's artillery commander, H. A. Du Pont, said of him in his well-known book on the expedition has been almost as damaging to his reputation as the southern charges, for the book appears to be both authoritative and objective. Du Pont believed that Hunter's campaign had been "unquestionably" valuable to the Union cause, and that the General could not have captured Lynchburg because of the arrival of Early's superior force and the Union army's desperate shortage of food and ammunition. But he strongly condemned Hunter for much unnecessary destruction of private property, and portrayed him at Lynchburg as a dazed and indecisive man, incapable of leading his army.[44] Yet Du Pont's book was written sixty years after the events it describes, and is by no means free of the errors which so often cast doubt on the reliability of reminiscences. While it may indeed reflect some judgments formed at the time, it can hardly fail to reflect others formed later. Du Pont may have been influenced, for example, by the fact that the published sources were overwhelmingly anti-Hunter. His judgments may also have been affected by the falling out between his cousin the Admiral and Hunter, and by his own pique at his failure to receive the recognition in Hunter's official report which he believed himself entitled to.[45]

That Hunter was sometimes curt and hard to deal with even Halpine conceded. But judgment in his case has been pronounced by the prosecution only; the defense has not yet been heard.

The expedition up the Valley to Lynchburg and the hungry flight through the mountains to the Ohio River was one of the great adventures of the Civil War, but instead of touching those who made it with glory and romance, it left them vulnerable to charges and suspicion of ill-advised and even dishonorable conduct. Halpine was angry. By way of contrast, his prospects in New York politics had never looked brighter, and he was more than ever determined to become a civilian.

But his last days in the army were by no means miserable. He was a great favorite with the officers and men with whom he lived; nobody could be more "populous," he wrote Margaret, adding that he was more rugged, hardier, and better looking than ever. And to Thurlow Weed he reported: "We have had more real fun on this raid—sometimes rather grim fun, but nevertheless of a beasty, manly nature—than I ever saw before in all my life. It will make a magnificent volume." [46]

On July 10, 1864, Halpine asked the War Department to accept his resignation for reasons of health, supporting his request with an endorsement from Hunter and a letter from Weed. This time there was no difficulty; his resignation was accepted, effective July 31. Like many another volunteer soldier rejoicing to find himself again a civilian, Halpine experienced an unexpected nostalgia when he put his uniform away for the last time. He expressed it in a poem, "Resigned," which *Harper's Monthly* featured on its first page in December.

> Never again call "Comrade"
> To the men who were comrades for years;
> Never to hear the bugles,
> Thrilling and sweet and solemn;
> Never again call "Brother"
> To the men we think of with tears;
> Never again to ride or march
> In the dust of the marching column.

CHAPTER 9

New York Citizen

HALPINE'S ENLISTMENT in the army in 1861 attracted no attention and was of little importance to anyone outside of his family. His resignation three years later, however, was considered sufficiently newsworthy to be noticed in both the national pictorial weeklies, *Frank Leslie's Illustrated Newspaper* (August 20), and *Harper's Weekly* (September 24). The article in *Harper's,* which summarized his military career, reprinted his "Song of the Soldiers," and pictured him in his lieutenant colonel's uniform, carefully avoided calling him by name, referring to him only as "Miles O'Reilly." The compliment proved that frustrated and disappointed as he had been in the army, he had not wasted his time. Walking the streets of New York once again as a civilian, he was no longer a man without a name. He was now a man so well known his name did not need to be mentioned.

Even so, his political career got off to a slow start. He received the nomination of the county Democratic organization for Clancy's old office of county clerk, but the Tammany Democrats were so hostile to him that he declined it to avoid splitting the party. His political judgment told him that Tammany's enmity would strengthen him with Republicans and independents, and work to his advantage in the long run. In the meantime, he was solaced by being admitted to the bar following a cursory examination by the justices of the New York Supreme Court, and by serving in still another appointive office, assistant district attorney.[1]

First and last, he was a newspaperman, and as the presidential election approached, he expressed his hostility toward the Lincoln administration by denouncing it in editorials in both the *Herald* and the *World.* Lincoln should be defeated, he declared, because he had perverted a just war to preserve the Union for the benefit of mankind into an unjust war for the benefit of the Negro. But, like other War Democrats, Halpine loved the Union more than he disliked Negroes, and he supported the administration's war at the same time that he opposed the administration. As Miles O'Reilly put it:

> The collud pusson—free or slave—
> We care no curse about,
> But for the flag our fathers gave
> We mean to fight it out. . . .[2]

The *Herald* had never been reluctant to criticize the Lincoln administration, and it shared Halpine's aversion for both Copperheads and "Niggerheads," a term which appeared frequently in its columns. Early in September Halpine believed that James Gordon Bennett was about ready to endorse the Democratic candidate, General George B. McClellan, a close friend of Sam Barlow. There were also other influential New Yorkers, men whom Lincoln looked upon as his loyal supporters, who were almost ready to announce for McClellan. If they did, the effect upon independent and undecided voters would be enormous. "Everything now looks bright and promising" for the Democrats, Halpine exclaimed to Barlow.[3]

But Lincoln kept Bennett in line by promising to take him more into his confidence and by holding out the possibility of a diplomatic appointment, and timely military victories undercut the other expected defections. Late in September Halpine himself began to hedge his bets, and while he continued to ridicule Lincoln in the *Herald* and *World,* he told Hay that the over-all effect of his "jocularities" would be to popularize the administration, and was even bold enough to ask that they be called to the President's attention! Hay shook his head in wonder. "My Dear Misguided Miles," he replied. "You are old enough to know better. I can only say to you as Shelley to St. Eldon—'I curse thee but I hate thee not.' "[4]

On New Year's Day, 1865, the *Herald* presented its readers the story of another of Halpine's fictional banquets, this one allegedly held the previous evening at the Maison Doree to honor Generals William Tecumseh Sherman and George H. Thomas. Sixty of the leading celebrities of the hour were present, including Vice-President-elect Andrew Johnson, Hunter, Dix, Averell, Weed, Barlow, and a suspiciously large number of Halpine's special friends. The cast was sufficiently star-studded to guarantee that a high percentage of readers would finish the story and respond sympathetically to its main appeal.

Its main appeal was in behalf of a new Soldiers' Home, and guest after guest arose to declare in speeches and toasts reflecting their particular styles and interests that a nation which honored generals like

Sherman and Thomas could not forget the men who had fought in the ranks, especially those who had been disabled. The existing Soldiers' Home outside Washington was totally inadequate. What was needed was a new institution located on good farm land in the salubrious mountains of New York or Pennsylvania, and large enough to be self-supporting. Halpine was too shrewd a showman to allow the pleas to become tedious, and as at the famous Miles O'Reilly Banquet, he varied the pace of the evening with jokes and songs, including one from strait-laced Governor John A. Andrew of Massachusetts, who requested that his Puritan constituents not be told about it:

> Fill the bumper high,
> Showing, without shrinking,
> Patriotic joy
> By patriotic drinking!

When he came to James T. Brady, a fixture at New York banquets, real and fictitious, Halpine changed the subject and denounced Secretary of State Seward for treating England's violations of international law as a subject for negotiation. Brady preferred to fight, and offered a toast to the Fenian Brotherhood, the radical organization of Irish nationalists about which Halpine would have more to say in the future. "The day of our war with England," Halpine had Brady exclaim, "enrolls every able-bodied true Irishman, both here and in Canada, under the banner of the Union." [5]

There is no reason to doubt the sincerity of Halpine's endorsement of the Soldiers' Home project. But he did not scruple against using his story of the banquet to ask a favor of one of the men honored by it. Less than a month after its publication he wrote to Sherman, expressing a desire to trade in the Division of the Mississippi, the agency comprising all of the military departments in the West of which Sherman was the commander. The three and one-half years he had spent in the army, said Halpine, were making it difficult for him to reestablish himself as a lawyer and journalist, and had cost him the sight of his right eye. He could apply directly to the Secretaries of War and the Treasury for the necessary trading permits, but did not wish to do so without Sherman's express approval. Did he have it? [6] In all probability Sherman, who was preparing to leave Savannah on his march northward through the Carolinas, declined this subtle request to act as sponsor of a business venture by ignoring it.

At the Sherman-Thomas Banquet Miles O'Reilly was neither present nor conspicuously absent. But he soon had opportunities to join

Governor Andrew in the display of patriotic joy by patriotic drinking. In mid-January, after the fall of Fort Fisher, guarding Wilmington, North Carolina, the last remaining port of the Confederacy, Miles and a large group of patriots staggered into a bar at 17th Street and Broadway (Halpine's favorite, perhaps) and simply took possession. Miles was singing for the fifth or sixth time his song "Sherry, Terry, and Porter—A Lyric of Mixed Liquors," suggested by the names of the victors at Fort Fisher—General Alfred H. Terry and Admiral David Dixon Porter—when the police arrived and took him away, The Boy protesting loudly that he was only amusing himself with a "pathriotic ditty," and threatening the police with confinement in Fort Lafayette when his friend the President heard what they were doing.[7]

"Bad luck to the man who is sober tonight," cried Miles three months later, when Union forces occupied Richmond and the war was almost over. At such a moment, even whiskey was inadequate as a means of self-expression.

> Och, murther! will none o' yez hould me, me dears!
>   Or 'tis out o' me shkin wid delight I'll be jumpin';
> Wid me eyes shwimmin' round in the happiest tears,
>   An' the heart in me breasht like a pistin-rod thumpin'![8]

The approaching end of the war and his months as a civilian served to modify Halpine's antagonism toward the Lincoln administration, and his respect for the President personally was apparent in the long article he wrote for the *Herald* on the Inauguration, March 4, 1865, and published the next day. Noting with what patience the President stood in the receiving line at the White House, his white gloves turning black from the touch of many hands, Halpine wrote, "Mr. Lincoln looked weary, but he looked well, and to one who commiserated [with] him for the infliction of courtesy he responded readily that he was 'a live man yet.' May the time be very far distant when he will not be able to say so."

The time when he could not say so was only six weeks distant. On April 17, two days after Lincoln's death, Halpine published an article in the *Herald* on his place in history. Gone now was the tone of condescension which had characterized earlier writings about Lincoln. The man he had criticized for weakness he now saw as the embodiment of American democracy. The rough spots of Lincoln's prairie mannerisms and speech, which had once amused and irritated him, now lost their abrasiveness and became democratic virtues. Lincoln was "as indigenous to our soil," Halpine declared, "as the cranberry crop, and as American in his fibre as the granite foundations of the Appalachian range."

Through him, the people of the United States had proved the vitality and validity of democratic principles, and this triumph would have a profound effect upon the next one hundred years in Europe, tipping the scales away from Caesarism, as represented by Napoleon III, toward republican self-government. Lincoln would therefore stand in the judgment of history as "the type-man of a new dynasty of nation rulers . . . for the whole civilized portion of the human family."

Two weeks later in the New York *Citizen,* Halpine attempted a summary evaluation of Lincoln's character:

> President Lincoln endeared himself to the people not by his intellectual force or brilliancy, but by the goodness, justice, honesty, and disinterested patriotism of his heart, combined with sound judgment, patient and earnest devotion to the public good, purity of motive, and simple, unaffected manners. He was pre-eminently a man of the people. Tender, forbearing, unwilling to inflict pain, if it could possibly be avoided, accessible to all, kind to all, independent, yet willing to learn, cautious yet steadfastly pursuing his great purpose in behalf of his country and humanity, he succeeded in winning the universal confidence of the nation in the soundness of his judgment, the purity of his motives, and the benevolence of his heart.

The change in Halpine's view of Lincoln was of course due in part to the emotional impact of the assassination. But that impact was not exclusively emotional, and in just the same way that it became easier to appreciate the significance of the Civil War in world history when the last battle was won, it became easier to take the measure of Lincoln after he was dead, after the distracting influences of partisanship and the conflicts of personality were removed. As Halpine put it in a poem, "The Lost Chief,"

> Pride found no idle space to spawn
> Her fancies in his busy mind;
> His worth, like health of air, could find
> No just appraisal till withdrawn.[9]

It was the North's victory as much as its response to Booth's derringer which transformed Lincoln. During most of the war when the outcome was in doubt, the leader selected by the people looked weak and inadequate. After victory he seemed strong and wise, and once he was dead it became possible even for Democrats to see and say so.

At the time of Lincoln's death, Halpine was busily engaged in taking over the editorship and management of his own weekly newspaper, the New York *Citizen,* formerly the organ of a prominent group of reform-minded New Yorkers who had organized the Citizen's Association. Attracted to Halpine by his articles against machine politics written while on General Dix's staff, the association had contacted him through its secretary, Robert B. Roosevelt. He wanted to meet Miles O'Reilly, Roosevelt wrote to Halpine on 26 April 1864. "I want him, that is the loan of him to help carry out his scheme of City reform as further elucidated by the Citizen's Association. Would you bring him to me at my office or let me know where I can meet him?" A meeting was arranged, and following Halpine's resignation from the army, a close friendship developed with the man he had once called a "Fifth Avenue noodle," for his efforts to get Dix to run for mayor of New York.

Born in 1829, the same year as Halpine, Robert B. Roosevelt was a son of the merchant-banker Cornelius V. Roosevelt, and the most public-spirited member of his family before the rise to political prominence of his nephew Theodore, who was born in the house next door on East 20th Street, New York, and became president of the United States. A large and handsome man with a dark full beard, Roosevelt was a War Democrat, an active anti-Wood, anti-Tweed reformer, and a strongly conservation-minded sportsman. Later in the century, he served in Congress, was United States minister to the Netherlands, treasurer of the Democratic National Committee, and twice mentioned as a presidential possibility by his party. "Everything he did," a member of the family later recalled, "was performed with gusto, together with a salting of humor and a peppering of eccentricity." [10] It is easy to see how he and Miles O'Reilly might become friends.

Before Halpine bought into the *Citizen,* it was a weekly tabloid of good intentions and little influence. Its intentions were clearly stated in each issue: "Honest, Economical, and Public Spirited City Government." It had only two questions to ask of each candidate for office: "Is he honest? Is he capable?" It was without influence, the veteran New York journalist, Frederic Hudson, told Halpine, because its publication was entirely subsidized by the Citizen's Association, and readers assumed that a free newspaper was not worth reading. When Halpine took it over, Hudson advised him, "Don't give away another copy. Don't throw away your brains, my dear boy. Sell your paper, if you only sell three copies, and you will have three readers at any rate." [11] Halpine took the advice, selling subscriptions first for $3.00 a year in advance, and then for $5.00. He also dropped the tabloid format, replacing it with pages the size of the *Times* and the *World,* and greatly expanded reader interest by adding literary, foreign and national news, art, music, and family departments. The public response was so encouraging that in June, 1865, the paper moved to new offices, adopted the over-sized sheets of the *Herald,* announced the appointment of a business manager ("for the brilliant Halpine . . . was as innocent and as ignorant as a babe in such matters," said Hudson), and declared its intention of becoming ultimately a daily newspaper.[12]

In May the public was notified that the *Citizen* had been transferred —on very generous terms, one feels sure—to Halpine, and the issue of May 13 bore his name as editor. In one of his first editorials, he announced that Miles O'Reilly would be a frequent contributor. "We have personal assurances from the Private—whom we have the honor of seeing every day, and who, in fact, is our 'guide, philosopher, and friend,' that after this week he will write for us regularly and make the *Citizen* his official organ."

The New York dailies, for whom Halpine had worked so long and for whom he continued to write, did not see the new weekly as a competitor, and were generous in publicizing it and in reprinting its most interesting stories. In June, for example, the *Times* reprinted a *Citizen* article which asserted that Secretary Stanton was opposed to a military trial for the conspirators in Lincoln's assassination. As civilians, Stanton was said to have argued before the cabinet, they should be tried in a civil court. But the contrary views of Judge Advocate Joseph Holt prevailed, the *Citizen* story continued, and President Johnson himself, not the Secretary of War, signed the order establishing the military court (over which, as a matter of interest, David Hunter presided). Like so many subsequent articles in the *Citizen,* the story was interesting and provocative, because Stanton was much criticized at the time for being the chief supporter of a military trial.[13]

Another example of Halpine's editorial daring was his call, only six weeks after Lincoln's death, for the return to the stage of Edwin Booth, who had voluntarily left it in a wave of humiliating revulsion against his name. Yet, asked Halpine, who besides the immediate Lincoln family had "more reason to execrate the crime which we all deplore?" The summer before, Halpine had spent a few days with Booth at the seashore home of William Stuart, proprietor of New York's Winter Garden Theater. He now reported that he had been impressed by Booth's respect for Lincoln and his support for the war as well, since the majority of actors "were the reverse of zealous in the national cause." A few months later, Halpine published a long article criticizing the quality of the New York theater, and lamenting the dearth of first-rate actors. He was in correspondence with Booth, and his encouragement may have been a factor in Booth's decision to return to the stage early in 1866.

In his efforts to build up the *Citizen,* Halpine did not hesitate to approach his old army and navy friends, or even his old navy enemy, Gustavus V. Fox, whom he had ridiculed nearly as much as Gideon Welles in the original Miles O'Reilly stories. Perhaps John Hay, who liked Fox and saw him frequently, brought the two men together during one of Halpine's visits to Washington. Or perhaps the end of Halpine's friendship with Admiral Du Pont recommended Du Pont's critics to him. The Admiral never did succeed in rehabilitating himself with the Navy Department or in securing another sea command, although the fact that his successor could not capture Charleston from the sea, either, did help to clear his name with those who had followed the controversy over the monitors. But Halpine had championed Du Pont when almost everyone else was attacking him, and he felt that his efforts had been insufficiently appreciated. How much prize money had Du Pont received from the capture of the *Atlanta?* Halpine inquired of Fox. In the Navy Department files, Fox could read a letter from Du Pont "confessing that but for my action there would not have been a monitor within at least 60 miles." But, Halpine continued, "generosity is not Du Pont's peculiar foible—indeed, I hear rather in the contrary. . . . He is not the first idol of brass with feet of clay." In performing some small favor for Halpine, Fox had taken "more trouble for me than *he* ever did in the course of his old brown-wigged life!"

Could Fox send some testimonial letters from the Navy Department for publication in the *Citizen?* When Fox answered that such endorsements were contrary to department rules, Halpine asked him to waive the rules. "Whether you oblige me or not, certain things that will gratify you will appear in a few weeks." And he added a postscript: "O'Reilly joins in my request. He says you owe me something for the capture of the *Atlanta.*" [14]

Another incident shows that Halpine was not overly scrupulous in his efforts to make the *Citizen* interesting. On Christmas Eve, 1864, Henry Wadsworth Longfellow sent a basket of wine to his friend the scientist Jean Rudolphe Louis Agassiz, together with an uncharacteristically light-hearted poem in French describing Agassiz and his friends enjoying the bottles. Somehow, Halpine managed to get a copy of the poem, "Noel," translated it into English, and asked Longfellow for permission to publish it in the *Citizen.* In reply, Longfellow wished Halpine good luck with his paper, but declined to allow him to print "Noel," because it was "of so private a nature that I shrink from seeing it in the papers." Halpine went ahead and published it, anyway. To make matters worse, he even altered one of the verses and worked himself into it.

Longfellow was of course angry, and Halpine apologized, conceding that he might have overstepped the bounds of propriety "to some extent." But so many of his friends had admired the poem, he explained, as "one of the prettiest social compliments ever paid by poetry to science," that he had not been able to resist the temptation to publish it.[15]

Hard work, imagination, and Halpine's willingness to do almost anything to make the *Citizen* a success, quickly turned it into a lively and controversial paper. In addition to standard reports of major news events at home and abroad, it carried a wide variety of interesting feature articles and serials. Book reviews and literary essays were presented in a column entitled "Miles O'Reilly's Book Table," a series of articles about New York editors—"Verbographs," Halpine called them—appeared at frequent intervals, and in a column headed "Table Talk at the Clubs," readers were given a taste of the Café Society gossip so popular in the next century. Among the books serialized were George Alfred Townsend's *Glimpses of War Life in the North,* which was later published as a book under a different title and dedicated to Halpine.[16] In his *White House Sketches,* William O. Stoddard included much of the material which he later used in his various books on Lincoln. In addition, there were Edwin De Leon's *Secret History of Confederate Diplomacy Abroad,* an anonymous account of *Rummaging Through Rebeldom* by a man said to have been on Jefferson Davis' staff, and various works by Robert Roosevelt on hunting, fishing, and conservation. His writers did not always obey the *Citizen*'s "General Order No. 1," which Halpine pulled out of *Lyrics by the Letter H.* and posted for their benefit,

> In short, be brief. Each added leaf
> Is so much to your reader's grief;
> The point is gone; the lightning's shone
> And dies while yet we labor on;
> True wit ne'er knows a second dawn, . . .[17]

But on the whole, the *Citizen* was a lively and informative newspaper. It kept him in touch with "Young America," John Hay wrote from Paris, 3 August 1865.

The most entertaining of the *Citizen*'s writers was Miles O'Reilly, whose penchant for getting into trouble did not forsake him. One of Halpine's brothers, William Henry Halpin, a professor of classics at Huron College, London, Canada, amused himself by translating his brother's popular verses into Latin. Halpine printed these translations in the *Citizen,* together with a letter accusing Miles of being a plagiarist. The songs of the war which O'Reilly had been passing off as his own, he charged, were in reality the works of certain minor poets of the Second Empire. Proof of the deception was furnished in the form of side-by-side publication of stanzas in their Latin originals and English translations. For weeks the controversy raged in perfect seriousness, as Miles defended himself with impressive but irrelevant arguments, such as his descent from Marcus Au-Relius. The controversy fooled many people, including some editors of the New York *Post,* and ended at last with Miles's dismissal from the *Citizen.* But he was back after a short interval, and was involved early in 1867 in a love affair with one of Roosevelt's nieces, Lucie Ellice.

O'Reilly's eye for pretty girls was apparently as keen as Halpine's, and after just two meetings with Lucie Ellice he offered her "My Toast," and called her "The First, Last, and Only Girl I Ever Loved."

> Oh, give me a ruff that once touched her throat,
> And I ask no gems from a royal palace;
> Give me a ribbon that once did float
> Where the swelling lines her form denote,
> Then send me to die in some land remote,
> My last thought—"Lucie Ellice!"

The following week, Roosevelt published "My Warning. A Reply to 'My Toast,' " in which he said of his ardent friend,

> He hath toasted and sung every girl he has met,
> And now would steal from me my only solace,
> The darling I've worshipped—my beauty! my pet!

Soon readers, including another Lucie Ellice from somewhere in the South (very likely a hoax) sent in their own poems of advice and warning, and for months the subject of Miles and his love occupied the *Citizen*'s subscribers.

Many *Citizen* columns were devoted to exposing political corruption, more blatant in New York than ever. The lobbyists who crowded the state capital and the city hall and simply bought the legislation they wanted were more dangerous to the American experiment in democratic government, Halpine declared, than the southern rebels recently defeated had been.

But many writers denounced corruption in government, and Halpine's editorials were probably less important in influencing public opinion than his poems, his "Ring Rhymes," published periodically in the *Citizen* and with great frequency just before elections. It gave New Yorkers a grim satisfaction to read Miles O'Reilly's verse-caricatures, like the one comparing Boss Tweed, whose girth had expanded about as rapidly as his political power, to a Suffolkshire pig ready for the knife. It was several years before he received it, but the "Ring Rhymes," which, like Thomas Nast's more famous cartoons, had made him and so many of his henchmen seem ridiculous or contemptible, deserve some credit for bringing him to the block. Unfortunately, most of the verses dealt with specific instances of corruption or with minor officials, and it is no longer possible to appreciate their humor or understand their allusions.[18]

The tensions of his character and the strain of getting out an informative and entertaining paper each week of course affected Halpine's always sensitive health. His headaches, he told Hay, felt as if two men were boring with gimlet and awl from the tympanum of his left ear to the center of his brain, and they worked away for days at a time. While the headaches lasted, he gave them his usual treatment and remained at home to be cared for by Margaret, often sending copy and instructions for the paper from his bed.[19]

To a man of his temperament, plagued by moodiness, by physical pains and psychological fears, by a relentless ambition to prove himself by adding wealth and position to the fame he had acquired, Margaret's steady devotion and personal tranquility were indispensable. He could not have continued without her, and occasionally he recognized it and said it in poems which must have represented recompense and fulfillment for her. "We have lived in vain," he cries out in despair after a melancholy look at his life in a poem published by *Harper's Weekly,* 11 November 1865. But it was "not quite so," for at the end he sees the words expressed by Margaret's eyes: "Oh, soul of my soul, if my love be a prize,/Then you have not lived in vain."

But when he was well, he would wonder if there were to be other prizes in life for him, and before long the worry would make him sick, and then he would begin to drink again.

CHAPTER 10

The Prison Life of Jefferson Davis

As a MEMBER of Halleck's staff and as a friend of Lincoln's secretaries, Halpine frequently visited the White House during the Civil War. Afterwards, he continued to visit it as an adviser to Andrew Johnson, whose reconstruction policies he publicized and supported.

The basic feature of President Johnson's reconstruction program as stated in his Proclamation of Amnesty, 29 May 1865, was forgiveness for the ex-rebels, who, with certain exceptions, were granted full pardons and restoration of their rights as citizens after taking an oath of loyalty to the United States. Those excepted from the presidential amnesty— high-ranking Confederate officials and large landowners—could apply to the President for special clemency, which, he assured them would be "liberally extended." It was very close to what Lincoln himself had promised back in December, 1863, and was designed to bring about that quick reunion which most Union supporters of both parties had favored during the war.

Once the fighting stopped, however, opposition quickly developed. It was one thing to subscribe during the war to the general principle of a peace of charity for all, malice towards none, and another to accept it as a policy after the war, with all its unforeseen ramifications. What many people had not fully understood before was that the policy of forgiveness meant that the same men who had rebelled against the United States and fought it for four terrible years would continue in their positions of political leadership in the southern states. Under the President's amnesty, they could simply lay down their arms, hold up their right hands (or apply for special pardons), and remain the rulers of the South. It was not just malice and a desire for revenge which caused many northerners to object. What had the war been about, anyway, if not to remove these very men from power? The Democrats could not hope to lead the nation in the postwar years unless their publicists could give a convincing answer to the question.

Halpine first met Andrew Johnson in the summer of 1865, when the President, in the absence of Congress, was proceeding on his own to reconstruct the Union. He approved of what Johnson was doing, and said so over a period of months in editorials in the *Citizen*. It was not pleasant, he conceded, to see men who had recently been the enemies of the United States being elected to political office, but what alternative was there? "So long as we extend any true form of representation to the South, how can such persons be excluded?" The war had been fought to validate the principles of representative government and majority rule, and northerners could not now deny those principles without making themselves as much the enemies of the United States as the rebellious southerners had been. The choices in reconstruction policy were clear, Halpine argued, drawing a historical parallel he found especially persuasive. "Either we must treat the South as Cromwell treated Ireland— uprooting all the ancient laws and proprietors of the soil, and replanting it with the families of his own soldiers, holding by military tenure and with sufficient garrisons to repress and keep in subjection an enslaved and utterly ruined people; or we must pass liberal acts of oblivion and amnesty, in favor of all who took part in the secession movement, only excluding those . . . who have been guilty of individual crimes placing them outside the laws of civilized warfare."

Johnson was grateful for the support, and in February, 1866, nominated Halpine, who had had so much trouble with military rank under a Republican administration, for promotion to both colonel and brigadier general. Ostensibly, the promotions were in recognition of Halpine's services at the battle of Piedmont, but in reality they were the President's way of showing his gratitude for Halpine's services in the battle of Reconstruction. Nothing but the privilege of using the military title was involved, but General Halpine was the last man to consider the honor an empty one! [1]

The President soon had further cause to be grateful, when Halpine served administrative interests with an influential book on Jefferson Davis.

Following his capture by Union forces in Georgia in May, 1865, Davis was imprisoned at Fort Monroe, Virginia. Because he was believed to have been involved in the assassination of Lincoln, he was at first treated badly. For a few days he was even forced to wear shackles, and for a somewhat longer time a light and a guard were kept always in his room. Virtually the only person who treated him with compassion was the army surgeon assigned to look after him, John J. Craven, a friend of Halpine's who had once been mentioned in the *Herald* as the physician attending another distinguished prisoner—Miles O'Reilly, of Morris Island. Craven treated Davis' various illnesses, interceded in his behalf with the commandant, General Nelson A. Miles, and conversed with him respectfully. Mrs. Craven and her daughter saw to it that the prisoner had clean clothes and good food. "I feel deeply indebted to Dr. Craven and the ladies of his family," Davis wrote to his wife. Varina Davis, too, was grateful. "I will teach my children to pray for dear Dr. Craven all his life," she promised. After meeting Craven and his family in New York following his discharge from the army, she wrote her husband, "God bless them and keep them, for all they have done for you in your hour of extreme agony." Davis' most recent biographer, Hudson Strode, goes so far as to say that "being able to converse with one kindly man like his sympathetic doctor undoubtedly saved Davis' life." For Dr. Craven, Jefferson Davis felt an "inexpressible gratitude." [2]

From May to December, 1865, when he had charge of Davis' health, Craven kept a diary and miscellaneous notes of his conversations with the rebel leader. Reminded of the best-seller written about Napoleon at St. Helena by his physician, the Irishman Barry O'Meara, Halpine asked his friend for permission to turn his material into a book, to be published under Craven's name.

The potential royalties of such a book were certainly an inducement; but Halpine was interested in more than money. He could see that a book about the treatment of Jefferson Davis by his Republican jailers would play an important role in the controversy over Reconstruction. Indeed, he told President Johnson, it would make "the most powerful campaign document ever issued in this country, . . . a document that could not but abate the fanaticism of the radicals . . . & strengthen & rally the conservative opinions of the country to your increased support." In addition, it would effectively neutralize an anti-Davis, anti-Democratic book expected from General Miles, who, as " 'a Boston boy' par excellence," was in favor of the Radical Republican program for Reconstruction. Was the President interested in a pro-Democratic book on Davis based on Craven's sources? asked Halpine. [3] The President was decidedly interested, and Halpine went promptly to work.

His major purpose in writing, he told Sam Barlow, who had many important southern contacts, was "to put the whole present plea of the South in the mouth of Mr. Davis, interpolating political matters from Southern sources in his real conversations with Dr. Craven which were chiefly on scientific & social subjects, though not altogether so." In order to make his interpolations authentic, Halpine asked Barlow to send him any Davis letters he might have, and to arrange an interview with

Richard Taylor, son of Zachary Taylor, an ex-major general in the Confederate Army, and once Jefferson Davis' brother-in-law.[4]

In addition to pleading for the South, Halpine wished to create popular sympathy for Davis himself, for by 1866 the charge that he was implicated in Lincoln's assassination had collapsed, and since there was no longer any disposition to proceed with a trial for treason, his continued imprisonment was an embarrassment to the administration. In May, at the time Halpine was rushing chapters of his manuscript to the publishers, President Johnson told Varina Davis that he would like to release her husband. "But we must wait," he said. "Our hope is to mollify the public to Mr. Davis." [5] The principal vehicle for the mollification of the public, *The Prison Life of Jefferson Davis,* by John J. Craven, M.D., was published the next month. Lest any reviewers overlook the parallel, O'Meara's book on Napoleon was cited on the title page.

Halpine's connection with the writing of *The Prison Life* was an open secret from the beginning, although what he wrote and why has never before been revealed. Several early reviewers identified him as the real author, and one described the book as pure fiction. It was "an artfully woven tissue of truth and falsehood," the critic declared, and was no more reliable than if it had been written entirely from newspaper stories and Halpine's imagination.[6] In 1868, the Charleston, South Carolina, *Mercury* published an article, supposedly based on a conversation with Halpine himself, which asserted that the book was Halpine's invention exclusively.[7] Certainly readers of the *Citizen* had no reason to doubt Halpine's authorship, for *The Prison Life* was for months advertised along with the *Life and Adventures of Miles O'Reilly* and *Baked Meats of the Funeral* in such a way as to indicate that Miles O'Reilly was the author of all three. Craven's name did not appear in the *Citizen* ads, all three books were published by Carleton, and all of them (and no others) were for sale at the *Citizen* office. When Craven admitted in 1875 that "many words, perhaps sentences" [8] of the book had been written by Halpine, it therefore came as a surprise to nobody, except those who knew how grossly the good doctor had understated the truth.

The Prison Life of Jefferson Davis was about as subtle and truthful as the other works of Miles O'Reilly. In an introductory chapter, Halpine had the audacity to state, "The book aims to introduce no discussion of any political questions connected with the late rebellion; nor to be a plea influencing public judgment, either for or against, the gentleman who was for so many months the Author's patient," and in his conclusion he even declared that although his notes of his conversations with Davis were imperfect, "it has been my conscientious effort to report him as he was, neither inventing any new sentiments to put in his mouth, or suppressing any material. . . . In many of the important political conversations, let me add, the words are as nearly as possible the exact language used by Mr. Davis."

The portrait drawn of Davis was a flattering one of a broken man who had staked and lost all for what he believed, who was reconciled to his defeat, and who stood feebly but erect before God and the American people. Although in bad health and a prisoner in the strongest fortress in North America, to which he had once been welcomed with all the impressive pomp due a United States Secretary of War, he was subjected to humiliation like shackling and the lack of privacy which should make the cheeks of all Americans burn with shame. Accused of unspeakable crimes of which his conscience was clear, he found solace in his Bible and prayer book, one or the other of which was virtually always in his hand. He felt no bitterness in his heart, wrote Halpine (in defiance of the fact). For Lincoln he had respect, recognizing his adversary's goodness of character, honesty of purpose, and freedom from avarice. Indeed, he had done what he could to combat efforts of the southern press during the war to make Lincoln seem abhorrent and contemptible.

Davis was a kindly man, considerate of his guards, worried about the health and safety of his wife and children, and concerned about the welfare of other prisoners. With crumbs from his own plate he was trying to domesticate a little mouse, "the only living thing he now had power to benefit," his doctor explained.

Halpine's Davis was, to say the least, brilliant intellectually. His memory was almost miraculous, "a single perusal of any passage that interested either his assent or denial enabling him to repeat it almost verbatim." As was only to be expected of a man with such a talent, his fund of knowledge was immense and detailed. He was an expert on history, literature, geology, botany, and human anatomy, on navigation and ship design, on ordnance, industry, and engineering, on birds and dogs and the Bible, and he liked to recite long passages from Milton.

He was also a man of breeding and good taste, unwilling to discourse on subjects on which he knew he and his physician disagreed, and refusing to speak ill of any man, even his most vindictive enemies. Mistaken in his devotion to the theory of state sovereignty (which, however, Halpine observed, had once been very widely held by the people of both sections), he had suffered terribly for his error. "If Mr. Davis has been guilty of any private crime, such as connivance with the assassination of Mr. Lincoln or unauthorized cruelties to our prisoners, no punishment can be too heavy for him; but let the fact of his guilt be established in fair and open trial. If, on the other hand, his only guilt has been rebellion," said Halpine, speaking for the administration, "let a great nation show the truest quality of greatness—magnanimity—by including him in the wide folds of that act of amnesty and oblivion, in which all his minor partners, civil and military, in the late Confederacy are now so wisely enveloped."

The time had come to recognize, the book's argument continued, that the man who had been so passionately reviled during the war was not utterly bad, that he possessed, in fact, great redeeming virtues. It was also time to admit "that no movement so vast, and eliciting such intense devotion on the part of its partisans as the late Southern rebellion, could have grown up into its gigantic proportions without containing many elements of truth and good." It was time for northerners to concede that southerners had been trapped in a dreadful dilemma back in 1861: if they remained loyal to their states, they were disloyal to the United States; if they remained loyal to the United States, they were disloyal to their states. The war was now over and its results accepted in good faith, and, as Jefferson Davis observed to Dr. Craven, "Every man's experience must teach him that quarrels between friends are best healed when they are healed most promptly."

As Davis saw it, the quarrel between North and South should be healed by the prompt renewal of all the rights, privileges, duties, immunities, and obligations prescribed for the states by the Constitution. The alternative to a complete restoration of rights was unthinkable, yet the Republicans were threatening the South with the kind of peace which Cromwell had imposed upon Ireland. Davis fully accepted the emancipation of the slaves, but believed it a great tragedy for the Negroes, and held freedom responsible for the deterioration of relations between the races in the South. Under slavery there had been no antagonism because there had been no rivalry. The closer the Negro was pushed toward political equality by the Republicans, the greater the conflict would become. Equality for Negroes, Halpine caused Davis to say, was the same "as if our horses were given the right of intruding into our parlors." Surely northerners, who had so often refused to grant the suffrage to their own Negroes, though the colored population was "not numerous enough in any district to decide the majority of a pound keeper," would not require it of the South, but would respect the Constitutional right of the southern states to decide the qualifications of voters for themselves.

The Prison Life of Jefferson Davis, wrote a reviewer in the Washington *Chronicle,* reads like "a Democratic speech in Congress." [9] Indeed it did.

Although the book "helped enormously," according to Hudson Strode,[10] in bringing about Davis' release from prison in May, 1867, it did not deepen Davis' gratitude and sense of obligation to Craven. In fact, it ended their friendship forever, and twenty years later when Craven, aging and in poor health, approached Davis, he felt it necessary to go through a third party. He had not intended to write a book when first put in charge of Davis, he asked this person to explain to his former patient. But upon hearing that General Miles was going to write an unfriendly book, he and his daughter had hurriedly prepared their own sympathetic manuscript, and succeeded in getting it to the publisher in only twenty days. In his haste, Craven asked shamelessly, had he perhaps written something offensive to Davis? Although Davis endorsed the intermediary's letter "rec'd. & answed.," [11] his reply has not been preserved. It is unlikely that he ever wrote to Craven.[12]

The fact was that *The Prison Life* was intolerably offensive to Davis. It was not just that, as Strode tells us, he "winced to read some expressions Craven had put into his mouth that were inconceivable to his nature or his breeding," while recognizing that it was the work of "an admiring friend." [13] It was not just that Craven had been indiscreet in making public details of Davis' health and private conversations. Considering the extent to which the book rehabilitated his reputation in the South and won him friends among his former enemies in the North, even a proper Victorian like Davis might have forgiven an admiring friend whose only offense was overly colorful writing and a few minor indiscretions. Davis winced when he read *The Prison Life,* and indeed whenever he thought of it, because it was not an "honest book," as Douglas Southall Freeman has called it,[14] but a dishonest book, cynically calculated to make money and political propaganda. It was bad enough for Davis to read lies about himself; it was much worse to see himself cited as their source.

At the request of a friend who was considering an answer to Craven, Davis in 1887 annotated his own copy of *The Prison Life,* though he protested that the subject was "always painful." [15] Rereading the book with a pencil in his hand, he made frequent use of question marks, exclamation points, "x's," and such expletives as "fabrication," "fiction," "this is absurd," "never said so," "the reverse of my opinion," "not mine," "new to me," "false," "bah," "not so," "all wrong," and "pshaw." What he objected to was very plainly not the material based upon Craven's diary, a few fragments of which have survived and been printed in parallel columns with the relevant passages of the text in an effort to demonstrate the book's authenticity.[16] What he disliked were those parts made up by Halpine.[17]

Of course he did not object unduly to minor exaggerations and lies about subjects no more consequential than his domestication of the little mouse (which he did not attempt to tame), his technical knowledge of birds (which he did not possess), his reception at Fort Monroe as Secretary of War (which he had never visited except as a prisoner), or his recitation of Milton (whom he had not memorized). But he did resent it when his own conduct and views of public policy and public figures were misrepresented. Of the shackling scene, long recognized as overdrawn, he wrote "fiction distorting fact," "fiction perverting fact," "coloring laid on," and "gross misrepresentation." He did not like to read that he had ever contemplated suicide, that he believed the United States had been justified in treating medicine as contraband of war, that he ever admitted Confederate surgeons had resorted too frequently to amputations because many of them had only half finished their educations in the North, or that he thought the Negro freedmen might be better off in the next generation. "My opinion was & is," he wrote, "that the next generation will be still worse off."

As president of the Confederacy, he had had no plans to establish a protectorate in Mexico, and he did not believe that those southerners who had fled south of the border after Appomattox had evaded an obligation to remain at home and share the miseries of defeat and subjugation. Quite the contrary. "[I] always sympathized with the brave soldiers of the Confedcy. who, when they could no longer serve their country[,] shrunk from witnessing its misery and humiliation as the victim of a sectional despotism."

He denied many things he was supposed to have said about individuals. He "made no such statements" regarding the factors which had caused him to make his original cabinet selections. He did not believe that McClellan could have taken Richmond during the 1862 peninsular campaign, had he only been adequately supported by the United States government, and he did not rejoice when he heard of McClellan's removal from command. Following two pages of favorable characterization and appreciation of Halpine's Confederate hero, Stonewall Jackson, Davis made this startling comment: "If the writer ever conversed with me of Genl. Jackson he must have heard quite the opposite of the above. It is most charitable to suppose that in this as in many other instances he has attributed to me the opinion of some one else, not knowing what I thought, and only careful to fill his book according to programme." He must have trembled with anger to read that David Hunter was "his beau ideal of the military gentleman—the soul of integrity, intrepidity, true Christian piety and honor," whose lack of success was due largely to his "unwillingness to bend to anything mean or sinister," but at the conclusion of this astonishing paragraph, Davis simply observed, "All this of a man whose atrocities had caused him to be put under ban."

Among the many opinions on matters of state erroneously ascribed to Davis by *The Prison Life* was his belief that "the utter failure of Confederate finance was the failure of the cause," and his conviction that it could have been avoided. There were in the South at the time of secession, Davis is said to have told Craven, three million bales of cotton which could have been purchased by the government at ten cents a pound, and rushed to Europe before the North could stop it. Within a year or two, this cotton would have been worth a billion dollars. "Such a sum," Davis was quoted by Halpine as saying, "would have more than sufficed all the needs of the Confederacy during the war; would have sufficed, with economic management, for a war of twice the actual duration." Of this theory and statement, widely accepted in the literature of the Civil War as truly his, Davis wrote, spacing his words over the several pages of text and connecting them with a line in the margin, "The grain of truth perverted and hidden by a bushel of fiction."

Because *The Prison Life* was known from the first to be something less than the honestly written memoir of John J. Craven, it has been rejected as an historical source by most historians. Yet some—Freeman, E. Merton Coulter, and Burton J. Hendrick, to give three eminent examples—have used it or praised it,[18] and Davis' biographers have been notably partial to it, although they have avoided analysis of Davis' annotated copy. Even Varina Davis, who must have known her husband's opinion of the book, gives it her official approval by quoting a substantial part of it in her *Jefferson Davis. A Memoir*.[19] Thus its falsifications have been spread, many of them becoming established truths.

The public has enjoyed reading *The Prison Life,* and had the opportunity to do so in French, German, and Italian translations, as well as in English editions published in 1905 and 1960. Halpine's share of the royalties from the first edition was said to have amounted to $7,000 within two years,[20] and Craven no doubt received a like amount. But the one who profited the most from *The Prison Life of Jefferson Davis* was the man who found it so repugnant it was painful to think about, and whose position in history would be a lesser one without it.

In helping to make it possible for him to release Davis from prison, Andrew Johnson also profited, and he showed his appreciation by consulting with Halpine on matters of mutual interest, especially the patronage. Sometimes Halpine's advice was followed, as it was in the case of the collector of the Port of New York, the most valuable patronage position at the disposal of the United States government.[21] Other times it was ignored, as it was in the case of the naval officer of the Port of New York, the second most valuable appointive office.

It was the responsibility of the naval officer to examine and countersign nearly all of the collector's actions. He was paid an annual salary of $4,950, but his office was worth between $30,000 and $100,000 in fees, and he was empowered to appoint many subordinate officials. Of course, like the collector, whose fees sometimes reached the then fantastic figure of $150,000 a year, he had to be generous to the party and persons to whom he owed his appointment, and to respond to their wishes in hiring. When the office became vacant in June, 1866, Halpine recommended the appointment of Deputy Naval Officer C. S. Franklin, whose selection, he told the President, would help to bring about that coalition of conservative Republicans and Democrats "which must take place if your administration is to be sustained." [22] When Johnson declined to appoint a Republican to such a lucrative post, Halpine recommended as his second choice the colorful and eccentric Major General Daniel Sickles. Anticipating a negative response to so unstable a figure, he was ready with a third name—his own. In support of himself, Halpine promised the backing of all the non-Radical Republican press of the country, and some of the Radical, including the New York *Tribune,* nearly all of the high-ranking officers of the army, all New York Democrats, except the Copperheads, and virtually all of the Fenians. And he reminded the President that "few names in the country are more widely known." [23]

For weeks, Halpine urged his own appointment, but in October, 1866, the office was awarded to John A. Dix, who soon resigned it and went to France as United States Minister. Relations between the Democratic President and the Republican senate became so hostile that no successor was chosen.

Dix, a War Democrat capable of attracting support from conservative Republicans, was precisely the kind of man Halpine wanted Johnson to appoint to domestic and diplomatic offices. But to allow him to fill so important a position as that of naval officer for only a few short weeks, after which the office was lost for good to the President and the party, only served to illustrate Johnson's ineptitude in the handling of the patronage. Miles O'Reilly would not have vacated the job so quickly!

In other ways, too, Johnson failed to use his vast patronage powers wisely. Instead of winning the support of moderate and conservative Republicans by retaining Lincoln appointees in office, Johnson acted as if he had been elected president in his own right, with a mandate from the people to replace Republicans with Democrats. Under the circumstances, the number of removals he made for partisan reasons was excessive, and had the effect of uniting the disunited Republicans against him. If he lost strength with his removals, he failed to gain it with his appointments, for too often his appointees—including a few Republicans—were men without significant political influence. Halpine was discouraged, and by September, 1866, was criticizing the President's patronage "blunders" in the *Citizen,* and attributing the rapid growth of Radicalism to them.

But he continued to support Johnson's efforts to bring about a quick and full restoration of southern Constitutional rights. When Horace Greeley denounced this policy as "Johnson's policy," Miles O'Reilly responded in the *Citizen,* September 8.

> *"His* policy," do you say?
> By Heaven, who says so lies in his throat!
> 'Twas *our* policy, boys, from our muster-day,
> Through skirmish and bivouac, march and fray—
> *"His* policy"—do you say?
>
> . . . .
>
> *"His* policy"—how does it hap?
> Has the old word "Union" no meaning, pray?
> What meant the "U.S." upon every cap?
> Upon every button, and belt, and strap?
> 'Twas *our* policy, all the way!

For the fact that only a year and a half after Appomattox "our policy" had indeed become "his policy," Andrew Johnson's lack of political finesse was in large part responsible, and Halpine knew it.

At about the same time that *The Prison Life of Jefferson Davis* moved Halpine into the inner circles of the collapsing Johnson administration, the Fenian Brotherhood, with which he had become identified, moved him temporarily back out by involving the United States in a diplomatic crisis with England. Founded in the United States in 1858 by John O'Mahony, the Fenians were devoted to the vague but dangerous-sounding objective of freeing Ireland from English oppression. To native-born Americans, already antagonistic to Irish immigrants, the Order seemed conspiratorial and anti-American, and its existence helped to restore in the early 1860's a sense of righteousness to their prejudices against the Irish which had been lacking since the nativist excesses of the middle 1850's. Tightly organized and disciplined, Fenianism was often equated during the war with Copperheadism, and the Fenian spirit was held responsible for the New York draft riots. Some of the fears about the character of the Brotherhood were laid to rest, and some new ones took their place early in May, 1865, when Halpine published a long article on the Fenians in the *Herald*. It was the first detailed and informed discussion of the organization ever presented to the public, and it must have found fascinated readers in England when it was reprinted later in the month in the London *Times*. Halpine credited it with infusing new life into the movement in America.

There was nothing secret about the Fenian Brotherhood in the United States, Halpine announced, and then proved it by revealing the names of virtually all of its officers, from Head Centre O'Mahony down to the leaders of State Centres and local Districts. Its branches in Ireland and Canada were indeed secret, but on the free soil of America there was no need for members to hide either their identities or their purpose. Their purpose was single and revolutionary—the establishment of a free and independent Ireland—but they worked to achieve this end, Halpine declared, without violating any of the laws of the United States. Contrary to what so many Americans believed, the Fenians were not subversive. As to the alleged link between Fenianism and Copperheadism, Halpine conceded that some members of the society had indeed been followers of antiwar leaders like Clement L. Vallandigham and the Wood brothers, Fernando and Benjamin. But the overwhelming majority had been loyal supporters of the Union, and many thousands of them had served in the United States Army.[24]

Although Halpine never stated publicly that he was himself a member of the Fenian Brotherhood and in November, 1866, told President Johnson that he was not, his love for Ireland and his hatred for England, as expressed in his novels published in the *Irish-American* during the 1850's, can only be described as Fenian in the extreme. After the outbreak of the Civil War he published in the New York *Leader* a poem promising "Old Ireland" that her sons abroad, now arming themselves, would soon come to her rescue. He was proud that the organization's charter song had been written (to the tune of a familiar Irish melody) by "a Fenian private soldier of the old Tenth Army Corps." But there was nothing funny about Miles O'Reilly's "Fenian Rallying Song," sung at regular monthly meetings and on special occasions. It was, on the contrary, an expression of dedicated and aggressive Irish nationalism, and it earnestly prayed for the day

When Yankee guns thunder
On Britain's coast, on Britain's coast,
And land, our green flag under,
The Fenian host, the Fenian host! [25]

The Fenians, exhilarated by the sense of outrage in the North at England's wartime violations of neutrality, hoped that war was imminent and that when it came the United States would ship to Ireland the arms and munitions needed for its liberation. But even if the grievances against England should be settled peacefully, a possibility they scorned with characteristic Celtic vehemence, they assumed that the surplus American arms they were now purchasing from the War Department could be sent to Ireland, just as England had allowed its citizens to sell arms to the Confederacy. Either way, the more optimistic of them could see freedom for Ireland in the near future.[26]

By early 1866 Secretary of State Seward's evident willingness to negotiate United States claims against England made war between the two nations unlikely. With arms and munitions being stockpiled, thanks to the cooperation of a United States government anxious not to offend Irish voters, some Fenians therefore clamored for immediate action; they would strike a blow for Ireland's freedom by attacking the English in Canada.

Such an attack, Halpine assured readers of the *Citizen* in 1866, was entirely feasible. Once a Canadian island or port was captured, the Fenians could issue letters of marque and prey upon British shipping as the English-built *Alabama* had so recently preyed upon American. Far from being repudiated by the people of the United States, he declared, mistaking anti-English sentiment for pro-Irish, the action would be supported by 99 percent of them. The cause of liberating Ireland was "one of the holiest that human life can be given to forward." It was worth 10,000 lives, or even 100,000, but unless the invasion had a real chance of success, it should not be undertaken.[27]

Divided into two major wings over the wisdom and utility of the attack on Canada, the Fenian Brotherhood was stunned in the spring of 1866 by the revelation of a scandalous misuse of funds by some of its most prominent leaders. It was a devastating blow to the members' morale, and the organization never really recovered. A portion of the activist wing, however, was unwilling to give up its plans for an attack on Canada, and in April some of them attempted and bungled an attack on Campobello Island, New Brunswick, close to the southeast corner of

Maine. The raid was such a fiasco that both British and American authorities believed there would be no more Fenian invasions of Canada, and dismissed the continuing talk of military action as mere braggadocio and blarney.[28]

It was not—not quite. For on June 1, some thousand Fenians, men who hated England not wisely but too much, crossed the international frontier near Buffalo without artillery and very nearly without supplies, skirmished briefly with the Canadian militia, and engaged in a few days of pointless pillaging. American officials, surprised by the foolhardy action, moved quickly enough to prevent reenforcements from being sent across the Niagara River, and, upon their return to the United States, arrested the Fenian adventurers.

Although Halpine had helped to whet Fenian appetites for an attack on Canada and therefore could not escape all responsibility for this one, he had not marched up the Shenandoah Valley at General Hunter's side for nothing. He knew that an invasion of hostile territory required planning, skillful leadership, an overwhelming superiority of force, and an ample supply of arms, munitions, and equipment. He had favored military action only when it had a reasonable chance of being successful, and he promptly denounced the attack as a folly and a crime. He was also very likely the New York *Herald*'s correspondent, previously sympathetic to the Fenians, who described the invaders as nothing more than "an armed mob, roving about wherever they pleased, robbing the homes, and insulting and abusing women and children." And in the Preface to his *Baked Meats* he referred to the Fenian Brotherhood as "that curious and erratic movement."

But if Halpine disavowed the Fenian raid as criminal and irresponsible, he nevertheless continued to believe that the cause of Irish freedom could be advanced by an invasion of Canada. He even went so far as to suggest to President Johnson that the new Head Centre, James Stephens, fresh from Ireland and convinced that the road to Irish freedom did not lead through Canada, was in reality a British agent.[29]

He also protested the vigorous anti-Fenian actions taken after the raid by the Johnson administration. After arresting the men who had actually engaged in the attack (and releasing them on nominal bail), the President authorized General George G. Meade, the victor at Gettysburg, to employ the land and naval forces of the United States to prevent any such expedition in the future. So much was only to be expected. But in addition, on June 5 the President ordered Attorney General James Speed to arrest "all prominent, leading, or conspicuous persons called 'Fenian' who you may have probable cause to believe have been guilty or may be guilty of violations of the neutrality laws of the United States." This was a very strong order indeed, one which could be interpreted so broadly as to include the President's friend and contact-man with the New York Irish, that outspoken advocate of a war with England and of a successful invasion of Canada, General Charles G. Halpine!

It was of course necessary for President Johnson to take action against the Fenians sufficiently strong to placate England and avoid breaking off the claims negotiations with which Seward was engaged. At the same time, the President had to be sufficiently restrained to avoid alienating the large Irish-American vote, estimated by Halpine to be close to 600,000, or nearly one-sixth of the 1864 electorate, which was certain to be an important factor in the fast-approaching congressional elections. Like so many other political problems, this one proved too delicate for the Johnson administration.

"I find the democratic Irish sentiment (not merely the Fenians proper, but the whole Irish element)," Halpine informed the President, "arrayed against Mr. Seward's foreign policy with a bitterness which makes it no longer safe for any man of prominence on the Irish side to attempt to stem." The Irish-Americans believed that Seward had given the Fenians tacit encouragement for the attack on Canada by making no objection to their purchase of arms from United States arsenals, and that when the attack took place he then betrayed them by closing the international border to the reenforcements they had to have to be successful. He was a pro-English toady. If he remained as secretary of state, Halpine warned Johnson, he would drive the Irish out of the Democratic party and into an alliance with the Radical Republicans, thus bringing ruin to Johnson himself.[30]

During the fall political campaign, Halpine loyally supported the Johnson-backed candidates in New York. When they were crushingly defeated, he explained it largely as a result of the Irish repudiation of Johnson's foreign policy. Unless Secretary of State Seward, whom he described as "the supple agent of the British Government," were replaced, he announced in the Citizen, the President could expect little support among the Irish for his domestic program.

If 1866 was a disastrous year for Johnson politically, it was a good year for Halpine. Although he had held many appointive positions in New York, it was not until 1866 that he ran for an elective office. Indeed, his popularity was such that he had a choice between two possibilities. The first was a seat in congress from the Ninth District of New

York, for which even the Tammany Democrats, whom he had fought
for so long, were willing to support him in order to defeat the Republican incumbent. The backing of both the Tammany and reform, or
Union, wings of the Democratic party made his election a virtual
certainty, but in July, two months before the official party nominations,
he was still unsure he wanted to go to the House of Representatives.
"My present purpose is *not* to go," he wrote to Syble, now sixteen years
old and mature enough to take an interest in her father's career, "though
you probably, would not object to figure in Washn. for a couple of
seasons as the young Princess of Feniandom—for the strongest pressure
on me to go is from the Fenian chiefs of both wings, & all over the
country."

The second possibility was the office of register of the County of
New York, less prestigious, perhaps, than a seat in Congress but much
more lucrative. As with the customhouse, where the moderate fees
authorized in earlier days brought great wealth to lucky collectors and
naval officers as the business of the port expanded, so the register's fees
for the recording of deeds, mortgages, and titles increased prodigiously
with the growth of New York City. By the middle 1860's, the register
collected a small fortune every year. At a time when the President of
the United States received $25,000 annually, and congressmen $8,000,
the register of New York made somewhere between $40,000 and
$90,000. He was, in fact, the best-paid elected official in the United
States.[31]

In August, as he considered the alternatives and made his decision,
Halpine had to recognize that his election as register was no sure thing.
Tammany Hall might back him for Congress, but the registership was
much too valuable to lose to an enemy without a fight. Should he try
for it anyway, or accept a safe seat in the House of Representatives?
The strain of indecision added to his habitual nervousness; he believed,
as he had so often in the past, that he was at the crossroads of his life,
that everything depended upon what he now did. The editorship of the
Citizen was demanding and nervewracking, and no longer so rewarding
as it had been. It seemed quite unlikely, furthermore, that the paper's
influence would increase very much in the future unless money could be
raised to turn it into a daily; he had taken it about as far as it could go
as a weekly. Did that mean he was traveling on a road which dead-ended
in obscurity? If only he had money. But if he gambled for money—for
the office of register—he might end up with nothing.

Margaret and the children had escaped the city's heat at the seashore, and in a room at the Astor House Halpine sought to escape the

harassment of his own uncertainties. When he recovered, he made his decision. He would run for register. "It is my last throw of these loaded dice," he wrote to Margaret late in August. "I am gaining strength in *every* way, & look forward to a happy & tranquil future. I feel that my great fight of life is drawing to its close & that the coming years will be full of happiness—or at least quiet. I have accomplished the first object of my life—a name & fame; & now think I shall not fail in the second. . . . Let me get an easy mind, & you will see me a different man."

For many months Halpine had hoped that a coalition of moderate Republicans and War Democrats might be formed to reconstruct the nation without trying to bring about a radical revolution in race relations in the South. Early in 1866 a National Union movement was organized with just such an objective, but Halpine withheld his support because of the prominence in it of Gideon Welles and William H. Seward—one an old enemy, the other a new. Such men, he felt, were no longer powers within their own party, and were merely trying to recoup their losses among the Democrats. They had little to offer. They were brigadiers without brigades, balloons without inflation, bankers without capital. The initiative in the new political coalition should come, he declared in the editorial columns of his paper, from the Democrats.

Halpine was right that Republicans like Welles and Seward had little to bargain with, and by August, when a National Union convention was held in Philadelphia, Democrats were in control of the movement. The interest of Republicans, therefore, faded away. Nevertheless, Halpine believed that the convention, which emphasized national unity by parading delegates from Massachusetts and South Carolina arm-in-arm, and by insisting that the Johnson governments of the South were entitled to representation in congress, was a success. "All hail Philadelphia!" he exclaimed in a poem.[32]

It was soon obvious that Philadelphia was nothing to hail, and that the National Union movement was still-born. But in New York, where the old parties made their usual nominations, Halpine was the beneficiary of just the kind of bi-partisan coalition he favored. He was nominated for register by both the Union Democrats and the Republicans, thanks to an hour-long speech in his behalf at the Republican convention by Horace Greeley.[33]

In addition to the support of the Republican political organization and Republican newspapers, Halpine's candidacy received much-publicized endorsements from influential New Yorkers like Peter Cooper, Robert Roosevelt and his brother, Theodore (the father of the future President), and from such military heroes as Meade, Dix, Hunter,

Averell, Sickles, and Admiral Farragut.[34] Among the major immigrant groups he was already popular, as one of his campaign ditties pointed out:

> All the Germans an' the Irish here
> For him have dhrawn the skean,
> For Von Halpine trinks zwei lager bier,
> And Miles he wears the green.

It proved to be an easy election, after all. Halpine beat the Tammany incumbent with 60 percent of the vote cast.

CHAPTER 11

Black Loyalty

AT NOON on New Year's Day, 1867, Halpine took over the duties and emoluments of his new office, and very soon afterwards began to lead the life of a man of wealth. He gained weight, bought the finest clothes, wore a large ring and a gold watch chain, and purchased an imposing brownstone house, 58 West 47th Street, in an upper-middle-class neighborhood. John Hay, back in the United States for a visit in June, breakfasted there with Robert Roosevelt from white bone china decorated with a bold emerald margin. Unless it was not yet on display, he was no doubt also called upon to admire the full-length oil portrait of New York's register in the uniform of a brigadier general. George Gerhard, for whom Ulysses S. Grant and many fashionable New Yorkers sat, was the artist. Halpine was "never more cynical or witty," Hay noted. "He said he had the Irish vote in his belly & both parties were plying him emetics for it. He was equally unblushing in regard to public and private matters." [1]

Two months later Hay wrote from Vienna, where he was United States *chargé d'affaires,* to thank Halpine for a flattering notice in the *Citizen* at the time of his departure, and to ask for a copy to send his mother. "She will read it & believe most of that article," he told his friend, "which can be said of no other mortal." At Paris Hay had called upon Minister Dix, who expected Halpine to come over for a visit. Halpine would love Vienna, Hay continued. "You would appreciate it better than I, as your judgments of female frailty are more Catholic than mine. The trail of the serpent is over them all. The Music is good & a great deal of it." [2]

With boyish pride, Halpine printed in the *Citizen* in March, 1867, an article about the mines of the Sierra-Nevada, including the "Miles O'Reilly Lode" near the headwaters of Walker Lake, the outcroppings of which were said to yield up to one-fourth their weight in copper and other metals. No doubt he asked questions about it of Sam Clemens,

fresh from literary triumphs on the Pacific coast, when they dined together just before the trip which produced *Innocents Abroad*.[3] Later in
the year, he published one of Mark Twain's satires in the *Citizen*.

The office of register was no mere sinecure, and Halpine was required to spend so much time in his office in the Hall of Records that
early in 1867 he sold his stock in the *Citizen* to a joint stock company.
Although he continued to be listed as Editor or Editor-in-Chief, most
of the responsibility for getting out the paper now devolved upon
Managing Editor Roosevelt and his assistants, J. F. Bailey and J. C.
Bayles. But Halpine spent as much time as he could at the *Citizen*
offices, and even during his illnesses continued to show the concern of
an editor-proprietor for the paper's composition. When what his doctor
called rheumatism in his shoulder and eye kept him at home for a while,
he sent instructions to Roosevelt to buy or write one good essay for the
front page every week. "This patchwork & amateur business is sad stuff
for a reliance, & it is very poor economy in the long run." He promised
to send in ten columns for the next issue, even if he had to dictate them
to a stenographer.[4]

As the chief proprietor of an influential weekly newspaper and the
holder of an elective office which was making him a rich man, Halpine
began to assert himself more aggressively at the highest levels of national
politics. The 1866 elections had been disastrous for the Democratic
party, and 1868 promised to be worse unless the Democratic Reconstruction program and the personality of Andrew Johnson were presented more favorably to the public. Like other unsuccessful presidents,
Johnson had been unable to reach the American people and explain
persuasively what he wished to accomplish. Too often when he tried, he
impressed northern audiences as being intemperate, stubborn, and
intolerant of opposition. It was up to his friends, therefore, to save him
from himself, and thereby save the Democratic party and the nation.
With the new authority and confidence he felt as a recognized political
leader, Halpine determined to try.

In February, 1867, he published a long article describing the President's position on one of the major issues of the Reconstruction controversy with Congress—the seating of the senators and representatives
sent to Washington by the southern states reorganized under Johnson's
amnesty program. Because these delegations were largely composed of
prominent ex-rebels, including the Vice-President of the Confederacy,
Confederate generals, cabinet members, and members of the Confederate
Congress, the Republican-controlled United States Congress had long
refused to seat them. In the spring of 1866, it passed the Fourteenth

Amendment, Section Three of which made ineligible to hold political office all officials who had violated previous oaths of loyalty to the Constitution by participating in the rebellion, unless Congress waived the proscription by a two-thirds vote. Nearly all of the political leaders of the South were affected.

In opposing the proposed Fourteenth Amendment and by stressing his belief that Congress was violating the Constitution by denying representation to the southern states, Johnson had made it seem as though he was opposed to all screening of members by Congress and favored the seating of anyone who was elected. Such was not at all the case, Halpine explained in his "Talk with the President," based upon a conversation held in the White House on February 20 and published in the *Citizen* three days later. The President conceded Congress' right to judge its own membership and to deny admission for any reasonable cause. He only believed that each elected senator and representative should be considered on his own individual record, and the southern states clearly informed that representation would not be denied to them when "proper" men were elected. "There are scores and hundreds of ambitious men of loyal record in every State," Halpine quoted the President as saying, "who would then be naturally forced to the surface." The President was as anxious as any Republican to see loyal men in Congress. But he strongly disapproved as unnecessary and unjust the attempt, through the Fourteenth Amendment and the soon-to-be-passed Reconstruction Act, to wipe out the southern state governments he had helped to establish and to create new ones in their place.

Following his presentation of the President's views on congressional representation, clearer and more sympathetic than most published before or since, Halpine sketched a flattering personal portrait. He had had direct contact with the three preceding presidents, he wrote, and Johnson's appearance and bearing were "more presidential" than any of them. There was something about him, too, Halpine continued, with an eye to alienated northern Democrats and those who thought Johnson drank too much, which was reminiscent of Stephen A. Douglas. Still, Johnson's skin and features were "wholly free from certain blemishes which at times told the story of our great Lost Leader's only folly." He was almost ashamed to have to write about such matters, Halpine concluded, but partisan passions had vilely slandered Andrew Johnson. The President was fatally wrong in some of his views and was cursed by more than the usual number of bad advisers, but he was a grave, decorous, hard-working, and self-sacrificing patriot.

The article was immediately republished in the big dailies in New

York and elsewhere, and Halpine told Johnson he expected it to be the most widely copied article of recent times. Such stories, he added, were more effective in spreading the President's views than dry official statements, and he asked for another interview so that he could report Johnson's thinking in a way to attract still more attention.[5] Johnson was delighted and arranged for a meeting on March 5. But this time he was not at all happy with Halpine's story and the attention it received.

Speaking freely because he was led to believe he would have a chance to revise what Halpine wrote before it was published, the President denounced the "aristocracy of money" which was coming to dominate the country, much as the aristocracy of slaveholders had dominated it before the war. The new aristocrats, whose power derived from their ownership of $3 billion of government securities, enriched themselves at the expense of the poor. For the bondholders, the people had no value but to yield up the "golden blood under the tax-gatherer's thumbscrew." As far as the people were concerned, the public debt was a burden to be paid off; but to the bondholders it was private property bringing in an annual income of $180 million. Since the proper annual expenses of the United States government in peacetime were about $60 million, the people were paying in interest on the debt enough to support three national governments! Sooner or later, the tax-oppressed people would ask, " 'How much was actually loaned to our Government during the civil war by these bondholders? . . .' You know what the popular answer must be," said the President, "—I do not say the right answer —'Less than half the amount they claim, for gold ranged at an average of one hundred premium while this debt was being incurred.' " Having asked the question and answered it, the people would refuse to pay any more on the debt.

The President wanted it understood that he did not favor a repudiation of the national debt, for the debt was a legal obligation. But, he warned, repudiation would certainly come unless his administration was supported in its efforts to reestablish respect for law and the U. S. Constitution. "The war of finance is the next war we have to fight," he said, "and every blow struck against my efforts to uphold a strict construction of the laws and the Constitution is in reality a blow in favor of repudiating the national debt."

The Reconstruction Act just passed over his veto, providing for the military occupation of the South, Johnson continued, was a step in the direction of repudiation. A congressional usurpation striking ten state governments out of existence, it set a precedent for lawlessness and disregard of constitutional obligations. By attempting to provide for the enfranchisement of a million ignorant and penniless Negroes, it also swelled the ranks of those who would soon demand repudiation.

There is little reason to doubt that Halpine reported the substance of the President's views accurately. Johnson had always been a battler against aristocratic privilege, and as an old Jacksonian Democrat it would have been natural for him to see the financiers of the Civil War as a new money power oppressing the people. But he already had enough enemies, and was embarrassed to see such vehemence in print. The certainty with which Halpine made him predict that the repudiation of the national debt would follow the abandonment of his Reconstruction program, farfetched as the argument was, could only have an unsettling effect, since his Reconstruction program had in fact been just abandoned. For the President even to mention the possibility of repudiation was considered reckless and irresponsible. Indeed, the House Judiciary Committee, later considering the subject of Johnson's impeachment and eager to find fault, was curious to know whether he had really expressed the views attributed to him, and called Halpine to testify. Yes, declared Halpine under oath, the President had indeed expressed the views attributed to him, but because he had been forced to return to New York immediately after the interview, due to the illness of his wife, he had been unable to clear the article with the President before its publication. Had Johnson seen an advanced copy of the text, Halpine admitted, he might have decided to call the conversation private and confidential.[6]

Without doubt, Halpine had committed an indiscretion, but it was probably nothing worse. For in a note written in *"Haste"* when he reached his room following the interview, he explained his sudden need to return to New York, and pressed hard for a patronage appointment of interest to the Roman Catholic Archbishop of New York.[7] Had he deliberately planned to betray Johnson's confidence by printing a story he knew would cause a minor sensation and embarrass the administration, he could hardly have expected to receive any presidential favors. And who knows—Margaret might really have been ill.

When the storm broke Halpine, unabashed, put his case to the President in positive terms. If the article was being criticized in some papers, it was being praised in others. The New York *Herald,* for one, had endorsed it "earnestly and cordially," and newspapers all over the country were reprinting it and commenting favorably upon it. "I have reason to believe," he continued, "that the change of public opinion [in favor of the administration] which I predicted, has already set in and is crystallizing around that article." To have given Johnson the promised opportunity to see and revise it before publication would have made him officially responsible for all that was said. It was true that many of Johnson's views had been "amplified & illustrated" in ways designed "to arrest public attention," but, on the whole, he concluded, "I believe the article has set more men thinking seriously of whither Congress has been hurrying us of late, than could have been achieved by any less potent instrumentality." [8]

The President was not angry for long, but he did not make the appointment desired by the Archbishop, and the next time he gave Halpine an interview he saw to it that he was cited only indirectly, as a man in "the very highest circles of Conservative politics" in Washington.

Johnson was in an irritable mood at this meeting in September, 1867, and seemed more anxious to denounce his congressional enemies and their recurring talk of impeachment than to allow Halpine or anyone else to present his side of the Reconstruction debate to the people. When Halpine left the White House after a two-hour tirade, he was pretty well convinced that neither the Democratic party nor the country could hope for leadership from such a man. The case for Johnsonian Reconstruction would have to be made without Johnson.[9]

Fundamentally, the President and Congress were divided in their attempts to reunite the nation by the same problem which had divided the parties and the sections in the first place—disagreement over the place of the Negro in American society. The jump from slavery to freedom was a very big one—big for blacks who had lived their lives in enforced debasement to make, and big for southern whites who believed the men they had debased were inferior beings to accept. But, although Lincoln had hinted that a temporary position somewhere between slavery and freedom might be worked out, no such middle ground was ever defined. By 1867 the choice seemed to be between extremes: either confer equal citizenship upon Negroes, or allow their freedom to be largely taken away by their former masters. For a variety of reasons, Congress and the Republicans favored the first alternative, and the President and the Democrats were willing to accept the second.

Repetition has made the arguments of the racial equalitarians familiar to twentieth-century Americans. But the counter-arguments of those Democrats who opposed the Republicans in the 1860's have been ignored or dismissed as mere racist bigotry. Bigoted Democrats there were in abundance—and dogmatic Republicans, too—but many of them were entirely respectable intellectually and morally, and deserve to be heard and judged by the facts and conditions of their own time. To ignore their point of view is to ignore assumptions, recognized and unrecognized, which for over a century have helped to shape American attitudes towards race.

To Halpine, a principal spokesman for those northern War Democrats who thought of themselves as moderates on the racial issue, the Republican attempt to bring about an immediate equality between whites and blacks was as reprehensible as slavery itself had been, and its advocates as much extremists as the old slave owners. "Extreme views are easy to maintain," Halpine observed, in one of his many *Citizen* articles dealing with race, "they require merely a wilful blindness to an adversary's arguments and an absolute devotion to fanaticism." In the United States, an enormous social change—the freeing of the slaves —had taken place within a very brief period of time. If abolitionists like Wendell Phillips and William Lloyd Garrison had predicted in 1861 that what happened in the next five years would take place in fifty, they would have been laughed at as mad men. Nevertheless, the revolutionary change had taken place, the Negro was free. Without doubt his elevation in the social and political scale was the next step, but society had to be given time to adjust to the fact of him as a free man before it could learn to think of him as an equal. "Old ideas must be eradicated," said Halpine, "old prejudices overcome, and many of those little influences that make up so much of common life be modified by the laws of time and change, before the new order of things is fully and finally established."

The chief argument of the Republicans in favor of enfranchising the Negroes and conferring other rights of citizenship upon them was the insistence that the nation owed them a debt of gratitude for their help in winning the war, and for their continued and unquestionable loyalty to the United States in a section of the country where most of the whites had been disloyal. Surely loyal black men were more entitled to be citizens, exclaimed the Republicans, than disloyal white men.

Halpine scoffed at the argument. The fact was, he said, that southern Negroes had been of more help to the Confederacy than to the Union. During the war they had served in the rebel commissary, ordnance, and hospital departments, they had helped build and repair roads, railroads, and fortifications, and, by remaining tractable laborers, they had raised the food and other products which sustained the rebellion.[10] When David Hunter gave them a chance to fight for their freedom in South Carolina, only a handful of men volunteered, the vast majority choosing to remain on their plantations. And when Hunter ordered a draft of able-bodied Negroes within the Union lines, most of them "commenced a general skedaddle, . . . rushing back into slavery rather than take service with arms against the rebellion." It was true that 200,000 Negroes had served in the Union Army, but considering that a victory for the United States would mean the end of slavery, the number was not so very great, after all. Every Negro who had carried a gun deserved to be given the ballot, Halpine continued, but it was absurd to enfranchise the whole race on the grounds that, to use Greeley's phrase, Negroes were the "loyal, hearty Unionists of the South." They had been, on the contrary, Halpine declared, "superbly loyal to the desperate fortunes of the White masters."

With southern white men off in the Confederate army, Halpine asked in March, 1867, why did the slaves not revolt? "One rousing Negro insurrection in any Southern State," he said, "would have terminated the recent civil war in its first year." Then he answered his own question. They did not revolt because their long and brutal conditioning as slaves kept them docile and apathetic. They were not to be condemned for their apathy, "but let us not deny that the apathy existed."

The truth of history, he wrote in his poem "Black Loyalty," was that the Negro, far from contributing to the Union victory, had assisted the rebellion by remaining the productive servant of his master, by resisting United States military service, and by failing to stage the uprising which would have caused the immediate and wholesale collapse of southern military operations.

> The White rebels came with a cheer,
> Their bayonets aslant and aglow,
> While the Black rebels slunk in the rear,
> Assisting (and freely) our foe.
>
> .   .   .   .
>
> To the Black rebel glory and power,
> To the White rebel chains and disgrace;
> Oh, madness, and worse, rules the hour—
> We are false to faith, wisdom, and race!
> To my heart with you, Longstreet and Hill,
> Johnston, Lee—every man in the fight—
> You were rebels, and bad ones, but still
> You share my misfortune—you're white.[11]

The poem attracted much attention in the press, and was answered by the Negro poet, Frances E. Watkins Harper, who reminded Miles

O'Reilly that at the beginning of the war General George B. McClellan had told the people of western Virginia he would crush any revolt of their slaves with "an iron hand."

> And when we sought to join your ranks,
>   And battle with you, side by side,
> Did men not curl their lips with scorn,
>   And thrust us back with hateful pride?
>
> And when at last we gained the field,
>   Did we not firmly, bravely stand,
> And help to turn the tide of death,
>   That spread its ruin o'er the land?
>
> We hardly think we're worse than those
>   Who kindled up this fearful strife,
> Because we did not seize the chance
>   To murder helpless babe and wife.
>
> And had we struck, with vengeful hand,
>   The rebel where he most could feel,
> Were you not ready to impale
>   Our hearts upon your Northern steel? [12]

And so the controversy raged. For Halpine and the Democrats, the conviction that the United States owed no debt of gratitude to any blacks except those who had actually borne its arms all but removed race as a factor in Reconstruction and made Republican policies seem oppressive and vengeful. "Be merciful to the South," Halpine pleaded in another poem. The trouble with Reconstruction was that the Democrats and Republicans could not agree on which South to be merciful to—the white South or the black South.

Like every other American politician dissatisfied with the course of political developments, Halpine looked to the next presidential election for the defeat of his enemies and the triumph of his principles. Johnson, he knew, was hopeless, but the Democratic party was not, and with the right man at the head of its ticket in 1868, he believed its program of mercy for the white South would yet prevail. The right man for the Democrats, Halpine was convinced, was Ulysses S. Grant. As the nation's most popular hero, Grant was of course irresistible to leaders of both parties. But Halpine and other Democrats thought that his terms to Lee at Appomattox made him ideologically one of them, and believed that he could reunite the sections and restore peace to the nation in the same way he had ended the war—generously and without bitterness. The trouble was that the Radicals also claimed he sympathized with their views, and until he committed himself definitely to one side or the other, neither could convincingly claim him for its own.

In August, 1867, Democratic prayers were apparently answered. President Johnson dismissed Secretary Stanton, who had been working against him more or less openly for months, and offered an *ad interim* appointment as secretary of war to Grant, who accepted it. Halpine immediately endorsed him for president, and Miles O'Reilly toasted him with a "Bumper to Grant." One of his best political verses, it celebrated the General's military victories, called upon him to lead the country he had saved, and predicted among other things that when he entered the White House there would be no more knuckling-under to England. A few months later, Horace Greeley gave so much publicity in the *Tribune* to four lines from the last verse that they became familiar in households all over the country, and were featured in Grant's political campaigns ever after:

> And if asked what state he hails from,
>   This our sole reply shall be
>   "From near Appomattox Courthouse,
>   With its famous apple tree."

It was probably in appreciation of this quatrain, with its reminder of the victory and the compassion which were the twin glories of Appomattox, that Grant presented Halpine with a gold pen inscribed, "The Pen of a Ready Writer." [13]

To hopeful Democrats, the fact that Grant had joined the Johnson administration, thus apparently endorsing the Democratic Reconstruction program, was a sign that the national political tide was at last turning in their favor. Halpine promised Johnson a heavy anti-Radical majority in the 1867 elections in New York, and was elated when his optimistic estimate was exceeded. The President was relieved, and a kind of quiet confidence that the worst was over permeated his letter to Halpine at the end of the year. "There is a redeeming spirit," wrote Johnson to the man who had tried to take his case to the public, "a returning sense of Justice on the part of the people, that will in the end, Save the Nation, and repair the wrongs which have been inflicted on those who have cared to act upon principle, and stood firmly by our great Charter of free Government. Come: I will be pleased to see you at any time, and confer freely and fully upon the pending difficulties." [14] Perhaps in such a mood the President told Halpine he intended to nominate him for another brevet promotion in the army. He never did so, but Halpine's friends later called him a major general and buried him in the uniform of one, anyway.[15]

Halpine, too, was optimistic. The political principles in which he believed and the leader in whom he believed had joined forces, and the kind of peace and reunion for which so many millions had fought and prayed would soon be realized. His own standing within the party was now national instead of local, and he would certainly be a major power in a new Democratic administration headed by Grant. Life had never been so satisfying, and he enjoyed his money and celebrity with vigor and good taste. He patronized New York's best restaurants and clubs, though he did not abandon the Bohemians at Pfaff's, and he had never been more entertaining or more popular. He spent and drank freely because he did nothing in moderation, and because he was immoderately happy. "Madame Le Comtesse D O'Reilly," he addressed a note to Margaret in December, 1867, explaining that he was dining at the Manhattan Club and would not be home for dinner. Most thrilling of all, he who had always feared that he would make a wreck of his life was just beginning to realize that he was, or might very well become, the most influential Irishman in America.

Then, in January, 1868, the man upon whom he had based his hopes handed the War Department back to Edwin M. Stanton, whose resignation the senate, acting under the Tenure of Office Act, had refused to accept. Grant's action amounted to an abandonment of the President, who had expected him to hold on to the position while the administration sought a judicial ruling, and it signified that if Grant made it to the White House it would not be as a Democrat, after all, but as a Radical Republican. Much to Greeley's delight, Halpine at once announced that he no longer believed the hero of Appomattox should be president. "The noted Miles O'Reilly," said Greeley in the *Tribune* on January 27, "who divides with Mr. [Elihu] Washburne the credit of being 'the original Grant man,' who has certainly written the best verses we have read upon the apple-tree, and is the prominent musical member of the Grant Club, now formally reads himself out of the party." He would be happy to read himself back in, Halpine replied in the *Citizen* on February 1, if Grant returned to the spirit of Appomattox. "But it is clear," he concluded, his disillusionment complete, "that the arena of politics is one far different from that of war, and requiring wholly different talents." He expressed his disappointment in a poem, "Farewell to Grant," but put the manuscript away and never published it.[16]

Although Halpine and Greeley used their newspapers to carry on a vigorous debate with each other over politics and Reconstruction, their disagreements, good for circulation, did not in the least affect their friendship, and at one dinner Greeley admitted to Halpine that he regretted the "necessity" for Grant to join the Radicals. It wasn't a necessity at all, Halpine interrupted, but an act of "bad faith & cowardice." [17]

For Halpine, the vacuum left by Grant's defection from the Democratic party was partially filled by Salmon P. Chase, who as chief justice presided over the impeachment trial of Andrew Johnson in the spring. "Hold the scales even," Halpine had written him in a poem at the beginning of the trial.[18] Chase did hold them even, and thereby completed the break with his old Radical friends which had begun soon after the end of the war. The break, in turn, raised the distinct possibility that Chase might be the man around whom Democrats and anti-Radical Republicans could rally. Who would have a better chance to defeat Grant? Halpine began to slant stories in Chase's favor in the *Citizen* and in the *Herald;* he was the author, he told Chase, of "nearly all" the *Herald*'s stories which mentioned his name. He also held out the possiblity of an endorsement of Chase by James Gordon Bennett himself, although that aging editor was "so fitful and uncertain that I could not bind myself for his continuing steadfast to this or any other programme." Chase, who was always delighted when others joined him in considering his prospects for the presidency, responded warmly, and sent Halpine periodic "strictly private" lists of points to be made in the press.[19]

The nomination by the Democrats of a Republican like Chase was dependent upon so many uncertainties that Halpine was by no means ready to commit himself to it. If the expected public revulsion against the impeachment of President Johnson and against Radicalism in general did in fact materialize, then it might not be necessary to go out of the party for a nominee to beat Grant. This possibility was in Halpine's mind when he contacted the former governor of New York, Horatio Seymour, now out of office and planning to stay out. "While it seemed to me that the Dem. ticket for Pres. must be beaten, I did not want you to run," Halpine told Seymour in April, with his usual excess of flattery, "but now it begins to look that we are going to win, and I want you to run above all things. In my judgment, you are by all odds the strongest Democrat that can be placed before the people: you are the only one for whom I wd. take the stump from now until November next, and speak in every large city of the Union to the Soldiers and Irish." Because Seymour had been blamed by much of the press for the severity of the anti-draft riots in New York, it would be necessary to choose some man whom the Radicals could not possibly brand a Copperhead—somebody very much like Halpine himself—to lead the campaign for the nomination. Although he would not be a member of the New York delegation to the nominating convention, Halpine believed he reached "a larger constituency daily than half a dozen Tammany Halls put together. May I go my old boots on you, or must I look in some other direction?" [20]

Seymour, who had already twice stated publicly that he would not be a candidate, told Halpine to look elsewhere. So did William Tecumseh Sherman, who wrote him from St. Louis: "I have long since made up my mind never, under any state of facts, to be drawn into politics." [21]

Another general to whom Halpine looked was Winfield Scott Hancock of Pennsylvania, who had substantial support among war veterans, northern Democrats, and the South. A Currier and Ives print, "The Democracy in Search of a Candidate," pictured Miles O'Reilly waving a shillelagh in the air with one hand and carrying under his other arm a large rooster with a major general's stars on its shoulders and the head of General Hancock. "Me friends," Miles is saying, "don't be going off on a wild goose-Chase. This fine cock under me arrum is the bird to bet on," while circling above, a goose topped by Chase's head replies, "Who said Goose? I aim to be an Eagle!" [22] But by the time the convention met in New York on July 4, Halpine favored a ticket of Chase and Hancock, with Hancock for the top position if Chase could not make it.

For Chase's failure to make it Halpine blamed the rivalry of Chase's fellow Ohioan, George Pendleton, McClellan's running mate in 1864, plus the unappeasable enmity of the Tammany Democrats. Hancock's chances were probably ruined by convention chairman Seymour, who used his gavel to adjourn a session just as Hancock's strength was building. Seymour had hoped that the Chase forces would rally the next day, but to his genuine dismay, the delegates conferred the nomination on Seymour himself, instead. [23]

Halpine believed that Seymour had "a rarer and more genial faculty for making and retaining friends than any other public man of our acquaintance, since the death of Douglas," and in his over-flattering April letter to the ex-Governor had called him "by all odds the strongest Democrat that can be placed before the people." But he did not really believe it, and said so publicly. Chase's nomination, he declared sadly in the *Citizen* on July 11, would have meant "an overwhelming certainty of success." Seymour's nomination improved Grant's chances "a hundred-fold." For Seymour was the Democrat most widely identified as the leader of the opposition to Lincoln, and was thus extremely vulnerable to Republican criticism. As Greeley put it in the *Tribune,* July 10, "If the Democratic Convention had been intent on selecting that candidate for President least likely to win Republican votes and most certain to arouse and intensify Republican opposition, it could not have hit the mark more exactly."

CHAPTER 12

The Astor House

IN ITS OWN self-advertisements, the *Citizen* described itself as "a first-class Family Paper, handsomely printed on fine white paper, and filled with choice and entertaining literature, by the best authors, including the songs and sketches of the universally popular 'MILES O'REILLY.' " In 1868, however, Miles made very few appearances in his own newspaper, though his "Three Sensational Books"—the two books of reprinted essays, hoaxes, and songs, and *The Prison Life of Jefferson Davis*—were still regularly offered for sale. Discerning readers also noted the reduced number of feature articles and the increased space devoted to unsigned literary reviews and serialized novels. For months cash prizes were offered for new subscriptions, and in April the single-issue price was lowered from ten to eight cents.

The *Citizen* declined in 1868 because Halpine's duties as register and his preoccupation with presidential politics made it increasingly difficult for him to give it much attention. Nor could he write for it with the same spirit as in the past. His readiest access to the public mind was through the character of Miles O'Reilly, whose songs and escapades were known far beyond the subscription list of the *Citizen*. But how was it possible for him to write on the issues of Reconstruction with Miles's carefree exuberance? Like other Democrats he believed that the Republicans, in blocking the admission to Congress of southern senators and representatives and in attempting to establish the civil equality of the white and black races, were betraying the objectives of the war for the most outrageous of partisan motives. Miles's light-heartedness, his joyful irreverence, his amusing and illuminating exaggerations, were silenced by more than his stammer. The fact was that The Boy was all but choked to death by the emotional intensity of Halpine's feelings, as Jehiel Stebbings had been slain by the bite of his satire. When Halpine needed him the most, Miles O'Reilly could not speak.

The frustration and discouragement were familiar. It was the fate of the comedian to suffer, Halpine told the Brooklyn businessman, Charles C. Yeaton, to whom he had dedicated *Baked Meats*. "The world will never understand that of all men, the saddest is the humorous man; that Grimaldi, with his paint & clown's dress off, makes up in the anguish of his closet for the grins & laughter of his broad feats in the circus." [1]

If Miles O'Reilly was no longer performing many broad feats for his public, Halpine was finding more anguish than ever in his closet. Plagued by prolonged periods of sleeplessness and recurrent attacks of brain fever and neuralgia, he was drinking so heavily and losing so much time, that he could no longer escape facing the fact that it was not only Miles O'Reilly who was failing him. At a time when he could influence a presidential election and either move ahead to the position of undisputed leadership of the Irish-Americans which was apparently within his reach, or fall away from it forever, he was failing himself. By June, his condition was so clearly desperate that with Margaret's tears strengthening his own wavering resolution, he undertook a desperate action. He took the pledge of total abstinence. [2] And he meant to keep it. This time he would really live the new life he had so often promised, for he knew that his role in Seymour's presidential campaign, as well as his own future, required it. Of course he did not know if he would be successful; he only knew that he had no choice but to try.

Seymour's only chance to defeat Grant was to convince devoted Union men in both parties that they could vote for him in good conscience. As one of the men best able to make the point, Halpine was slated to attend a strategy meeting at Seymour's home in Utica in mid-August, and to be on the stump almost continually after September 4, speaking in every large city in the North.

Of course he did not need to be told what to say. He would skip over Seymour's wartime record, and talk instead about his integrity, his Lincolnian purity of heart, his reasonableness, his vast experience in political office, and his demonstrated ability to work harmoniously with others, precisely the qualities now most needed in a president. Naturally, he would refrain from attacking Grant, although he might point out (as he already had at least once) that political leadership required quite different training and experience than military leadership. He might even remind his audiences of the well-known failures of political generals, and allow them to draw their own inferences about military politicians. But mostly he would talk about the war, and about the gallantry of the common soldiers who had endured so much. He would point out that all of the great objectives of the war had been achieved, the Union preserved, the slaves freed. It was time, he would say, to restore representative government to the South and to abandon the foolish attempt to bring about a revolution in race relations. How many white soldiers, after all, had fought to make blacks their equals? Stimulated by responsive crowds, Private Miles O'Reilly would find his voice again, and create an emotional bond with his audiences by singing some of his best-loved songs, "Sambo's Right to Be Kilt," "The Canteen," "The Song of the Soldiers." In a close election, the Private just might elect the Commander-in-Chief! [3]

Contemplating the tour at the end of July, some of Halpine's optimism returned. "It begins to look to me now," he said, *"very strongly* (though it looked otherwise at first) that Seymour is to win, and Grant to be badly beaten." Of course, prospects could change two or three times before November, but Grant had committed "the monstrous blunder against which I so often warned him," of joining the Radicals instead of remaining above politics. Grant still enjoyed wide surface popularity, but Halpine told his mother, who had returned to Ireland, that he could feel an undertow of public sentiment towards Seymour.

He also told her of his own bright prospects. Once again, a seat in Congress from the Ninth District was his for the asking, and this time he was tempted to take it. A United States representative's salary was much less than he was presently making, but Congress met for an average of only six months a year, and a seat in it would be a good springboard to a diplomatic appointment in Italy or Russia, or to the New York offices of surveyor or collector, both of which paid as much or more than the registership and required less work. From Seymour, he could get a good appointment any time he wanted it. From Grant, too, he could get a desirable position, for the Republicans would be anxious to get him off the floor of Congress "if it became my cue to 'be as nasty as I could be.' "

With the pride of the self-made man, Halpine described for his mother the extent of his social success in America. His family vacationed at Long Branch, New Jersey, at such a fashionable resort that the children had to be dressed up all day. He had recently joined the New York Yacht Club, and would sail in Bennett's schooner, *Dauntless,* in the August regatta. After the campaign, he would go with Roosevelt to the Sportsman's Club, near Narragansett Bay. Syble was vacationing in the White Mountains with "the Partridges of Fifth Avenue," who were "enormously rich," and with, among others, Sam Ward, who was "not only a millionaire but also a poet of no mean pretensions." Although not pretty, Syble was bright, graceful, attractive, and full of poise and self-assurance. Halpine joked that Horace Greeley, of whom the whole family was more fond all the time, was "madly in love" with her. Phil Sheridan was "captivated" by her, and she was "as free with Gen. Grant (who also took a great fancy to her), leaning on his arm, as with any other gentleman." When Horatio Seymour, who might be the next President of the United States, came to New York City in September, he would stay at the Halpine home.[4]

Like a good Irishman, Halpine was putting roots into the earth. He now owned a plantation near Nottoway Courthouse, Virginia, and was having it extensively remodeled. Broad piazzas, he reported to Syble, were being built around both houses, the smaller of which might do for her honeymoon with Horace Greeley. The framework for the six-room addition to the big house was up, and the planking and plastering would be completed in August.[5]

The pressures and demands upon his time never ceased. The Sixty-Ninth New York planned a reunion at the end of July, and invited him to preside and read a poem. He would always be happy to speak before his old regiment, of course, especially in an election year, but it was more than ordinarily important for him to be there and to make a good impression, because Horace Greeley would attend and speak for the Republicans. Yet up to the day before the meeting not a word had been put to paper. He was accustomed to being harried, and he habitually wrote in frantic, last-minute surges against foreclosing deadlines. But there is little wonder that sleeplessness so often accompanied his weariness. He suffered, so he said, from his father's old complaint of "insomnies." Still, he finished his "Lines for the Day"—130 of them—in time. His major theme was that the men of the Irish Brigade had not fought to make the South another Ireland.[6]

At about the time of the Sixty-Ninth's reunion, Halpine met J. C. Derby, the publisher of *Lyrics by the Letter H.*, aboard the night boat to Albany, and spent the voyage entertaining him with songs and witty cynicism. He had never seen Halpine more clever or high-spirited, thought Derby as they parted. A few days later the publisher read that Halpine was dead.[7]

All his life, Halpine had compensated with simple nervous energy for the sleeplessness and bad health his intemperate habits and restless personality inflicted upon him, and had used whiskey as a means of maintaining an equilibrium between his sharply fluctuating moods. But now, having taken the pledge, he could no longer find an easy escape from his tensions, and he began to suffer the tortures of deprivation and withdrawal. Unable to drink himself into tranquility, he drew upon his brief training in medicine at Trinity University, and began to resort to more dangerous potions.

On Friday, July 31, Halpine worked at the *Citizen* office until mid-afternoon, when fatigue and one of his merciless headaches drove him home to bed. He returned in the evening, lay down on a sofa in his office, and inhaled a few drops of ether sprinkled on a handkerchief. (It is easy to imagine that Margaret's ministrations at home had been cancelled out by the children, back from the seashore and noisy about it.) Feeling better between eleven o'clock and midnight, he and William L. Alden, a staff member, took a Sixth Avenue car to their homes. Halpine told Alden that he was planning a trip to Long Branch the next afternoon with Peter B. Sweeny. At the office in the morning, he said his headache was better, and again spoke of his trip to Long Branch.

To John Savage, his Deputy Register, he told a different story. Around noon, he sent Savage a note at the Hall of Records, asking that his carpetbag be sent to the *Citizen* office, because he was taking a trip to Rockaway, Long Island, with James T. Brady.[8] Exhausted, depressed, desperate for whiskey, he was really going to the Astor House, alone.

There were times when Halpine hated life and wished himself rid of it with the same excessive passion with which at other times he embraced it. His spirits were often either too high or too low to be contained within conventional limits, and when suffering from headaches, brain fever, and his obsessive fears, he had more than once contemplated suicide. In sober moments, of course, he rejected the idea. "Life is not like a commission that we can resign when disgusted with the service," he had made Jefferson Davis say to Dr. Craven. "Taking it by your own hand is a confession of judgment to all that your worst enemies can allege."

He did not check into the Astor House late Saturday afternoon to commit suicide but to escape his terrible craving for whiskey, to find relief, to get some sleep. He had progressed far beyond the point where he could make a simple choice between keeping his pledge of total abstinence and beginning to drink again; he knew that if he weakened this time he would be unable to shrug off his self-recriminations with a joke and another drink, as he had so often in the past. He had now to make the ultimate decision of his life, to master his dependence upon liquor and go on to the position of prestige and power of which he had always dreamed, or to succumb completely to it and sink into the failure—complete, debasing, and unredeemable—which had so long haunted him. He was a sick man, and probably he feared that he did not possess the strength to decide his own fate, that it was too late for him, that he was doomed. In his carpetbag there were three vials, containing from one to three ounces of chloroform. As he closed the door of his room behind him and opened his bag, he probably did not care whether the chloroform killed him or merely let him get some sleep.

He is reported to have spent a restless night, and indeed intervals of agitated pacing must have alternated with intervals of benumbing stupor. Sunday afternoon, out of chloroform and almost out of his mind with desire for peace and unconsciousness, he sent a prescription signed by his family doctor to the hotel physician, Charles Y. Swan, for another half ounce. Dr. Swan, fearful that the guest in Room 130 did not understand the power of the drug, sent him only a quarter of an ounce, filling up the bottle with alcohol. Expectantly, Halpine poured the solution upon a towel, lay down, and inhaled deeply. He was unconscious briefly. Slowly and matter of factly realizing that the solution was too weak for him, he jumped to his feet in an agony of frustration. He would go to sleep if it were the last thing he ever did!

Straightening his clothes, he went to the hotel office, cashed a check, and sent to Hudnut's Drug Store—it was in the *Herald's* building, nearby—for an entire pint of the anesthesia. When it arrived, he poured most of it on his towel, and lay down on the bed.

Shortly after 8:00 P.M., a waiter opened the door to his room, took one horrified look, and ran for Dr. Swan. "He was struggling a great deal when I found him," the doctor stated at the inquest, "and his face was almost livid, with a very weak pulse. He was in a state of collapse; he was cold, and his breath was short and stertorous, and his outward appearance betokened great interior excitement." In addition to the pint bottle of chloroform, nearly empty, Dr. Swan found the four empty vials. During the war, he said, half an ounce was considered enough for the amputation of an arm or leg.

For over three hours, the doctor labored to keep his patient alive. But at about ten minutes after midnight, Charles G. Halpine finally went to sleep.[9]

Obituaries are often extravagant, and Halpine's undoubtedly reflected the emotions of newspapermen mourning the loss of a friend. Even so, they confirm the kind of friend and the kind of man he was. Warm gregariousness, boisterous passions, and a prodigious capacity for work were prominent qualities of his character, as wit, cleverness, cultivation, and a thorough mastery of his profession were of his mind. His friends

were awed, perhaps excessively, by his brilliance, and saddened by the
abandon with which he squandered his gifts. Influenced by the strength
and charm of his personality, by the eminence and intimacy of his contacts in public life, and by his involvement with so many wartime and
postwar controversies, they did not doubt that he had made a mark in
his time, or that he would have gone on to greater fame and power in
the future. His faults, as Robert Roosevelt said, harmed himself alone
(Margaret and the children aside), and though he was by no means free
of lapses from moral principle his death removed a powerful voice for
honest government in New York and made the triumph of the notorious
Tweed Ring, just about to begin its great era of organized looting, that
much easier.

His successor as register of New York was Patrick H. Jones, an interim appointee of the Republican governor of the state, Reuben E.
Fenton. Generals Grant and Sheridan and other prominent men had
petitioned Fenton to appoint a man who would turn over the fees collected for the rest of the year to Margaret. It is possible that Jones did
so, though he flatly rejected a plea from Roosevelt not to remove Halpine's friends from various patronage positions.[10]

The Republicans did not hold the registership for long, for in the
November elections the Republican candidate, none other than Horace
Greeley, was badly beaten by a Tammany Democrat, and the office be-
came one of the major sources of income for Boss Tweed's spoilsmen.

There was also bad election news in the Ninth Congressional District, which Halpine had believed so confidently he could carry for himself. In a three-man race his friend John Savage was badly beaten by the
incumbent, Fernando Wood, running for reelection with the support of
Tammany Hall. Even the Citizen's Association, which had struggled for
so long against corruption in New York, was allowed to fall into Tammany's hands by its much respected but elderly and easily duped president, Peter Cooper. It ceased to be a reforming organization, and was
denounced by the *Citizen,* once its official organ.[11]

Before long the *Citizen,* too, felt Halpine's absence—and Miles
O'Reilly's. Although Robert Roosevelt tried to continue publishing it as
"a high toned family paper," he soon found it necessary to merge with
a literary periodical, *The Round Table.* As the *Citizen and Round Table*
it lasted with declining influence into the 1870's.[12]

Halpine did not have the luck of the Irish. But he did have Margaret,
and it was Margaret's love and faith in him which preserved the letters
and manuscripts which have helped to make it possible at last to tell his
story. In fact, it was Margaret who made it possible for him to have a

story to tell. For it is difficult to imagine how even so talented a man as Halpine, whose temperament fluctuated so wildly between the extremes of joy and despair and who so readily permitted himself the indulgence of his weaknesses, could have achieved anything at all without the loving and steadfast support she provided him. In what was one of his very last poems—it was published in the *Citizen* on July 28—Halpine described her in the healthful fullness and beauty of her maturity, and called her "My Every Day Love."

> She reads aloud—'tis pleasant,
>   That voice's silvery stream—
> The more so, as at present
>   My volume is her theme.
> So indeed, in mind and person,
>   In fortune and degree,
> The girl that I make my verse on
>   Is just the girl for me.

Margaret was indeed just the girl for Halpine. Perhaps he was lucky, after all.

Notes to the Chapters

CHAPTER 1 Carpetbagger, pp. 1–15

1. "Biographical Sketch," *The Poetical Works of Charles G. Halpine,* Robert B. Roosevelt, ed. (New York: Harper & Brothers, 1869), p. lv.

2. On Nicholas John Halpin, see *Dictionary of National Biography,* VIII, 1007.

3. Nicholas J. Halpin to Charles, n.d., probably 1838. The letter is owned by the Halpine family, Annapolis, Maryland.

4. Halpine to James Russell Lowell, 1 March 1866, Lowell Papers.

5. Affidavit signed by William J. Lane Milligan, 21 April 1883, Halpine Papers.

6. Margaret M. Halpine, "Life of Charles Graham Halpine," typescript copy of manuscript in the Halpine Papers, p. 4.

7. Typescript, n.d., Halpine Papers.

8. There is no comprehensive study of the *Carpet-Bag,* but see Franklin J. Meine, "American Comic Periodicals. No. 1—The *Carpet-Bag,*" *Collector's Journal,* IV, No. 2 (October–December 1933), 411–13.

9. *Fifty Years Among Authors, Books and Publishers* (New York: Carleton, 1884), p. 412.

CHAPTER 2 A Literary Swiss, pp. 16–32

1. He wrote two sonnets describing his nightmare-like feelings and thanking "Paul Creyton," Trowbridge's pseudonym, for nursing him. "Scrapbook of *Carpet-Bag* and Other Poems," Halpine Papers.

2. "Paul Creyton" to Halpine, 30 April 1854, Halpine Papers. Unless otherwise indicated, all correspondence both to Halpine and to members of his family is part of the Halpine Papers, Huntington Library.

3. Prospectus of Halpine, Williamson & Co., New York, 1853, Halpine Papers; Halpine to Margaret, 11 January 1853.

4. *Poetical Works,* pp. 64–65.

5. In her "Life," p. 8.

6. Originally published in the *Tribune,* 13 June 1854, the poem was republished in "Private Miles O'Reilly" (Charles G. Halpine), *Baked Meats of the Funeral* (New York: Carleton, 1866), pp. 130–32.

7. *Fitz-James O'Brien. A Literary Bohemian of the Eighteen-Fifties* (Boulder: University of Colorado Press, 1944), pp. 84–85.

8. *Henry J. Raymond and the New York Press for Thirty Years* (Hartford, Conn.: A. S. Hale, 1870), p. 143.

9. *Fifty Years*, pp. 426–27.

10. *Masterpieces of Wit and Humor* (n.p., 1903), p. 107, and Trowbridge, "Recollections," p. 357.

11. Frederic Hudson, *Journalism in the United States from 1690 to 1872* (New York: Harper & Brothers, 1873), p. 620.

12. *Poetical Works*, pp. 138–40.

13. *Sir Dudley's Heir; or, A Glance at the Early Life of Mary Doyle, the Wexford Heroine; Lord Edward's Guard; or, the Foster Brothers of Kildare. An Episode of the Last Great Irish Insurrection; The Willows of the Golden Vale. A Page from Ireland's Martyrology;* and *The Shamrock in Italy; or, Mountcashel's Brigade.*

14. *Bartle Byrne; A Biography: Being Some Passages of Interest in the Life of An Adopted Citizen* (but unfortunately not of Halpine's); *Us Here; or, A Glimpse Behind Know-Nothingism in One of the Rural Districts;* and *The Title Deeds; or, the Wife's Secret.*

15. *E.g., Dictionary of American Biography,* and John D. Hayes and Doris D. Maguire, "Charles Graham Halpine: Life and Adventures of Miles O'Reilly," *New-York Historical Society Quarterly,* LI, No. 4 (October 1967), 330–31.

16. This biographical data is from the New York *Times,* 2 July 1864.

17. Oscar H. Harpel, *Poets and Poetry of Printerdom* (Cincinnati: Oscar H. Harpel, 1875), p. 301.

18. See Gustavus Myers, *The History of Tammany Hall* (New York: Boni & Liveright, 1917), pp. 190, 209; Homer Adolph Stebbins, *A Political History of the State of New York, 1865–1869* (New York: Columbia University Press, 1913), p. 196n; and Allan Nevins and Milton Halse Thomas, eds., *The Diary of George Templeton Strong* (New York: Macmillan, 1952), II, 373–75.

19. Mathew Hale Smith, *Sunshine and Shadow in New York* (Hartford, Conn.: J. B. Burr, 1868), p. 660. Halpine's commission as commissioner of deeds, signed by Clancy as county clerk, is in the Halpine Papers.

20. *E.g.,* Halpine to Weed, 10 February 1860 and 10 March 1860, Weed Papers.

21. Greeley's letter is reprinted in James Parton, *The Life of Horace Greeley* (Boston: Fields, Osgood, 1869), pp. 481–86. See also Glyndon G. Van Deusen, *Thurlow Weed: Wizard of the Lobby* (Boston: Little, Brown, 1947), pp. 253–54.

22. Willard L. King, *Lincoln's Manager. David Davis* (Cambridge: Harvard University Press, 1960), pp. 145, 179; Swett to Lincoln, n.d. [probably 25 May 1860], Lincoln Papers.

23. Halpine to Greeley, 16 June 1860, Greeley Papers; Halpine to Weed, 15 June 1860, Weed Papers.

24. The closeness of their relationship is suggested in Halpine's letters to Weed on 18 September 1860 and 21 September 1860, Weed Papers.

CHAPTER 3   Adjutant, pp. 33–43

1. Thurlow Weed Barnes, *Memoir of Thurlow Weed* (Boston: Houghton, Mifflin, 1884), p. 341. Halpine is not listed as an officer of the Sixty-Ninth in D. P. Conyngham, *The Irish Brigade* (New York: Wm. McSorley, 1867).

2. The story is told in Margaret M. Halpine, "Life," pp. 15–16, and the New York *Times,* 3 May 1861.

3. Halpine to Edwin D. Morgan, 25 January 1864, Morgan Papers; Halpine to Weed, 21 May 1861, Weed Papers; Halpine to Margaret, 24 May 1861.

4. Hunter's letters to Lincoln, 20 October 1860 and 18 December 1860, are in the Lincoln Papers; biographical data is in David Hunter, *Report of the Military Services of Gen. David Hunter* (New York: D. Van Nostrand, 1873).

5. 28 September 1861, in Roy P. Basler, ed., *The Collected Works of Abraham Lincoln* (New Brunswick: Rutgers University Press, 1953), IV, 513.

6. Halpine to Weed, 17 October 1861, Lincoln Papers.

7. Halpine to Greeley, 10 October 1861, Greeley Papers.

8. *Official Records, War of the Rebellion,* Ser. I, III, 540–49.

9. The best pro-Fremont account is Allan Nevins, *The War for the Union* (New York: Scribner's, 1959), I, 374–82.

10. Lincoln to Hunter, 24 October 1861, Collected Works, V, 1–2; *Official Records,* Ser. I, III, 567.

11. Halpine to Henry W. Halleck, 14 March 1862, in *Official Records,* Ser. I, VIII, 615–17.

12. Hunter to Lincoln, 23 December 1861, Lincoln Papers; Lincoln to Hunter, 31 December 1861, *Collected Works,* V, 84–85.

13. *Official Records,* Ser. I, VIII, 428–29, 450–51.

14. Lincoln to Hunter and Lane, 10 February 1862, *Collected Works,* V, 131. For the controversy between Hunter and Lane, see Wendell Holmes Stephenson, *The Political Career of General James H. Lane* (Topeka: Kansas State Printing Plant, 1930), pp. 113–22.

15. *Official Records,* Ser. I, VIII, 831.

16. Lincoln to Edwin M. Stanton, 31 January 1862, *Collected Works,* V, 115–16; Salmon P. Chase, *Inside Lincoln's Cabinet,* David Donald, ed. (New York: Longmans, Green, 1954), p. 50; Jay Monaghan, *Civil War on the Western Border, 1854–1865* (Boston: Little, Brown, 1955), p. 252.

17. *Official Records,* Ser. I, VIII, 553, 555, 559; Ulysses S. Grant, *Personal Memoirs* (New York: Webster, 1885), I, 316.

CHAPTER 4   Getting High, pp. 44–60

1. See Thomas Wentworth Higginson, *Army Life in a Black Regiment* (Boston: Beacon Press, 1962), p. 97. There are many interesting pictures in Robert Carse, *Department of the South. Hilton Head Island in the Civil War* (Columbia, S.C.: State Printing Co., 1961).

2. Charles G. Halpine, "The Marching Soldier. His Joys and Sorrows. A Lecture," unpublished manuscript, n.d., Halpine Papers. Frank Moore, ed., *Rebellion Record* (New York: G. P. Putnam, 1861–68), IV, 462–63.

3. Affidavit of E. Whitney, M.D., 21 May 1862, in *Congressional Record*, 48 Cong., 1st Sess., 13 June 1884, p. 5124; *Official Records*, Ser. I, XIV, 359.

4. Halpine manuscript, "The Marching Soldier," Halpine Papers.

5. *Official Records*, Ser. I, VI, 176–77; Dudley Taylor Cornish, *The Sable Arm: Negro Troops in the Union Army, 1861–1865* (New York: W. W. Norton, 1966), pp. 18–19.

6. *Official Records*, Ser. III, II, 29–30, and Ser. I, XIV, 341.

7. 19 May 1862, *Collected Works*, V, 222–23.

8. Hunter, *Report of the Military Services*, p. 18. Lincoln's statement is part of his proclamation of May 19.

9. *Official Records*, Ser. III, II, 31, 50–60; James M. McPherson, *The Struggle for Equality* (Princeton: Princeton University Press, 1964), pp. 195–96. For a full discussion of the experiment, which was intended to serve as a pilot project for the turning of slaves into free laborers elsewhere in the South, see Willie Lee Rose, *Rehearsal for Reconstruction* (Indianapolis: Bobbs-Merrill, 1964).

10. "Army Discipline," unpublished manuscript, n.d., Halpine Papers.

11. As quoted in Rose, *Rehearsal*, p. 188.

12. *Congressional Globe*, 37 Cong., 2nd Sess., pp. 2620–21.

13. Halpine, *Baked Meats*, pp. 180–82.

14. *Official Records*, Ser. III, II, 196–98.

15. *Congressional Globe*, 37 Cong., 2nd Sess., pp. 3121, 3125–26.

16. Chase, *Inside Lincoln's Cabinet*, 21 July 1862, p. 96.

17. *Official Records*, Ser. III, II, 292, and Ser. I, XIV, 347–48.

18. *Official Records*, Ser. III, II, 152 and Ser. I, XIV, 377–78; Cornish, *Sable Arm*, pp. 79–80.

19. *Official Records*, Ser. III, II, 695; Cornish, *Sable Arm*, pp. 84–86; McPherson, *Struggle for Equality*, pp. 197–98.

20. [Charles G. Halpine,] *The Life and Adventures . . . of Private Miles O'Reilly* (New York: Carleton, 1864), p. 57, and *Baked Meats*, p. 192.

21. Hunter's letter is copied in Halpine to Weed, 29 July 1862, Weed Papers.

22. The request is in Halpine to Weed, 29 July 1862, Weed Papers.

23. Halpine to Hay, 28 July 1862, Hay Papers.

24. Earl Schenk Miers, ed., *Lincoln Day by Day. A Chronology* (Washington, D.C.: Lincoln Sesquicentennial Commission, 1960), 8 December 1862, III, 154.

25. *Baked Meats*, pp. 103–11.

26. New York *Citizen*, 13 October 1866.

27. *Anecdotes of Public Men* (New York: Harper & Brothers, 1873), pp. 272–73.

28. Halpine to Weed, 28 August 1862, Weed Papers.

29. Greeley to Halpine, 31 August 1862, Halpine Papers.

30. Charles A. Dana, *Recollections of the Civil War* (New York: Collier Books, 1963), p. 38.

31. In John Hay, *Lincoln and the Civil War in the Diaries and Letters of . . . ,* Tyler Dennett, ed. (New York: Dodd, Mead, 1939), p. 56n.

32. Chase, *Inside Lincoln's Cabinet*, pp. 172–73.

CHAPTER 5   The Butchered Bull, pp. 61–75

1. Shillaber to Halpine, 8 February 1863.

2. *Life and Adventures,* pp. 234–35.

3. "Two Weeks at Port Royal," *Harper's New Monthly Magazine,* XXVII (June, 1863), 117; Halpine to Miss M. L. Brooks, 18 June 1863, Mary P. Robinson Collection.

4. Fox to Samuel F. Du Pont, 3 June 1862, *Confidential Correspondence of Gustavus Vasa Fox, Assistant Secretary of the Navy, 1861–1865,* Robert Means Thompson and Richard Wainwright, eds. (New York: DeVinne Press, 1918), I, 127, and 5 August 1862, 144; *Official Records of the Union and Confederate Navies* . . . , Ser. I, XIII, 503. See also John D. Hayes, " 'Captain Fox—*He Is* the Navy Department,' " *United States Naval Institute Proceedings,* Vol. 91, No. 9 (September 1965), 64–71.

5. 3 June 1862, *Confidential Correspondence,* I, 126.

6. *Official Records, Navy,* Ser. I, XIV, 3–4.

7. John G. Nicolay and John Hay, *Abraham Lincoln. A History* (New York: Century, 1890), VII, 65, 77; Gideon Welles, *Lincoln and Seward* (New York: Sheldon, 1874), pp. 199–200; Madeline Vinton Dahlgren, *Memoir of John A. Dahlgren* (Boston: J. R. Osgood, 1882), p. 390.

8. Halpine to Sidney Howard Gay, 30 April 1863, Gay Papers.

9. The complete letter is in *Life and Adventures,* pp. 11–24.

10. This first public mention of Miles O'Reilly is in *Life and Adventures,* pp. 19–22.

11. Hunter to Lincoln, 22 May 1863, Lincoln Papers. The letter is in Halpine's hand.

12. *Official Records,* Ser. I, XIV, 599.

13. As quoted in *Baked Meats,* pp. 194–201.

14. *Official Records,* Ser. I, XIV, 448–49.

15. *Official Records,* Ser. III, II, 695.

16. The poem is published in a different and fictional context in *Life and Adventures,* pp. 55–56.

17. *Official Records,* Ser. III, III, 177.

18. The letters are in *Official Records,* Ser. I, XIV, 456–57, 462–63, and Ser. III, III, 740.

19. Cornish, *Sable Arm,* p. 149; E. Merton Coulter, "Robert Gould Shaw and the Burning of Darien, Georgia," *Civil War History,* V, No. 4 (December, 1959), 367–68.

20. The letter is in *Harper's Weekly,* 3 September 1870, p. 563.

21. *Official Records,* Ser. I, XIV, 466–67.

22. *Official Records,* Ser. I, XIV, 469.

23. Coulter, "Burning of Darien," p. 371; *Official Records,* Ser. I, XIV, 464.

24. Hunter reported the conversation in a letter to Halpine, 21 July 1863.

25. As quoted in Hay, *Lincoln and the Civil War,* p. 72.

26. Frederick Phisterer, *New York in the War of the Rebellion* (Albany, N.Y.: Lyon, 1912), I, 39; Halpine to his mother, reviewing his career, 27 July 1868.

CHAPTER 6   Private Miles O'Reilly, pp. 76–93

1. See *Diary of a Union Lady, 1861–1865,* Harold Earl Hammond, ed. (New York: Funk & Wagnalls, 1962), pp. 183, 185, 248, and Joseph M. Hernon, Jr., "The Irish Nationalists and Southern Secession," *Civil War History,* XII, No. 1 (March, 1966), 43.

2. Edward Robb Ellis, *The Epic of New York City* (New York: Coward-McCann, 1966), p. 315.

3. Strong, *Diary,* III, 341, 345, 352.

4. John Adams Dix, *Memoirs* (New York: Harper & Brothers, 1883), II, 74–92.

5. Halpine to Lincoln, 19 September 1863, Lincoln Papers; Lincoln to Stanton, 30 September 1863, *Collected Works,* VI, 490.

6. Halpine to Du Pont, 3 September 1863, Du Pont Papers.

7. The story is reprinted in *Life and Adventures,* pp. 25–39.

8. Halpine to Weed, 8 September 1863 and 10 September 1863, Weed Papers.

9. In his five-volume memoir, *Retrospections of an Active Life* (New York: Baker & Taylor, 1909–13), Bigelow does not mention Weed's services in France.

10. (Indianapolis: Bobbs-Merrill, 1945), pp. 199, 203.

11. The story is in *Life and Adventures,* pp. 40–51.

12. 9 October 1863, Du Pont Papers.

13. *Life and Adventures,* p. 57.

14. This installment of the saga of Miles O'Reilly was not published in the *Herald,* which printed "Sambo's Right To Be Kilt" as part of a different story on 17 January 1864.

15. *Life and Adventures,* pp. 73–113.

16. *Life and Adventures,* p. 61.

17. *Life and Adventures,* pp. 117–51.

18. Halpine to Hay, 12 November 1863, Hay Papers.

19. Halpine to Dix, 20 October 1863, Dix Papers.

20. The petition, dated 7 November 1863, is in the Lincoln Papers; Lincoln's response is in *Collected Works,* VII, 5, 5n.

21. Halpine to Hay, 24 November 1863, Hay Papers.

22. Miers, *Lincoln Day By Day,* 26 November 1863, III, 223.

23. The story is in *Life and Adventures,* pp. 154–97.

24. Halpine to Dix, 7 December 1863, Dix Papers.

CHAPTER 7   The Bogus Proclamation, pp. 94–106

1. Many of them may be read in Halpine Scrapbook No. 1, Library of Congress.

2. Carleton to Halpine, 15 March 1864.

3. Halpine to Hay, 24 November 1863, Hay Papers; Hay to Halpine, n.d. [early December, 1863].

4. *Official Records, Navy,* Ser. I, XIV, 282.

5. Halpine to Du Pont, 15 January 1864, Du Pont Papers.

6. The exchange of letters is in *Official Records,* Ser. I, XXVIII, 190–91.

7. *Official Records, Navy,* Ser. I, XIII, 750, and XIV, 261–62. See also H. A. Dupont, *Rear-Admiral Samuel Francis Du Pont* (New York: National Americana Society, 1926), p. 284.

8. Halpine to Morgan, 21 January 1864, Morgan Papers.

9. Halpine to Hay, 21 January 1864, Hay Papers, Library of Congress.

10. Greeley to Lincoln, 18 January 1864, Lincoln Papers.

11. Halpine to Gay, 25 January 1864, Gay Papers.

12. Hunter to Halpine, 18 December 1863.

13. Connes to Halpine, 27 February 1864, and Hunter to Halpine, 10 March 1864.

14. The National Archives and Records Service, General Services Administration, has been unable to locate a copy of the revised Rules and Articles of War, though a copy was received in the adjutant general's office on 16 February 1864. Elmer O. Parker for Robert W. Krauskopf, chief, army and navy branch, to William Hanchett, 20 April 1966.

15. Halpine to Nicolay, 11 February 1864, Nicolay Papers.

16. New York *Herald,* 9 January 1864. Halpine was almost certainly the author of the article describing these practices.

17. Spinola was allowed to resign. See the New York *Herald,* 11 January 1864, and Ezra J. Warner, *Generals in Blue* (Baton Rouge: Louisiana State University Press, 1964), pp. 467–68.

18. State of New York, Senate Doc. No. 93, April 1864, p. 18; New York *Times,* 16 April 1864.

19. Hunter to Halpine, 17 March 1864.

20. Halpine to Samuel L. M. Barlow, 5 April 1864, Barlow Papers.

21. Halpine to Barlow, 5 April 1864, Barlow Papers.

22. Barlow to Montgomery Blair, 23 October 1863, Lincoln Papers.

23. *Official Records,* Ser. III, IV, 386–87, 388.

24. The original copy of the order is in the Barlow Papers.

25. Robert S. Harper, *Lincoln and the Press* (New York: McGraw-Hill, 1951), p. 298.

26. *Official Records,* Ser. III, IV, 390–91.

27. *Official Records,* Ser. III, IV, 392–93.

28. As quoted in Hudson, *Journalism in the United States,* pp. 67–74.

CHAPTER 8   Hunter's Expedition, pp. 107–30

1. *Official Records,* Ser. I, XXXVII, Pt. 1, 500, 507, 535–36, 543, 561.

2. 13 July 1864. For ease in reading, the dates of Halpine's entries in his diary will not be given in the text unless they have special interest or significance. The unpublished manuscript is of course in the Halpine Papers.

3. *Official Records,* Ser. I, XXXVII, Pt. 1, 516–17.

4. *Official Records,* Ser. I, XXXVII, Pt. 1, 517.

5. Charles H. Lynch, *The Civil War Diary, 1862–1865, of* . . . (Hartford, Conn.: privately printed, 1915), p. 62.

6. *Official Records*, Ser. I, XXXVII, Pt. 1, 528.

7. David Hunter Strother, *A Virginia Yankee in the Civil War. The Diaries of* . . . , Cecil D. Eby, Jr., ed. (Chapel Hill: University of North Carolina Press, 1961), pp. 235–36; Halpine Diary, 30 May. It is not clear whether there was a second attack in Newton. See Marshall Moore Brice, *Conquest of a Valley* (Charlottesville: University of Virginia Press, 1965), p. 19.

8. *Baked Meats*, p. 337.

9. *Official Records*, Ser. I, XXXVII, Pt. 1, 517–18.

10. Halpine Diary, 27 May 1864, 30 May 1864; *Baked Meats*, pp. 300–301

11. *Official Records*, Ser. I, XXXVII, Pt. 1, 518, 546, 555–56.

12. Lynch, *Diary*, 30 May 1864, p. 64.

13. *Baked Meats*, pp. 306–307.

14. Strother, *A Virginia Yankee*, p. 243.

15. Hunter had been chairman of the commission which tried and convicted Porter.

16. Strother, *Virginia Yankee*, p. 248.

17. Halpine Diary, 5 June 1864, and letter to Margaret, 8 June 1864. Hunter's official report of casualties agreed in essentials with Halpine's estimates, and added that the Confederates lost as many more men through desertion and straggling. *Official Records*, Ser. I, XXXVII, Pt. 1, 94–95.

18. *Official Records*, Ser. I, XXXVII, Pt. 1, 95.

19. Strother, *Virginia Yankee*, p. 248.

20. Strother, *Virginia Yankee*, pp. 251–52; Halpine to Margaret, 8 June 1864.

21. *Official Records*, Ser. I, XXXVII, Pt. 1, 96–97.

22. *Baked Meats*, pp. 312–13.

23. *Baked Meats*, pp. 309–11. For the controversy over the burning of Letcher's house, see F. N. Boney, *John Letcher of Virginia* (University: University of Alabama Press, 1966), pp. 294–95.

24. On 6 June 1864. *Official Records*, Ser. I, XXXVII, Pt. 1, 598.

25. *E.g.,* Jubal A. Early, *A Memoir of the Last Year of the War* (Lynchburg: C. W. Button, 1867), p. 380n; Edley Craighill, "Lynchburg, Virginia, in the War Between the States," *The Iron Worker*, XXIV, No. 2 (Spring 1960), 2; and Edward J. Stackpole, *Sheridan in the Shenandoah* (Harrisburg, Pa.: Stackpole, 1961), p. 33.

26. George E. Pond, *The Shenandoah Valley in 1864* (New York: Jack Brussel, n.d. [1959]), p. 31; *Official Records*, Ser. I, XXXVII, Pt. 1, 633.

27. Strother, *Virginia Yankee*, pp. 249–50.

28. Even so, Grant suggested to Hunter on 6 June 1864 that he make exactly such a move, joining force with General Philip Sheridan, who would move west to meet him. But Sheridan was turned back at Trevillian Station on June 12, and Hunter did not receive Grant's letter until his expedition was over, anyway. *Official Records*, Ser. I, XXXVII, Pt. 1, 598; Pond, *Shenandoah Valley*, p. 43.

29. *Baked Meats*, pp. 340–41.

30. *Baked Meats*, pp. 343–44; Halpine Diary, 17 June 1864; Strother, *Virginia Yankee*, p. 264.

31 Stackpole, *Sheridan in the Shenandoah*, p. 39, and Craighill, "Lynchburg," p. 9, refer to the noise as a ruse; Brice, *Conquest of a Valley*, does not.

32. Halpine Diary; H. A. Du Pont, *The Campaign of 1864 in the Valley of Virginia and the Expedition to Lynchburg* (New York: National Americana Society, 1925), pp. 75–77, 79–80.

33. Halpine Diary, 21 June 1864; *Baked Meats,* pp. 364–66.

34. *Baked Meats,* p. 367.

35. Du Pont, *Campaign of 1864,* p. 91; Lynch, *Diary,* 22 June 1864, p. 83.

36. *Baked Meats,* pp. 373–74; Halpine Diary, 25 June 1864; Pond, *Shenandoah Valley,* p. 40.

37. Early, *Memoir,* p. 48n. These sentences are unaccountably missing from Frank E. Vandiver's edition of Early's *War Memoirs* (Bloomington: Indiana University Press, 1960), which prints the rest of the same passage.

38. The letter is in *Southern Historical Society Papers,* VIII, No. 5 (May 1880), 215–16.

39. Thomas A. Ashby, *The Valley Campaigns, Being the Reminiscences of a Non-Combatant* (New York: Neale Publishing Co., 1914), p. 278; Cecil D. Eby, Jr., "David Hunter: Villain of the Valley," *Iron Worker,* XXVIII, No. 2 (Spring, 1964), p. 1, and *"Porte Crayon,"* *The Life of David Hunter Strother* (Chapel Hill: University of North Carolina Press, 1960), p. 140; Charles M. Blackford, "The Campaign and Battle of Lynchburg," *Southern Historical Society Papers,* XXX (1902), 303.

40. *Official Records,* Ser. I, XXXVII, Pt. 2, 332–33.

41. *Baked Meats,* pp. 309–13, 332, 335, 359–60.

42. Hunter to Halpine, 25 October 1864, 20 June 1865, and 17 November 1865.

43. Edward H. Phillips, *The Shenandoah Valley in 1864* (Charleston, S.C.: The Citadel, 1965), p. 13.

44. Du Pont, *Campaign of 1864,* pp. 83–86, 95.

45. Du Pont, *Campaign of 1864,* pp. 95–97. Du Pont believed that Hunter was ungrateful to other officers, as well.

46. Halpine to Weed, 14 July 1864, Weed Papers.

CHAPTER 9 New York Citizen, pp. 131–42

1. *Poetical Works,* p. xvi. Other notices of Halpine's discharge from the army are in Halpine Scrapbook No. 1, Library of Congress.

2. *Baked Meats,* p. 48.

3. Halpine to Barlow, 8 September 1864, Barlow Papers.

4. Halpine to Hay, n.d. (October 1864), Hay Papers; Hay to Halpine, 21 October 1864.

5. The story of the banquet is in *Baked Meats,* pp. 6–41.

6. Halpine to Sherman, 20 January 1865, Sherman Papers.

7. *Baked Meats,* pp. 42–48.

8. *Baked Meats,* pp. 87–89.

9. *Baked Meats,* pp. 100–102.

10. Karl Schriftgiesser, *The Amazing Roosevelt Family, 1613–1942* (New York: W. Funk, 1942), pp. 159–67. See also Allen Churchill, *The Roosevelts: American Aristocrats* (New York: Harper & Row, 1965), pp. 116–17.

11. Hudson, *Journalism in the United States,* p. 426.

12. New York *Citizen,* 4 March 1865 and 17 June 1865.

13. Stanton's most recent biographers say he favored a military trial. Benjamin P. Thomas and Harold Hyman, *Stanton: The Life and Times of Lincoln's Secretary of War* (New York: Knopf, 1962), pp. 423–24.

14. Halpine to Fox, 24 February 1865, 10 April 1865, 26 May 1865, Fox Papers.

15. Halpine to Longfellow, 14 April 1865 and 14 August 1865, Longfellow Papers; Longfellow to Halpine, 24 April 1865. Longfellow published the original French version of his poem in the *Atlantic Monthly*, October, 1865. The lines which Halpine altered described one member of the Christmas party who, "In his Burgundy patois viley/Stammered—worse than Miles O'Reilly."

16. George Alfred Townsend, *Campaigns of a Non-Combatant* (New York: Blelock, 1866). The dedication read: "To 'Miles O'Reilly,' Who saw the war as vividly as he sang it; and whose aims for the peace that ensued, are even nobler than the noble influence he exerted during the struggle, these chapters are inscribed by his friend and colleague."

17. *Lyrics by the Letter H.*, pp. 189–91. The poem is also in *Poetical Works*, pp. 217–18.

18. *E.g.,* see *Poetical Works*, pp. 261, 343.

19. Halpine to Hay, 16 December 1864, Hay Papers. Halpine to Townsend, 6 July 1865, 5 October 1865, Townsend Papers.

CHAPTER 10   The Prison Life of Jefferson Davis, pp. 142–59

1. The nominations were confirmed on 10 April 1866. *Journal of the Executive Proceedings of the Senate*, XIV, Pt. 2, 593, 605, 717.

2. *Jefferson Davis, Private Letters, 1823–1889*, Hudson Strode, ed. (New York: Harcourt, Brace & World, 1966), pp. 243, 245, 182, 168; Hudson Strode, *Jefferson Davis, Tragic Hero* (New York: Harcourt, Brace & World, 1964), p. 272.

3. Halpine to Johnson, 20 March 1866, Johnson Papers.

4. Halpine to Barlow, 23 April 1866, Barlow Papers.

5. As quoted in Strode, *Tragic Hero*, p. 284.

6. Mrs. M. B. Clarke, "Puritan Peculiarities," *Land We Love*, I, No. 6 (October 1866), 409.

7. As reported in Chester D. Bradley, "Dr. Craven and The Prison Life of Jefferson Davis," *Virginia Magazine of History and Biography*, LXII, No. 1 (January 1954), 55–56.

8. As quoted in Bradley, "Dr. Craven," p. 89.

9. As quoted in the New York *Citizen*, 30 June 1866.

10. In Davis, *Private Letters*, p. 168.

11. Mrs. John T. Brodnax to Davis, 13 March 1887, in *Jefferson Davis, Constitutionalist. His Letters, Papers and Speeches*, Dunbar Rowland, ed. (Jackson, Miss.: Department of Archives and History, 1923), IX, 534–35. Davis' endorsement is dated 17 March 1887.

12. He probably never saw Craven following his release from prison, either. Robert McElroy, *Jefferson Davis* (New York: Harper & Brothers, 1937), II, 582, states that Craven accompanied Davis from Fort Monroe to Richmond, but he meant Craven's successor, Dr. George Cooper.

13. Strode, *Tragic Hero*, p. 288.

14. Douglas Southall Freeman, *The South to Posterity* (New York: Scribner's, 1939), p. 55.

15. Davis to C. W. Frazer, 21 July 1887, *Letters, Papers and Speeches,* IX, 583. It is possible that Davis annotated his copy at an earlier date.

16. See Bradley, "Dr. Craven," pp. 61–64.

17. The annotated copy is at Tulane University.

18. E. Merton Coulter, *The South During Reconstruction* (Baton Rouge: Louisiana State University Press, 1947), p. 176; Burton J. Hendrick, *Statesmen of the Lost Cause* (New York: Literary Guild of America, 1939), pp. 188, 204–205.

19. Varina Howell Davis, *Jefferson Davis, A Memoir* (New York: Belford Co., 1890), pp. 659–95.

20. See Bradley, "Dr. Craven," p. 56.

21. Halpine was among those who recommended Henry A. Smythe, a New York banker, who was nominated and confirmed. Halpine to Johnson, 21 March 1866, Johnson Papers. For a detailed discussion of the pressures and candidates involved in this appointment, see Lawanda Cox and John H. Cox, *Politics, Principle, and Prejudice, 1865–1866* (Glencoe, Ill.: The Free Press, 1963), pp. 113–23.

22. Halpine to Johnson, 16 June 1866, Johnson Papers.

23. Halpine to Johnson, 24 July 1866, Johnson Papers.

24. The article is reprinted in *Baked Meats,* pp. 208–51.

25. *Baked Meats,* pp. 212–13.

26. See Brian Jenkins, *Fenians and Anglo-American Relations during Reconstruction* (Ithaca: Cornell University Press, 1969), p. 26, and William D'Arcy, *The Fenian Movement in the United States: 1858–1886* (Washington, D.C.: Catholic University of America Press, 1947), 63–65.

27. Especially provocative articles were published in the *Citizen* on 3 February 1866 and 19 May 1866.

28. Jenkins, *Fenians,* pp. 140–42.

29. Halpine to Johnson, 24 July 1866. Johnson Papers.

30. Halpine to Johnson, 15 November 1866. Johnson Papers.

31. Clippings in Halpine Scrapbook No. 2, Library of Congress, estimate the register's income at between $40,000 and $70,000. In a letter to Margaret, 29 August 1866, Halpine said the office was worth $70,000 to $90,000 a year.

32. On the National Union movement and convention, see Eric L. McKitrick, *Andrew Johnson and Reconstruction* (Chicago: University of Chicago Press, 1960), pp. 410–20.

33. Greeley's effort is referred to in a letter from Halpine to his mother, 27 July 1868.

34. Halpine Scrapbook No. 2, Library of Congress.

CHAPTER 11 Black Loyalty, pp. 160–72

1. Hay, *Lincoln and the Civil War,* p. 287.

2. Hay to Halpine, 26 August 1867.

3. The dinner is referred to in Mark Twain to John McComb, 8 June 1867, a typescript copy of which is in the Mark Twain Papers.

4. Halpine to Bayles, 29 April 1867, Bayles Papers.

5. Halpine to Johnson, 25 February 1867, Johnson Papers.

6. New York *Citizen,* 23 March 1867, and 4 January 1868.

7. Halpine to William G. Moore, private secretary to President Johnson, 5 March 1867, Moore Papers.

8. Halpine to Johnson, 13 March 1867. Despite the stir raised at the time by Halpine's report of the interview, it has been all but ignored by historians. A recent exception is Kenneth M. Stampp, *The Era of Reconstruction, 1865–1877* (New York: Knopf, 1965), p. 57.

9. Halpine expressed his discouragement with Johnson to George Templeton Strong, who recorded it in his *Diary,* IV, 150–51.

10. James H. Brewer, *The Confederate Negro. Virginia's Craftsmen and Military Laborers, 1861–1865* (Durham, N.C.: Duke University Press, 1969), supports Halpine's assertion that the blacks made a major contribution to the Confederate war effort.

11. *Poetical Works,* pp. 87–88. The poem was originally published in the *Citizen,* 21 September 1867.

12. Mrs. Harper's verse was published in the Philadelphia *Press,* 16 October 1867, and reprinted in the *Citizen,* 26 October 1867.

13. Owned by the Halpine family, Annapolis, Maryland.

14. Johnson to Halpine, 26 December 1867.

15. Halpine's friend, Thomas Francis Meagher, also called himself a major general without legal authority. Robert G. Athearn, *Thomas Francis Meagher* (Boulder: University of Colorado Press, 1949), p. 146.

16. The manuscript, marked "Not published," is in the Halpine Papers.

17. The conversation is reported in Halpine to Chase, 1 April 1868, Chase Papers.

18. *Poetical Works,* pp. 116–17.

19. One such list is referred to in Halpine to Chase, 1 April 1868, Chase Papers.

20. Halpine to Seymour, 2 April 1868, Seymour Papers.

21. Sherman to Halpine, 8 July 1868.

22. Harry T. Peters, *Currier & Ives. Printmakers to the American People* (Garden City: Doubleday, Doran, 1942), plate 155.

23. For a description of the convention, see Herbert Eaton, *Presidential Timber. A History of Nominating Conventions, 1868–1960* (Glencoe, Ill.: The Free Press, 1964), pp. 1–19.

CHAPTER 12   The Astor House, pp. 173–80

1. Halpine to Yeaton, 12 January 1868, Yeaton Papers.

2. According to an undated clipping (probably August, 1868), apparently from the *Christian Union,* in the Barlow Papers.

3. The election was indeed close. Grant received 52.7 percent of the popular vote, winning by narrow margins in seven northern states, without which he would have lost to Seymour.

4. Halpine to his mother, 27 July 1868.

5. Halpine to Syble, 28 July 1868.

6. Greeley published the poem in the *Tribune,* 4 August 1868.

7. Derby, *Fifty Years,* pp. 430–31.

8. New York *Times,* 7 August 1868. Substantially the same information was published in the obituaries published by the other New York newspapers.

9. Reports of the circumstances of Halpine's death were carried in all the major daily and weekly newspapers. The most comprehensive obituaries, in addition to the New York *Times* article cited, were in the New York *Tribune* and the New York *Herald,* 4 August 1868. Stories about the inquest and funeral followed on subsequent days. Miscellaneous clippings may be found in the Halpine Papers in the Huntington Library and in the Halpine Scrapbooks in the Library of Congress. Robert Roosevelt's "Biographical Sketch" of Halpine in *Poetical Works* is substantially the obituary he wrote for the *Citizen,* 8 August 1868.

10. New York *Times,* 23 August 1868; New York *Citizen,* 29 August 1868.

11. New York *Citizen,* 26 September 1868. See also Allan Nevins, *Abram S. Hewitt, with Some Account of Peter Cooper* (New York: Octagon Books, 1967), p. 268.

12. Frank Luther Mott, *A History of American Magazines, 1865–1885* (Cambridge: Harvard University Press, 1938), p. 324.

Bibliography

MANUSCRIPTS

Samuel L. M. Barlow Papers, Huntington Library.
J. C. Bayles Papers, Yale University Library.
James Gordon Bennett Papers, Library of Congress.
Salmon P. Chase Papers, Historical Society of Pennsylvania and University of Virginia Library.
John A. Dix Papers, Columbia University Library.
Samuel Francis Du Pont Papers, Eleutherian Mills Historical Library.
Gustavus V. Fox Papers, New-York Historical Society.
Sidney Howard Gay Papers, Columbia University Library.
Horace Greeley Papers, New York Public Library.
Charles G. Halpine Papers, Huntington Library and Library of Congress.
John Hay Papers, Brown University and Library of Congress.
Andrew Johnson Papers, Library of Congress.
Ward Hill Lamon Papers, Huntington Library.
Abraham Lincoln Papers, Library of Congress.
Henry Wadsworth Longfellow Papers, Harvard College Library.
James Russell Lowell Papers, Harvard College Library.
William G. Moore Papers, Norcross Collection, Massachusetts Historical Society.
Edwin D. Morgan Papers, New York State Library.
John G. Nicolay Papers, Library of Congress.
Charles Nordhoff Papers, University of Virginia Library.
Mary P. Robinson Collection, New York Historical Society.
William H. Seward Papers, University of Rochester Library.
Horatio Seymour Papers, Yale University Library.
William T. Sherman Papers, Library of Congress.
George Alfred Townsend Papers, Yale University Library.
Mark Twain Papers, University of California, Berkeley.
Thurlow Weed Papers, University of Rochester Library.
Charles C. Yeaton Papers, Historical Society of Pennsylvania.

OFFICIAL RECORDS, DIARIES, LETTERS, MEMOIRS

Ashby, Thomas A., *The Valley Campaigns, Being the Reminiscences of* . . . New York: Neale Publishing Co., 1914.

Barnes, Thurlow Weed, *Memoir of Thurlow Weed*. Boston: Houghton Mifflin, 1884.

Bigelow, John, *Retrospections of An Active Life*. New York: Baker & Taylor, 1909–13. 5 vols.

Chase, Salmon P., *Inside Lincoln's Cabinet. The Civil War Diaries of* . . . David Donald, ed. New York: Longmans, Green, 1954.

Craven, John J., *Prison Life of Jefferson Davis*. New York: Carleton, 1866.

Dahlgren, Madeline Vinton, *Memoir of John A. Dahlgren*. Boston: J. R. Osgood, 1882.

Dana, Charles A., *Recollections of the Civil War*. New York: Collier Books, 1963.

Davis, Jefferson, Constitutionalist. His Letters, Papers, and Speeches. Jackson, Miss.: Department of Archives and History, 1923. 10 vols.

——, *Private Letters, 1823–1889*. Hudson Strode, ed. New York: Harcourt, Brace & World, 1966.

Davis, Varina, *Jefferson Davis, A Memoir by His Wife*. New York: Belford Co., 1890.

Derby, J. C., *Fifty Years Among Authors, Books and Publishers*. New York: Carleton, 1884.

Diary of a Union Lady, Harold Earl Hammond, ed. New York: Funk & Wagnalls, 1962.

Dix, John Adams. *Memoirs*. New York: Harper & Brothers, 1883. 2 vols.

Du Pont, H. A. *The Campaign of 1864 in the Valley of Virginia and the Expedition to Lynchburg*. New York: National Americana Society, 1925.

Du Pont, Samuel Francis. *A Selection from His Civil War Letters*. John D. Hayes, ed. Ithaca, New York: Cornell University Press, 1969. 3 vols.

Early, Jubal. *A Memoir of the Last Year of the War for Independence in the Confederate States of America*. Lynchburg: C. W. Button, 1867.

——. *War Memoirs. Autobiographical Sketch and Narrative of the War Between the States*. Frank E. Vandiver, ed. Bloomington: Indiana University Press, 1960.

Forney, John W. *Anecdotes of Public Men*. New York: Harper & Brothers, 1873.

Fox, Gustavus Vasa. *Confidential Correspondence of* . . . Robert Means Thompson and Richard Wainwright, eds. New York: DeVinne Press, 1918. 2 vols.

Garfield, James A. *The Wild Life of the Army: Civil War Letters*. Frederick D. Williams, ed. East Lansing: Michigan State University Press, 1964.

Grant, Ulysses S. *Personal Memoirs.* New York: Webster, 1885. 2 vols.

Greeley, Horace. *The American Conflict.* Hartford: O. D. Case, 1864–66. 2 vols.

[Halpine, Charles G.] *Baked Meats of the Funeral.* New York: Carleton, 1866.

——. *The Life and Adventures of Private Miles O'Reilly.* New York: Carleton, 1864.

——. *Lyrics by the Letter H.* New York: J. C. Derby, 1854.

——. *The Patriot Brothers; or, The Willows of the Golden Vale,* Dublin: A. M. Sullivan, n.d. [1869].

——. *The Poetical Works of* . . . Robert B. Roosevelt, ed. New York: Harper & Brothers, 1869.

Harpel, Oscar H. *Poets and Poetry of Printerdom.* Cincinnati: Oscar H. Harpel, 1875.

Hay, John. *Lincoln and the Civil War in the Diaries and Letters of* . . . Tyler Dennett, ed. New York: Dodd, Mead, 1939.

Higginson, Thomas Wentworth. *Army Life in a Black Regiment.* Boston: Beacon Press, 1962.

Hunter, David. *Report of the Military Services of* . . . New York: D. Van Nostrand, 1873.

Journal of the Executive Proceedings of the Senate, XIV. Washington, D.C., 1887.

Lincoln, Abraham. *Collected Works.* Roy P. Basler, ed. New Brunswick: Rutgers University Press, 1953. 9 vols.

Lee, Henrietta E. "Letter to General David Hunter on the Burning of Her House," *Southern Historical Society Papers,* VIII, No. 5 (May, 1880).

Lynch, Charles H. *The Civil War Diary, 1862–1865, of* . . . Hartford, Conn.: privately printed, 1915.

State of New York. *Senate Document No. 93.* Albany, 1864.

Official Records of the Union and Confederate Armies, the War of the Rebellion. Washington, D.C.: Government Printing Office, 1880–1901. 130 vols.

Official Records of the Union and Confederate Navies, the War of the Rebellion. Washington, D.C.: Government Printing Office, 1894–1914. 30 vols.

The Rebellion Record. Frank Moore, ed. New York: G. P. Putnam, 1861–63; D. Van Nostrand, 1864–68. 11 vols.

Smith, Mathew Hale. *Sunshine and Shadow in New York.* Hartford: J. B. Burr, 1868.

Strong, George Templeton. *The Diary of* . . . Allan Nevins and Milton Halsey Thomas, eds. New York: Macmillan, 1952. 4 vols.

Strother, David Hunter. *A Virginia Yankee in the Civil War. The Diaries of* . . . Cecil D. Eby, Jr., ed. Chapel Hill: University of North Carolina Press, 1961.

Townsend, George Alfred. *Campaigns of a Non-Combatant.* New York: Blelock, 1866.

BOOKS

Athearn, Robert G. *Thomas Francis Meagher. An Irish Revolutionary in. America*. Boulder: University of Colorado Press, 1949.

Boney, F. N. *John Letcher of Virginia*. University: University of Alabama Press, 1966.

Brewer, James H. *The Confederate Negro. Virginia's Craftsmen and Military Laborers, 1861–1865*. Durham, N.C.: Duke University Press, 1969.

Brice, Marshall Moore. *Conquest of a Valley*. Charlottesville: University of Virginia Press, 1965.

Carse, Robert. *Department of the South. Hilton Head in the Civil War*. Columbia, S.C.: State Printing Co., 1961.

Churchill, Allen. *The Roosevelts: American Aristocrats*. New York: Harper & Row, 1965.

Conyngham, D. P. *The Irish Brigade and Its Campaigns*. New York: Wm. McSorley, 1867.

Cornish, Dudley Taylor. *The Sable Arm*. New York: W. W. Norton, 1966.

Coulter, E. Merton. *The South During Reconstruction, 1865–1877*. Baton Rouge: Louisiana State University Press, 1947.

Cox, Lawanda, and Cox, John H. *Politics, Principle, and Prejudice, 1865–1866*. Glencoe, Ill.: The Free Press, 1963.

D'Arcy, William. *The Fenian Movement in the United States: 1858–1886*. Washington, D.C.: Catholic University of America Press, 1947.

Du Pont, H. A. *Rear-Admiral Samuel Francis Du Pont, United States Navy, A Biography*. New York: National Americana Society, 1926.

Eaton, Herbert. *Presidential Timber. A History of Nominating Conventions, 1868–1960*. Glencoe, Ill.: The Free Press, 1964.

Eby, Cecil D., Jr. *"Porte Crayon," The Life of David Hunter Strother*. Chapel Hill: University of North Carolina Press, 1960.

Ellis, Edward Robb. *The Epic of New York City*. New York: Coward-McCann, 1966.

Freeman, Douglas Southall. *The South to Posterity*. New York: Scribner's, 1939.

Harper, Robert S. *Lincoln and the Press*. New York: McGraw-Hill, 1951.

Hendrick, Burton J. *Statesmen of the Lost Cause*. New York: Literary Guild of America, 1939.

Hudson, Frederic. *Journalism in the United States*. New York: Harper & Brothers, 1873.

Jenkins, Brian. *Fenians and Anglo-American Relations during Reconstruction*. Ithaca: Cornell University Press, 1969.

King, Willard L. *Lincoln's Manager. David Davis*. Cambridge: Harvard University Press, 1960.

McElroy, Robert. *Jefferson Davis, the Real and the Unreal.* New York: Harper & Brothers, 1937.

McKitrick, Eric L. *Andrew Johnson and Reconstruction.* Chicago: University of Chicago Press, 1960.

McPherson, James M. *The Struggle for Equality. Abolitionists and the Negro in the Civil War and Reconstruction.* Princeton: Princeton University Press, 1964.

Mandelbaum, Seymour J. *Boss Tweed's New York.* New York: John Wiley & Sons, 1965.

Masterpieces of Wit and Humor. Intro. by Robert J. Burdette, n.p., 1903.

Maverick, Augustus. *Henry J. Raymond and the New York Press.* Hartford, Conn.: A. S. Hale, 1870.

Miers, Earl Schenck, ed.-in-chief. *Lincoln Day by Day. A Chronology.* Washington, D.C.: Lincoln Sesquicentennial Commission, 1960, 3 vols.

Monaghan, Jay. *Civil War on the Western Border.* Boston: Little, Brown, 1955.

——. *Diplomat in Carpet Slippers.* Indianapolis: Bobbs-Merrill, 1945.

Mott, Frank Luther. *A History of American Magazines, 1865–1885.* Cambridge: Harvard University Press, 1938.

Myers, Gustavus. *The History of Tammany Hall.* New York: Boni & Liveright, 1917.

Nevins, Allan. *Abram S. Hewitt, with Some Account of Peter Cooper.* New York: Octagon Books, 1967.

——. *Fremont, Pathmarker of the West.* New York: Longmans, Green, 1955. 2 vols.

——. *The War for the Union,* Vol. I, *The Improvised War, 1861–1862.* New York: Scribner's, 1959.

Nicolay, John G., and Hay, John. *Abraham Lincoln. A History.* New York: Century, 1890. 10 vols.

Parton, James. *The Life of Horace Greeley.* Boston: Fields, Osgood, 1869.

Peters, Harry T. *Currier & Ives. Printmakers to the American People.* Garden City, N.Y.: Doubleday, Doran, 1942.

Phillips, Edward H. *The Shenandoah Valley in 1864.* Charleston, S.C.: The Citadel, 1965.

Phisterer, Frederick. *New York in the War of the Rebellion.* Albany: Lyon, 1912. 6 vols.

Pond, George E. *The Shenandoah Valley in 1864.* New York: Jack Brussel, n.d. [1959].

Rose, Willie Lee. *Rehearsal for Reconstruction: The Port Royal Experiment.* Indianapolis: Bobbs-Merrill, 1964.

Schriftgiesser, Karl. *The Amazing Roosevelt Family.* New York: W. Funk, 1942.

Stackpole, Edward J. *Sheridan in the Shenandoah.* Harrisburg, Pa.: Stackpole, 1961.

Stampp, Kenneth M. *The Era of Reconstruction, 1865–1877.* New York: Knopf, 1965.

Stebbins, Homer Adolph. *A Political History of the State of New York, 1865–1869.* New York: Columbia University Press, 1913.

Stephenson, Wendel Holmes. *The Political Career of General James H. Lane.* Topeka: Kansas State Printing Plant, 1930.

Strode, Hudson. *Jefferson Davis, Tragic Hero.* New York: Harcourt, Brace & World, 1964.

Talman, James J. *Huron College, 1863–1963.* London, Canada: Huron College, 1963.

Thomas, Benjamin P., and Hyman, Harold. *Stanton: The Life and Times of Lincoln's Secretary of War.* New York: Knopf, 1962.

Van Deusen, Glyndon G. *Thurlow Weed: Wizard of the Lobby.* Boston: Little, Brown, 1947.

Warner, Esra J. *Generals in Blue.* Baton Rouge: Louisiana State University Press, 1964.

Wolle, Francis. *Fitz-James O'Brien. A Literary Bohemian of the Eighteen-Fifties.* Boulder: University of Colorado Press, 1944.

ARTICLES

Barbee, David Rankin. "Dr. Craven's 'Prison Life of Jefferson Davis'—An Exposé," *Tyler's Quarterly Historical and Genealogical Magazine,* XXXII (April, 1951), 282–95.

Blackford, Charles M. "The Campaign and Battle of Lynchburg," *Southern Historical Society Papers,* XXX (1902), 279–314.

Bradley, Chester D. "Dr. Craven and the Prison Life of Jefferson Davis," *Virginia Magazine of History and Biography,* LXII, No. 1 (January, 1954), 50–94.

Clarke, Mrs. M. B. "Puritan Peculiarities," *Land We Love,* I, No. 6 (October, 1866), 406–409.

Coulter, E. Merton. "Robert Gould Shaw and the Burning of Darien, Georgia," *Civil War History,* V, No. 4 (December, 1959), 363–73.

Craighill, Edley. "Lynchburg, Virginia, in the War Between the States," *The Iron Worker,* XXIV, No. 2 (Spring, 1960), 1–13.

Eby, Cecil D., Jr. "David Hunter: Villain of the Valley. The Sack of the Virginia Military Institute," *The Iron Worker,* XXVIII, No. 2 (Spring, 1964), 1–9.

Hayes, John D. " 'Captain Fox—*He* Is the Navy Department,' " *United States Naval Institute Proceedings,* Vol. 91, No. 9 (September, 1965), 64–71.

Hayes, John D., and Maguire, Doris D. "Charles Graham Halpine: Life and

Adventures of Miles O'Reilly," *New York Historical Society Quarterly,*
   LI, No. 4 (October, 1967), 326–44.
Hernon, Joseph M., Jr. "The Irish Nationalists and Southern Secession,"
   Civil War History, XII, No. 1 (March, 1966), 43–53.
Meine, Franklin J. "American Comic Periodicals. No. 1—The *Carpet-Bag,*"
   Collector's Journal, IV, No. 2 (October–December, 1933), 411–13.
Trowbridge, John T. "Recollections of 'Miles O'Reilly,' " *Independent,* LV
   (February 12, 1903), 357–59.

Index

popularity and symbolism of, 86–87; celebrates Union victories, 134; writes for *Citizen,* 137, 139–40, 173
Milligan, Margaret G. *See* Halpine, Margaret Milligan
Mitchell, John: 4
Monaghan, Jay: 81
Monitor: 44, 64
Monitors, controversy over: 64–65, 66–67, 74, 79, 80, 83
Montgomery, James: 72, 73
Morgan, Edwin D.: 97
Morris Island, S.C.: 68, 74, 144
Morny, Duke de: 81–82
Mosby, John Singleton: 108
Mount Crawford, Va.: 114
Mozart Hall: 29, 88, 89
Murdoch, Frank H.: 57

Nahant: 95, 97
Napoleon III: 80, 81
Nast, Thomas: 141
National Republican (Washington): 58, 59
National Union movement: 158
Naval officer, Port of New York: 151
Negro soldiers: initial War Department policy on, 47–48; Hunter recruits, 48–51; prejudice in North, 51, 69–70; reaction against in South, 69, influence of "Sambo's Right To Be Kilt," 69–71, 83–84
Nesmith, James W.: 57
Newcastle, Va.: 122
New Market, Va.: 106, 111, 113, 115
News (New York): 86
Newtown, Va.: 109
New York anti-draft riots: 76–77
Nicaragua: 27
Nicolay, John G.: 36, 56, 57, 66, 100
Nordhoff, Charles: 64

Oakford, Charles: 57
O'Brien, FitzJames: 21–22, 23, 57
O'Connell, Daniel: 3, 4
O'Mahony, John: 152
O'Sullivan, John L.: 8

Pendleton, George: 172
Pfaff's Restaurant: 24, 170
Phillips, Wendell: 166
Piedmont, Va., Battle of: 115–16, 143
Pierce, Edward L.: 49
Pierce, Franklin: 9, 92

Pomeroy Circular, the: 99
Pope, John: 115
"Port Crayon." *See* Strother, David Hunter
Port Republic, Va.: 115
Port Royal, Va. *See* Department of the South
Porter, FitzJohn: 115
Post (Boston): 17
Post (New York): 9
Press (Philadelphia): 58
Price, Sterling: 39, 40
Punch: 3
Putnam's Monthly: 21

Raymond, Henry J.: 1, 24, 31, 81
Raymond, Mrs. Henry J.: 64
Read, Buchanan: 57
Republican (Savannah): 45
Reconstruction controversy: 142, 161–69, 173
Rockingham Reporter (Harrisonburg, Va.): 114
Rodgers, C. R. P.: 65, 78, 96
Rolla, Mo.: 37, 40
Roosevelt, Cornelius V.: 136
Roosevelt, Robert B.: 1, 2, 24, 89, 136, 139, 140, 158, 160, 161, 175, 179
Roosevelt, Theodore: 158
Round Table (New York): 179

Saint Helena Island, S.C.: 49
Salem, Va.: 120, 121
Saxton, Rufus B.: 52–53, 69
Savage, John: 5, 30, 46–47, 57, 98, 117, 177, 179
Savannah, Ga.: 45, 47, 96
Scott, Winfield: 9, 80
Sedalia, Mo.: 38, 40
Seward, William H.: 30–31, 154, 156, 158
Seymour, Horatio: 75, 171–72, 174, 176
Seymour, Truman: 60
Shaffer, J. W.: 42
Shaw, Robert Gould: 72
Shenandoah Valley: 107, 113, 124–25
Sheridan, Philip: 128, 176, 179
Sherman, William T.: 128, 132, 133, 172
Shillaber, Benjamin P.: 6, 10, 14, 15, 19, 22, 61, 70
Sickles, Daniel: 151, 159
Sigel, Franz: 106, 108, 111